INTRODUCTORY MATHEMATICAL ANALYSIS

6 TH EDITION

STUDENT SOLUTIONS MANUAL

INTRODUCTORY
MATHEMATICAL ANALYSIS
For Business, Economics, and the Life and Social Sciences

Ernest F. Haeussler, Jr.
The Pennsylvania State University

Richard S. Paul
The Pennsylvania State University

Prentice Hall, Englewood Cliffs, New Jersey 07632

Editorial/production supervision: Lynda Santamaria
Cover design: Suzanne Behnke
Manufacturing buyer: Paula Massenaro

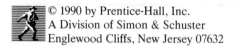
Printed in the United States of America

10   9   8   7   6   5   4   3   2

ISBN 0-13-501446-8

Prentice-Hall International (UK) Limited, *London*
Prentice-Hall of Australia Pty. Limited, *Sydney*
Prentice-Hall Canada Inc., *Toronto*
Prentice-Hall Hispanoamericana, S.A., *Mexico*
Prentice-Hall of India Private Limited, *New Delhi*
Prentice-Hall of Japan, Inc., *Tokyo*
Simon & Schuster Asia Pte. Ltd., *Singapore*
Editora Prentice-Hall do Brasil, Ltda., *Rio de Janeiro*
Prentice-Hall, Inc., *Englewood Cliffs, New Jersey*

Contents

v

Preface

This student supplement to *Introductory Mathematical Analysis:* FOR BUSINESS, ECONOMICS, AND THE LIFE AND SOCIAL SCIENCES, 6TH EDITION provides solutions to every other odd-numbered problem (1, 5, 9, ...) in every exercise set in the text. [For drill-type problems that basically involve one step, just the answer is given.]

If you attempt to solve one of these problems and are not successful, this manual should be useful. It is designed specifically to show you how to set up the problem and to allow you to check any resulting manipulations. Every effort has been made to ensure that this supplement is helpful to you; sufficient details and intermediate steps are included so that you can readily see how the correct answer can be found. Although many problems can be solved in a variety of ways, usually the most direct and natural method, consistent with the text, is shown.

INTRODUCTORY
MATHEMATICAL ANALYSIS

Algebra Refresher

1. true; -2 is a *negative integer.*

5. true, because $5 = \frac{5}{1}$.

9. true, because 0 and 6 are integers and $6 \neq 0$. Note: $\frac{0}{6} = 0$.

1. false, because 0 does not have a reciprocal.

5. true; $-x + y = y + (-x) = y - x$.

9. false: left side is $x + y + 5$; right side is $x + y + x + 5$

-1-

13. associative

17. definition of subtraction

21. $5a(x + 3) = (5a)x + (5a)(3) = 5ax + (3)(5a)$
$$= 5ax + (3\cdot5)(a) = 5ax + 15a$$

25. $x[(2y + 1) + 3] = x[2y + (1 + 3)] = x[2y + 4]$
$$= x(2y) + x(4) = (x\cdot2)y + 4x$$
$$= (2x)y + 4x = 2xy + 4x$$

EXERCISE 0.4

1. $-2 + (-4) = -6$

5. $7 - (-4) = 7 + 4 = 11$

9. $7(-9) = -(7\cdot9) = -63$

13. $-(-6 + x) = -(-6) - x = 6 - x$

17. $\frac{-2}{6} = -\frac{2}{6} = -\frac{1}{3}$

21. $3[-2(3) + 6(2)] = 3[-6 + 12] = 3[6] = 18$

25. $3(x - 4) = 3(x) - 3(4) = 3x - 12$

29. $8\left(\frac{1}{11}\right) = \frac{8\cdot1}{11} = \frac{8}{11}$

33. $\dfrac{2}{3} \cdot \dfrac{1}{x} = \dfrac{2 \cdot 1}{3 \cdot x} = \dfrac{2}{3x}$

37. $\dfrac{7}{y} \cdot \dfrac{1}{x} = \dfrac{7 \cdot 1}{y \cdot x} = \dfrac{7}{xy}$

41. $\dfrac{3}{10} - \dfrac{7}{15} = \dfrac{9}{30} - \dfrac{14}{30} = \dfrac{9 - 14}{30} = \dfrac{-5}{30} = -\dfrac{5 \cdot 1}{5 \cdot 6} = -\dfrac{1}{6}$

45. $\dfrac{2}{3} - \dfrac{5}{8} = \dfrac{16}{24} - \dfrac{15}{24} = \dfrac{16 - 15}{24} = \dfrac{1}{24}$

49. not defined (we cannot divide by 0)

EXERCISE 0.5

1. $(2^3)(2^2) = 2^{3+2} = 2^5 \ (= 32)$

5. $\dfrac{x^2 x^6}{y^7 y^{10}} = \dfrac{x^{2+6}}{y^{7+10}} = \dfrac{x^8}{y^{17}}$

9. $(2x^2 y^3)^3 = 2^3 (x^2)^3 (y^3)^3 = 8x^{2 \cdot 3} y^{3 \cdot 3} = 8x^6 y^9$

13. $\dfrac{(x^3)^6}{x(x^3)} = \dfrac{x^{3 \cdot 6}}{x^{1+3}} = \dfrac{x^{18}}{x^4} = x^{18-4} = x^{14}$

17. $\sqrt[5]{-32} = -2$

21. $(100)^{1/2} = \sqrt{100} = 10$

25. $(32)^{-2/5} = \dfrac{1}{(32)^{2/5}} = \dfrac{1}{(\sqrt[5]{32})^2} = \dfrac{1}{(2)^2} = \dfrac{1}{4}$

29. $\sqrt{32} = \sqrt{16 \cdot 2} = \sqrt{16}\sqrt{2} = 4\sqrt{2}$

33. $\sqrt{16x^4} = \sqrt{16}\sqrt{x^4} = 4x^2$

37. $(9z^4)^{1/2} = \sqrt{9z^4} = \sqrt{3^2(z^2)^2} = \sqrt{3^2}\sqrt{(z^2)^2} = 3z^2$

41. $\dfrac{x^3y^{-2}}{z^2} = x^3 \cdot y^{-2} \cdot \dfrac{1}{z^2} = x^3 \cdot \dfrac{1}{y^2} \cdot \dfrac{1}{z^2} = \dfrac{x^3}{y^2z^2}$

45. $(3t)^{-2} = \dfrac{1}{(3t)^2} = \dfrac{1}{9t^2}$

49. $\sqrt{x} - \sqrt{y} = x^{1/2} - y^{1/2}$

53. $(8x - y)^{4/5} = \sqrt[5]{(8x - y)^4}$

57. $2x^{-2/5} - (2x)^{-2/5} = \dfrac{2}{x^{2/5}} - \dfrac{1}{(2x)^{2/5}} = \dfrac{2}{\sqrt[5]{x^2}} - \dfrac{1}{\sqrt[5]{(2x)^2}}$

$\qquad\qquad\qquad\qquad = \dfrac{2}{\sqrt[5]{x^2}} - \dfrac{1}{\sqrt[5]{4x^2}}$

61. $\dfrac{4}{\sqrt{2x}} = \dfrac{4}{(2x)^{1/2}} = \dfrac{4(2x)^{1/2}}{(2x)^{1/2}(2x)^{1/2}} = \dfrac{4\sqrt{2x}}{2x} = \dfrac{2\sqrt{2x}}{x}$

65. $\dfrac{\sqrt{32}}{\sqrt{2}} = \sqrt{\dfrac{32}{2}} = \sqrt{16} = 4$

69. $2x^2y^{-3}x^4 = 2x^6y^{-3} = \dfrac{2x^6}{y^3}$

73. $\dfrac{2^0}{(2^{-2}x^{1/2}y^{-2})^3} = \dfrac{1}{2^{-6}x^{3/2}y^{-6}} = \dfrac{2^6y^6}{x^{3/2}} = \dfrac{64y^6 \cdot x^{1/2}}{x^{3/2} \cdot x^{1/2}} = \dfrac{64y^6x^{1/2}}{x^2}$

77. $3^2(27)^{-4/3} = 3^2(3^3)^{-4/3} = 3^2(3^{-4}) = 3^{-2} = \dfrac{1}{3^2} = \dfrac{1}{9}$

81. $\sqrt{x}\sqrt{x^2y^3}\sqrt{xy^2} = x^{1/2}(x^2y^3)^{1/2}(xy^2)^{1/2}$

$$= x^{1/2}(xy^{3/2})(x^{1/2}y)$$

$$= x^2y^{5/2}$$

85. $\dfrac{(x^2)^3}{x^4} \div \left[\dfrac{x^3}{(x^3)^2}\right]^{-2} = \dfrac{x^6}{x^4} \div \dfrac{(x^3)^{-2}}{(x^6)^{-2}} = x^2 \div \dfrac{x^{-6}}{x^{-12}}$

$$= x^2 \div x^{-6-(-12)} = x^2 \div x^6 = \dfrac{x^2}{x^6} = \dfrac{1}{x^4}$$

89. $\left(\dfrac{2x^2y}{3y^3z^{-2}}\right)^2 = \left(\dfrac{2x^2z^2}{3y^2}\right)^2 = \dfrac{2^2(x^2)^2(z^2)^2}{3^2(y^2)^2} = \dfrac{4x^4z^4}{9y^4}$

EXERCISE 0.6

1. $8x - 4y + 2 + 3x + 2y - 5 = 11x - 2y - 3$

5. $\sqrt{x} + \sqrt{2y} + \sqrt{x} + \sqrt{3z} = 2\sqrt{x} + \sqrt{2y} + \sqrt{3z}$

9. $\sqrt{x} + \sqrt{2y} - \sqrt{x} - \sqrt{3z} = \sqrt{2y} - \sqrt{3z}$

13. $3(x^2 + y^2) - x(y + 2x) + 2y(x + 3y)$

$= 3x^2 + 3y^2 - xy - 2x^2 + 2xy + 6y^2 = x^2 + 9y^2 + xy$

17. $-3\{4x(x + 2) - 2[x^2 - (3 - x)]\}$

$= -3\{4x^2 + 8x - 2[x^2 - 3 + x]\}$

$= -3\{4x^2 + 8x - 2x^2 + 6 - 2x\}$

$= -3\{2x^2 + 6x + 6\}$

$= -6x^2 - 18x - 18$

21. $(x + 3)(x - 2) = x^2 + (3 - 2)x + 3(-2) = x^2 + x - 6$

25. $(x + 3)^2 = x^2 + 2(3)x + 3^2 = x^2 + 6x + 9$

29. $(\sqrt{2y} + 3)^2 = (\sqrt{2y})^2 + 2(\sqrt{2y})(3) + 3^2 = 2y + 6\sqrt{2y} + 9$

33. $(x^2 - 3)(x + 4) = x^2(x + 4) - 3(x + 4)$

$= x^3 + 4x^2 - 3x - 12$

37. $x\{3(x - 1)(x - 2) + 2[x(x + 7)]\}$

$= x\{3(x^2 - 3x + 2) + 2[x^2 + 7x]\}$

$= x\{3x^2 - 9x + 6 + 2x^2 + 14x\}$

$= x\{5x^2 + 5x + 6\}$

$= 5x^3 + 5x^2 + 6x$

41. $(x + 5)^3 = x^3 + 3x^2(5) + 3x(5)^2 + 5^3$

$= x^3 + 15x^2 + 75x + 125$

45. $\dfrac{z^2 - 4z}{z} = \dfrac{z^2}{z} - \dfrac{4z}{z} = z - 4$

49.

$$\begin{array}{r} x \\ x + 3\overline{)x^2 + 3x - 1} \\ \underline{x^2 + 3x} \\ -1 \end{array}$$

Ans. $x + \dfrac{-1}{x + 3}$

53.

$$\begin{array}{r} t + 8 \\ t - 8\overline{)t^2 + 0t + 0} \\ \underline{t^2 - 8t} \\ 8t + 0 \\ \underline{8t - 64} \\ 64 \end{array}$$

Ans. $t + 8 + \dfrac{64}{t - 8}$

EXERCISE 0.7

1. $6x + 4 = 2(3x + 2)$

5. $8a^3bc - 12ab^3cd + 4b^4c^2d^2 = 4bc(2a^3 - 3ab^2d + b^3cd^2)$

9. $p^2 + 4p + 3 = (p + 3)(p + 1)$

13. $z^2 + 6z + 8 = (z + 4)(z + 2)$

17. $2x^2 + 12x + 16 = 2(x^2 + 6x + 8) = 2(x + 4)(x + 2)$

21. $6y^2 + 13y + 2 = (6y + 1)(y + 2)$

25. $x^{2/3}y - 4x^{8/3}y^2 = x^{2/3}y(1 - 4x^2y^2) = x^{2/3}y[1^2 - (2xy)^2]$
$$= x^{2/3}y(1 + 2xy)(1 - 2xy)$$

29. $(4x + 2)^2 = [2(2x + 1)]^2 = 2^2(2x + 1)^2 = 4(2x + 1)^2$

33. $(x^3 - 4x) + (8 - 2x^2) = x(x^2 - 4) + 2(4 - x^2)$

$$= x(x^2 - 4) - 2(x^2 - 4)$$

$$= (x^2 - 4)(x - 2)$$

$$= (x + 2)(x - 2)(x - 2)$$

$$= (x - 2)^2(x + 2)$$

37. $x^3 + 8 = x^3 + 2^3 = (x + 2)(x^2 - 2x + 4)$

41. $(x + 3)^3(x - 1) + (x + 3)^2(x - 1)^2$

$$= (x + 3)^2(x - 1)[(x + 3) + (x - 1)]$$

$$= (x + 3)^2(x - 1)[2x + 2]$$

$$= (x + 3)^2(x - 1)[2(x + 1)]$$

$$= 2(x + 3)^2(x - 1)(x + 1)$$

45. $x^4 - 16 = (x^2)^2 - 4^2$

$$= (x^2 + 4)(x^2 - 4)$$

$$= (x^2 + 4)(x + 2)(x - 2)$$

49. $x^4 + x^2 - 2 = (x^2 + 2)(x^2 - 1) = (x^2 + 2)(x + 1)(x - 1)$

EXERCISE 0.8

1. $\dfrac{x^2 - 4}{x^2 - 2x} = \dfrac{(x + 2)(x - 2)}{x(x - 2)} = \dfrac{x + 2}{x}$

5. $\dfrac{6x^2 + x - 2}{2x^2 + 3x - 2} = \dfrac{(3x + 2)(2x - 1)}{(x + 2)(2x - 1)} = \dfrac{3x + 2}{x + 2}$

9. $\dfrac{(2x - 3)(2 - x)}{(x - 2)(2x + 3)} = \dfrac{(2x - 3)(-1)(x - 2)}{(x - 2)(2x + 3)} = \dfrac{(2x - 3)(-1)}{2x + 3}$

$\qquad\qquad\qquad\qquad = \dfrac{3 - 2x}{2x + 3}$

13. $\dfrac{x^2}{6} \div \dfrac{x}{3} = \dfrac{x^2}{6} \cdot \dfrac{3}{x} = \dfrac{3x^2}{6x} = \dfrac{x}{2}$

17. $\dfrac{4x}{3} \div 2x = \dfrac{4x}{3} \cdot \dfrac{1}{2x} = \dfrac{4x}{6x} = \dfrac{2}{3}$

21. $\dfrac{\dfrac{x - 5}{x^2 - 7x + 10}}{x - 2} = (x - 5) \cdot \dfrac{x - 2}{x^2 - 7x + 10}$

$\qquad\qquad = (x - 5) \cdot \dfrac{x - 2}{(x - 2)(x - 5)}$

$\qquad\qquad = (x - 5) \cdot \dfrac{1}{x - 5} = 1$

25. $\dfrac{x^2 + 7x + 10}{x^2 - 2x - 8} \div \dfrac{x^2 + 6x + 5}{x^2 - 3x - 4}$

$= \dfrac{x^2 + 7x + 10}{x^2 - 2x - 8} \cdot \dfrac{x^2 - 3x - 4}{x^2 + 6x + 5}$

$= \dfrac{(x + 5)(x + 2)}{(x - 4)(x + 2)} \cdot \dfrac{(x - 4)(x + 1)}{(x + 5)(x + 1)}$

$= 1$

29. $\dfrac{x^2}{x + 3} + \dfrac{5x + 6}{x + 3} = \dfrac{x^2 + 5x + 6}{x + 3}$

$\qquad\qquad = \dfrac{(x + 3)(x + 2)}{x + 3}$

$\qquad\qquad = x + 2$

33. L.C.D. $= p^2 - 1$

$$1 - \frac{p^2}{p^2 - 1} = \frac{p^2 - 1}{p^2 - 1} - \frac{p^2}{p^2 - 1}$$

$$= \frac{p^2 - 1 - p^2}{p^2 - 1} = \frac{-1}{p^2 - 1}$$

$$= \frac{1}{1 - p^2}$$

37. $x^2 - x - 2 = (x - 2)(x + 1)$ and $x^2 - 1 = (x + 1)(x - 1)$,

so L.C.D. $= (x - 2)(x + 1)(x - 1)$.

$$\frac{1}{(x - 2)(x + 1)} + \frac{1}{(x + 1)(x - 1)}$$

$$= \frac{x - 1}{(x - 2)(x + 1)(x - 1)} + \frac{x - 2}{(x + 1)(x - 1)(x - 2)}$$

$$= \frac{(x - 1) + (x - 2)}{(x - 2)(x + 1)(x - 1)} = \frac{2x - 3}{(x - 2)(x + 1)(x - 1)}$$

41. $(1 + x^{-1})^2 = \left(1 + \frac{1}{x}\right)^2 = \left(\frac{x}{x} + \frac{1}{x}\right)^2 = \left(\frac{x + 1}{x}\right)^2 = \frac{(x + 1)^2}{x^2}$

$$= \frac{x^2 + 2x + 1}{x^2}$$

45. Multiplying the numerator and denominator of the given fraction by x gives

$$\frac{1 + \frac{1}{x}}{3} = \frac{\left(1 + \frac{1}{x}\right)x}{3x} = \frac{x + 1}{3x}$$

49. L.C.D $= \sqrt{x + h} \cdot \sqrt{x}$.

$$\frac{2}{\sqrt{x + h}} - \frac{2}{\sqrt{x}} = \frac{2\sqrt{x}}{\sqrt{x + h}\sqrt{x}} - \frac{2\sqrt{x + h}}{\sqrt{x}\sqrt{x + h}}$$

$$= \frac{2\sqrt{x} - 2\sqrt{x + h}}{\sqrt{x}\sqrt{x + h}}$$

53. $\dfrac{\sqrt{2}}{\sqrt{3} - \sqrt{6}} = \dfrac{\sqrt{2}}{\sqrt{3} - \sqrt{6}} \cdot \dfrac{\sqrt{3} + \sqrt{6}}{\sqrt{3} + \sqrt{6}}$

$$= \dfrac{\sqrt{2}(\sqrt{3} + \sqrt{6})}{3 - 6}$$

$$= \dfrac{\sqrt{6} + \sqrt{12}}{-3}$$

$$= - \dfrac{\sqrt{6} + 2\sqrt{3}}{3}$$

57. $\dfrac{1}{x + \sqrt{5}} = \dfrac{1}{x + \sqrt{5}} \cdot \dfrac{x - \sqrt{5}}{x - \sqrt{5}}$

$$= \dfrac{x - \sqrt{5}}{x^2 - 5}$$

1

Equations

1. $9x - x^2 = 0$.

    $9(1) - (1)^2 \overset{?}{=} 0$

    $9 - 1 \overset{?}{=} 0$

    $8 \neq 0$

    1 does not satisfy the equation.

    $9(0) - (0)^2 \overset{?}{=} 0$

    $0 - 0 \overset{?}{=} 0$

    $0 = 0$

    0 satisfies the equation.

5. $x(7 + x) - 2(x + 1) - 3x = -2$. Setting $x = -3$ gives

    $(-3)(7 - 3) - 2(-3 + 1) - 3(-3) \overset{?}{=} -2$

    $-3(4) - 2(-2) + 9 \overset{?}{=} -2$

    $-12 + 4 + 9 \overset{?}{=} -2$

    $1 \neq -2$

    Thus -3 does not satisfy the equation.

9. Squaring both sides; equivalence *not* guaranteed

13. Multiplying both sides by x-1; equivalence *not* guaranteed

17. $4x = 10$. Dividing both sides by 4 gives $x = \frac{10}{4} = \frac{5}{2}$.

21. $-5x = 10 - 15$, $-5x = -5$. Dividing both sides by 5 gives

$x = \frac{-5}{-5} = 1$.

25. $7x + 7 = 2(x + 1)$, $7x + 7 = 2x + 2$, $5x + 7 = 2$, $5x = -5$,

$x = \frac{-5}{5} = -1$

29. $\frac{x}{5} = 2x - 6$, $x = 5(2x - 6)$, $x = 10x - 30$, $30 = 9x$,

$x = \frac{30}{9} = \frac{10}{3}$

33. $q = \frac{3}{2}q - 4$. Multiplying both sides by 2 gives $2q = 3q - 8$,

$-q = -8$, $q = 8$

37. $\frac{2y - 3}{4} = \frac{6y + 7}{3}$. Multiplying both sides by 12 gives

$3(2y - 3) = 4(6y + 7)$, $6y - 9 = 24y + 28$, $-18y = 37$,

$y = -\frac{37}{18}$

41. $\frac{x + 2}{3} - \frac{2 - x}{6} = x - 2$. Multiplying both sides by 6 gives

$2(x + 2) - (2 - x) = 6(x - 2)$, $2x + 4 - 2 + x = 6x - 12$,

$3x + 2 = 6x - 12$, $2 = 3x - 12$, $14 = 3x$, $x = \frac{14}{3}$

45. $\frac{3}{2}(4x - 3) = 2[x - (4x - 3)]$, $3(4x - 3) = 4[x - 4x + 3]$,

     $12x - 9 = -12x + 12$, $24x = 21$, $x = \frac{21}{24} = \frac{7}{8}$

49. $p = 8q - 1$, $p + 1 = 8q$, $q = \frac{p + 1}{8}$

53. $S = \frac{n}{2}(a_1 + a_n)$, $2S = n(a_1 + a_n)$, $2S = na_1 + na_n$,

     $2S - na_n = na_1$, $a_1 = \dfrac{2S - na_n}{n}$

57. $y = a(1 - by)x$, $y = ax(1 - by)$, $y = ax - abxy$,

     $y + abxy = ax$, $y(1 + abx) = ax$, $y = \dfrac{ax}{1 + abx}$

EXERCISE 1.2

1. $\frac{5}{x} = 25$. Multiplying both sides by x gives $5 = 25x$, $x = \frac{5}{25}$,

     $x = \frac{1}{5}$ (which checks)

5. $\dfrac{4}{8 - x} = \frac{3}{4}$, $4(4) = 3(8 - x)$, $16 = 24 - 3x$, $3x = 8$, $x = \frac{8}{3}$

9. $\dfrac{1}{p - 1} = \dfrac{2}{p - 2}$, $p - 2 = 2(p - 1)$, $p - 2 = 2p - 2$, $p = 0$

13. $\dfrac{3x - 2}{2x + 3} = \dfrac{3x - 1}{2x + 1}$, $(3x - 2)(2x + 1) = (3x - 1)(2x + 3)$,

     $6x^2 - x - 2 = 6x^2 + 7x - 3$, $1 = 8x$, $x = \frac{1}{8}$

17. $\frac{-4}{x - 1} = \frac{7}{2 - x} + \frac{3}{x + 1}$.

Multiplying both sides by $(x - 1)(2 - x)(x + 1)$ gives

$$-4(2 - x)(x + 1) = 7(x - 1)(x + 1) + 3(x - 1)(2 - x)$$

$$-4(-x^2 + x + 2) = 7(x^2 - 1) + 3(-x^2 + 3x - 2)$$

$$4x^2 - 4x - 8 = 4x^2 + 9x - 13$$

$$-13x = -5$$

$$x = \frac{5}{13}$$

21. $\sqrt{x + 6} = 3$, $(\sqrt{x + 6})^2 = 3^2$, $x + 6 = 9$, $x = 3$ (checks)

25. $\sqrt{\frac{x}{2} + 1} = \frac{2}{3}$. Squaring both sides: $\frac{x}{2} + 1 = \frac{4}{9}$, $\frac{x}{2} = -\frac{5}{9}$, $x = -\frac{10}{9}$, which checks.

29. $(x - 3)^{3/2} = 8$, $[(x - 3)^{3/2}]^{2/3} = 8^{2/3}$, $x - 3 = 4$, $x = 7$, which checks.

33. $\sqrt{z^2 + 2z} = 3 + z$. Squaring both sides gives

$z^2 + 2z = (3 + z)^2$, $z^2 + 2z = 9 + 6z + z^2$, $-9 = 4z$,

$z = -\frac{9}{4}$, which checks.

37. $r = \frac{2mI}{B(n + 1)}$. Multiplying both sides by $n + 1$ gives

$r(n + 1) = \frac{2mI}{B}$, $n + 1 = \frac{2mI}{rB}$, $n = \frac{2mI}{rB} - 1$

EXERCISE 1.3

1. $x^2 - 4x + 4 = 0$, $(x - 2)^2 = 0$, $x - 2 = 0$, $x = 2$

5. $(x - 3)(x + 1) = 0$.
   $x - 3 = 0$ or $x + 1 = 0$
   $x = 3$ or $x = -1$.

9. $(x - 2)(x + 2) = 0$.
   $x - 2 = 0$ or $x + 2 = 0$
   $x = 2$ or $x = -2$

13. $4x^2 + 1 = 4x$, $4x^2 - 4x + 1 = 0$, $(2x - 1)^2 = 0$,
    $2x - 1 = 0$, $2x = 1$, $x = \frac{1}{2}$

17. $-x^2 + 3x + 10 = 0$, $x^2 - 3x - 10 = 0$, $(x - 5)(x + 2) = 0$.
    $x - 5 = 0$ or $x + 2 = 0$
    $x = 5$ or $x = -2$

21. $x(x - 1)(x + 2) = 0$.
    $x = 0$ or $x - 1 = 0$ or $x + 2 = 0$
    $x = 0$ or $x = 1$ or $x = -2$

25. $6x^3 + 5x^2 - 4x = 0$, $x(6x^2 + 5x - 4) = 0$,
    $x(2x - 1)(3x + 4) = 0$.
    $x = 0$ or $2x - 1 = 0$ or $3x + 4 = 0$
    $x = 0$ or $x = \frac{1}{2}$ or $x = -\frac{4}{3}$

29. $p(p - 3)^2 - 4(p - 3)^3 = 0.$ Factoring out $(p - 3)^2$ gives

$(p - 3)^2[p - 4(p - 3)] = 0,$ $(p - 3)^2(12 - 3p) = 0,$

$3(p - 3)^2(4 - p) = 0.$

$p - 3 = 0$ or $4 - p = 0$

$p = 3$ or $p = 4$

33. $4x^2 - 12x + 9 = 0.$ $a = 4, b = -12, c = 9.$

$x = \dfrac{-b \pm \sqrt{b^2 - 4ac}}{2a}$

$= \dfrac{-(-12) \pm \sqrt{144 - 4(4)(9)}}{2(4)} = \dfrac{12 \pm \sqrt{0}}{8} = \dfrac{12 \pm 0}{8} = \dfrac{3}{2}.$

37. $4 - 2n + n^2 = 0,$ $n^2 - 2n + 4 = 0.$ $a = 1, b = -2, c = 4.$

$n = \dfrac{-b \pm \sqrt{b^2 - 4ac}}{2a} = \dfrac{-(-2) \pm \sqrt{4 - 4(1)(4)}}{2(1)} = \dfrac{2 \pm \sqrt{-12}}{2},$

so there are no real roots.

41. $2x^2 - 3x = 20,$ $2x^2 - 3x - 20 = 0.$ $a = 2, b = -3, c = -20.$

$x = \dfrac{-b \pm \sqrt{b^2 - 4ac}}{2a}$

$= \dfrac{-(-3) \pm \sqrt{9 - 4(2)(-20)}}{2(2)} = \dfrac{3 \pm \sqrt{169}}{4} = \dfrac{3 \pm 13}{4}.$

$x = \dfrac{3 + 13}{4} = \dfrac{16}{4} = 4$ or $x = \dfrac{3 - 13}{4} = \dfrac{-10}{4} = -\dfrac{5}{2}$

45. $x^2 = \dfrac{x + 3}{2},$ $2x^2 = x + 3,$ $2x^2 - x - 3 = 0,$

$(2x - 3)(x + 1) = 0.$

$2x - 3 = 0$ or $x + 1 = 0$

$x = \dfrac{3}{2}$ or $x = -1$

49. $\frac{6x + 7}{2x + 1} - \frac{6x + 1}{2x} = 1$.

Multiplying both sides by the L.C.D., $2x(2x + 1)$, gives

$2x(6x + 7) - (2x + 1)(6x + 1) = 1(2x)(2x + 1)$,

$12x^2 + 14x - (12x^2 + 8x + 1) = 4x^2 + 2x$,

$6x - 1 = 4x^2 + 2x$, $\quad 0 = 4x^2 - 4x + 1$, $\quad 0 = (2x - 1)^2$,

$2x - 1 = 0$, $\quad 2x = 1$, $\quad x = \frac{1}{2}$

53. $\frac{y + 1}{y + 3} + \frac{y + 5}{y - 2} = \frac{14y + 7}{(y + 3)(y - 2)}$. Multiplying both sides by

the L.C.D., $(y + 3)(y - 2)$, gives

$(y + 1)(y - 2) + (y + 5)(y + 3) = 14y + 7$,

$y^2 - y - 2 + y^2 + 8y + 15 = 14y + 7$,

$2y^2 + 7y + 13 = 14y + 7$, $\quad 2y^2 - 7y + 6 = 0$,

$(2y - 3)(y - 2) = 0$, $\quad y = 3/2$ or $y = 2$. But $y = 2$ does

not check. The solution is $y = \frac{3}{2}$.

57. $\sqrt{x + 2} = x - 4$, $\quad x + 2 = (x - 4)^2$, $\quad x + 2 = x^2 - 8x + 16$,

$0 = x^2 - 9x + 14$, $0 = (x - 7)(x - 2)$, $\quad x = 7$ or $x = 2$.

Only $x = 7$ checks.

61. $\sqrt{x + 7} = 1 + \sqrt{2x}$, $\quad (\sqrt{x + 7})^2 = (1 + \sqrt{2x})^2$,

$x + 7 = 1 + 2\sqrt{2x} + 2x$, $\quad 6 - x = 2\sqrt{2x}$. Squaring both

sides again gives $(6 - x)^2 = 4(2x)$, $\quad 36 - 12x + x^2 = 8x$,

$x^2 - 20x + 36 = 0$, $\quad (x - 18)(x - 2) = 0$, $\quad x = 18$ or $x = 2$.

Only $x = 2$ checks.

65. $\sqrt{x + 5} + 1 = 2\sqrt{x}$, $(\sqrt{x + 5} + 1)^2 = (2\sqrt{x})^2$,

   $x + 5 + 2\sqrt{x + 5} + 1 = 4x$, $2\sqrt{x + 5} = 3x - 6$,

   $(2\sqrt{x + 5})^2 = (3x - 6)^2$, $4(x + 5) = 9x^2 - 36x + 36$,

   $0 = 9x^2 - 40x + 16$, $0 = (9x - 4)(x - 4)$, $x = \frac{4}{9}$ or $x = 4$.

   Only $x = 4$ checks.

69. Given $c = \frac{A}{A + 12}d$ and $c = \frac{A + 1}{24}d$, we set $\frac{A}{A + 12}d = \frac{A + 1}{24}d$.

   Dividing both sides by d and then multiplying both sides
   by $24(A + 12)$ give

$$24A = (A + 12)(A + 1)$$

$$24A = A^2 + 13A + 12$$

$$0 = A^2 - 11A + 12$$

   From the quadratic formula,

$$A = \frac{11 \pm \sqrt{121 - 48}}{2} = \frac{11 \pm \sqrt{73}}{2} = \frac{11 \pm 8.54}{2}.$$

   Thus $A = \frac{11 + 8.54}{2} = \frac{19.54}{2} = 9.77$ or

$$A = \frac{11 - 8.54}{2} = \frac{2.46}{2} = 1.23,$$

   which are not extraneous. Rounding these answers gives
   1 year and 10 years.

CHAPTER 1 - REVIEW PROBLEMS

1. $4 - 3x = 2 + 5x$, $2 = 8x$, $x = \frac{2}{8} = \frac{1}{4}$

5. $2 - w = 3 + w$, $-2w = 1$, $w = -\frac{1}{2}$

9. $2\left(4 - \frac{3}{5}p\right) = 5$, $8 - \frac{6}{5}p = 5$, $-\frac{6}{5}p = -3$, $-6p = -15$, $p = \frac{5}{2}$

13. $\frac{2x}{x - 3} - \frac{x + 1}{x + 2} = 1$.   Multiplying both sides by the L.C.D.,

$(x - 3)(x + 2)$, gives

$(x - 3)(x + 2)\left[\frac{2x}{x - 3} - \frac{x + 1}{x + 2}\right] = (x - 3)(x + 2)[1]$,

$2x(x + 2) - (x - 3)(x + 1) = (x - 3)(x + 2)$,

$2x^2 + 4x - (x^2 - 2x - 3) = x^2 - x - 6$,

$2x^2 + 4x - x^2 + 2x + 3 = x^2 - x - 6$,

$x^2 + 6x + 3 = x^2 - x - 6$, $7x = -9$, $x = -\frac{9}{7}$

17. $5q^2 = 7q$, $5q^2 - 7q = 0$, $q(5q - 7) = 0$.   Thus $q = 0$ or

$5q - 7 = 0$, from which $q = 0$, $7/5$

21. $3x^2 - 5 = 0$, $3x^2 = 5$, $x^2 = \frac{5}{3}$, $x = \pm\sqrt{\frac{5}{3}} = \pm\frac{\sqrt{15}}{3}$

25. $-3x^2 + 5x - 1 = 0$, $3x^2 - 5x + 1 = 0$.   Using the quadratic

formula with $a = 3$, $b = -5$ and $c = 1$ gives

$x = \frac{-b \pm \sqrt{b^2 - 4ac}}{2a} = \frac{-(-5) \pm \sqrt{25 - 4(3)(1)}}{2(3)} = \frac{5 \pm \sqrt{13}}{6}$

29. $\frac{6w + 7}{2w + 1} - \frac{6w + 1}{2w} = 1$.   Multiplying both sides by the

L.C.D., $(2w + 1)(2w)$, gives

$2w(6w + 7) - (2w + 1)(6w + 1) = (2w + 1)(2w)$,

$12w^2 + 14w - (12w^2 + 8w + 1) = 4w^2 + 2w$,

$6w - 1 = 4w^2 + 2w$, $0 = 4w^2 - 4w + 1$, $0 = (2w - 1)^2$,

$2w - 1 = 0$, $2w = 1$, $w = 1/2$

33. $\sqrt{2x + 5} = 5$, $(\sqrt{2x + 5})^2 = 5^2$, $2x + 5 = 25$, $2x = 20$, $x = 10$, which checks.

37. $\sqrt{y} + 6 = 5$, $\sqrt{y} = -1$, which has no solution because the square root of a real number cannot be negative.

41. $x + 2 = 2\sqrt{4x - 7}$, $(x + 2)^2 = (2\sqrt{4x - 7})^2$,

$x^2 + 4x + 4 = 4(4x - 7)$, $x^2 + 4x + 4 = 16x - 28$,

$x^2 - 12x + 32 = 0$, $(x - 4)(x - 8) = 0$, $x = 4$ or $x = 8$

MATHEMATICAL SNAPSHOT - CHAPTER 1

1. (a) $100 + $100(0.114) = $111.40

(b) $1 + $1(0.135) = $1.135

(c) $100 \cdot \dfrac{1 \text{ lb}}{\$1} = 100 \text{ lb}$

(d) $111.40 \cdot \dfrac{1 \text{ lb}}{\$1.135} \approx 98.15 \text{ lb}$

(e) $g = \dfrac{98.15 - 100}{100} = -0.0185 = -1.85\%$ (a loss of 1.85%)

(f) $g = \dfrac{y - i}{1 + i} = \dfrac{0.114 - 0.135}{1 + 0.135} \approx -0.0185 = -1.85\%$

2

Applications of Equations and Inequalities

1. Let q = number of units for $50,000 profit.

$$Profit = Total\ Revenue - Total\ Cost$$
$$50,000 = 3q - (2.20q + 95,000)$$
$$50,000 = 0.80q - 95,000$$
$$145,000 = 0.8q$$
$$\frac{145,000}{0.8} = q$$
$$q = 181,250$$

5. Let p = selling price. Then profit = 0.2p.

$$selling\ price = cost + profit$$
$$p = 3.40 + 0.2p$$
$$0.8p = 3.40$$
$$p = \frac{3.40}{0.8} = \$4.25$$

9. Let n = number of room applications sent out.

$$0.95n = 76, \quad n = \frac{76}{0.95} = 80$$

13. Let q = number of cartridges sold to break even.

$$\text{total revenue} = \text{total cost}$$
$$19.95q = 14.95q + 8000$$
$$5q = 8000$$
$$q = 1600$$

17. Revenue = (number of units sold)(price per unit). Thus

$$400 = q\left[\frac{80 - q}{4}\right]$$
$$1600 = 80q - q^2$$
$$q^2 - 80q + 1600 = 0$$
$$(q - 40)^2 = 0$$
$$q = 40.$$

21. Let n = number of $20 increases. Then at the rental charge of 400 + 20n dollars per suite, the number of suites that can be rented is 50 - 2n. The total of all monthly rents is (400 + 20n)(50 - 2n), which must equal 20,240.

$$20,240 = (400 + 20n)(50 - 2n)$$
$$20,240 = 20,000 + 200n - 40n^2$$
$$40n^2 - 200n + 240 = 0$$
$$n^2 - 5n + 6 = 0$$
$$(n - 2)(n - 3) = 0$$
$$n = 2, 3$$

Thus the rent should be either $400 + 2($20) = $440 or $400 + 3($20) = $460.

25. Setting supply equal to demand gives $2p - 8 = 300 - 2p$,

    $4p = 308$, $p = 77$.

29. Original volume $= (10)(5)(2) = 100$ cm^3. Volume cut from

    bar $= 0.28(100) = 28$ cm^3. Volume of new bar $= 100 - 28 =$

    72 cm^3. Let x = number of centimeters by which the length

    and width are each reduced. Then

    $$(10 - x)(5 - x)2 = 72$$
    $$(10 - x)(5 - x) = 36$$
    $$x^2 - 15x + 50 = 36$$
    $$x^2 - 15x + 14 = 0$$
    $$(x - 1)(x - 14) = 0$$
    $$x = 1 \text{ or } 14$$

    Because of the length and width of the original bar, we

    reject x = 14 and choose x = 1. The new bar has length

    $10 - x = 10 - 1 = 9$ cm and width is $5 - x = 5 - 1 = 4$ cm.

33. Let n = number of acres sold. Then n + 20 acres were

    originally purchased at a cost of 7200/(n + 20) each.

    The price of each acre sold was 30 + [7200/(n + 20)].

    Since the revenue from selling n acres is \$7200 (the

    original cost of the parcel), we have

    $$n\left[30 + \frac{7200}{n + 20}\right] = 7200$$
    $$n\left[\frac{30n + 600 + 7200}{n + 20}\right] = 7200$$
    $$n(30n + 600 + 7200) = 7200(n + 20)$$
    $$30n^2 + 7800n = 7200n + 144{,}000$$
    $$n^2 + 20n - 4800 = 0$$
    $$(n + 80)(n - 60) = 0, \quad n = -80 \text{ or } n = 60.$$

    We choose n = 60 (since n > 0).

EXERCISE 2.2

1. $3x > 12$, $x > \frac{12}{3}$, $x > 4$

    ⟶
    4

5. $-4x \geq 2$, $x \leq \frac{2}{-4}$, $x \leq -\frac{1}{2}$

    ⟵
    $-1/2$

9. $3 < 2y + 3$, $0 < 2y$, $0 < y$, $y > 0$

    ⟶
    0

13. $3(2 - 3x) > 4(1 - 4x)$, $6 - 9x > 4 - 16x$, $7x > -2$, $x > -\frac{2}{7}$

    ⟶
    $-2/7$

17. $x + 2 < \sqrt{3} - x$, $2x < \sqrt{3} - 2$, $x < \frac{\sqrt{3} - 2}{2}$

    ⟵
    $\frac{\sqrt{3} - 2}{2}$

21. $\frac{9y + 1}{4} \leq 2y - 1$, $9y + 1 \leq 8y - 4$, $y \leq -5$

    ⟵
    -5

25. $\frac{1 - t}{2} < \frac{3t - 7}{3}$, $3 - 3t < 6t - 14$, $-9t < -17$, $t > \frac{17}{9}$

    ⟶
    $17/9$

29. $\frac{2}{3}r < \frac{5}{6}r$, $4r < 5r$, $0 < r$, $r > 0$

33. $0.1(0.03x + 4) \geq 0.02x + 0.434$,

    $0.003x + 0.4 \geq 0.02x + 0.434$, $-0.017x \geq 0.034$, $x \leq -2$

EXERCISE 2.3

1. Let q = number of units sold.

$$\text{Profit} > 0$$
$$\text{Tot. Rev.} - \text{Total Cost} > 0$$
$$20q - (15q + 600,000) > 0$$
$$5q - 600,000 > 0$$
$$5q > 600,000$$
$$q > 120,000$$

At least 120,001 must be sold.

5. Let q be the required number of magazines. Then cost of publication is q(0.65). Revenue from dealers is 0.60q and from advertising it is 0.10(q - 10,000)(0.60). Thus

$$\text{Profit} \geq 0$$
$$\text{Total Revenue} - \text{Total Cost} \geq 0$$
$$0.60q + 0.10(q - 10,000)(0.60) - 0.65q \geq 0$$
$$0.01q - 600 \geq 0$$
$$0.01q \geq 600$$
$$q \geq 60,000$$

At least 60,000 magazines are required.

9. Let q be the number of units sold this month at $4.00
   each.   Then 2500 - q will be sold at $4.50 each.
$$4q + 4.5(2500 - q) \geqq 10,750$$
$$-0.5q + 11,250 \geqq 10,750$$
$$500 \geqq 0.5q$$
$$1000 \geqq q$$
The maximum number of units is 1000.

13. Let c be the cost (in dollars) of a ticket.
$$1000 + 0.40(800c) \leqq 2440$$
$$320c \leqq 1440$$
$$c \leqq 4.50$$
Thus the dean could charge at most $4.50 per ticket.
With this charge, the amount left for expenses is
$$800(4.50) - [1000 + 0.40(800)(4.50)] = \$1160.$$

EXERCISE 2.4

1. $|-13| = 13$

5. $\left|3\left(-\frac{5}{3}\right)\right| = |-5| = 5$

9. $|2 - \sqrt{5}| = -(2 - \sqrt{5})$ because $2 - \sqrt{5} < 0$.

13. $|p_1 - p_2| \leqq 2$

17. $\left|\frac{x}{3}\right| = 2$, $\frac{x}{3} = \pm 2$, $x = \pm 6$

21. $|5x - 2| = 0$, $5x - 2 = 0$, $x = \frac{2}{5}$

25. $|x| < 4$, $-4 < x < 4$

29. $|x + 7| < 2$, $-2 < x + 7 < 2$, $-9 < x < -5$

33. $|5 - 2x| \leq 1$, $-1 \leq 5 - 2x \leq 1$, $-6 \leq -2x \leq -4$, $3 \geq x \geq 2$, which may be rewritten as $2 \leq x \leq 3$.

37. $|x - \mu| > h\sigma$. Either $x - \mu > h\sigma$, or $x - \mu < -h\sigma$. Thus either $x > \mu + h\sigma$ or $x < \mu - h\sigma$.

CHAPTER 2 – REVIEW PROBLEMS

1. $3x - 8 \geq 4(x - 2)$, $3x - 8 \geq 4x - 8$, $-x \geq 0$, $x \leq 0$

5. $3p(1 - p) > 3(2 + p) - 3p^2$, $3p - 3p^2 > 6 + 3p - 3p^2$, $0 > 6$, which is false for all x. There is no solution.

9. Multiplying both sides by 8 gives $2s - 24 \leq 3 + 2s$, $0 \leq 27$, which is true for all s. Thus $-\infty < s < \infty$

13. $|4t - 1| < 1$, $-1 < 4t - 1 < 1$, $0 < 4t < 2$, $0 < t < \frac{1}{2}$

17. Let x be the number of issues with decline, and $x + 48$ be the number of issues with increase.
$$x + (x + 48) = 1132, \quad 2x = 1084, \quad x = 542$$

MATHEMATICAL SNAPSHOT - CHAPTER 2

1. $t = 2l - 4 = 2\left(2\frac{1}{2}\right) - 4 = 1$ hour

5. An appropriate formula for this situation is

$$\frac{t}{4} + \frac{l - \frac{lc}{60} - t}{2} = 1.$$

Letting $l = 3$ and $c = 8$ gives

$$\frac{t}{4} + \frac{3 - \frac{3(8)}{60} - t}{2} = 1$$

$$t + 2\left(3 - \frac{2}{5} - t\right) = 4$$

$$-t + \frac{26}{5} = 4$$

$$t = \frac{6}{5} \text{ hr} = 1 \text{ hr and } 12 \text{ min.}$$

Functions
and Graphs

1. The denominator is zero when x = 0. Any other real number
    can be used for x.   <u>Ans.</u> all real numbers except 0

5. Any real number can be used for t. <u>Ans.</u> all real numbers

9. We exclude values of y for which $y^2 - y = 0$,
    $y(y - 1) = 0$, y = 0 or 1.
    <u>Ans.</u> all real numbers except 0 and 1

13. f(x) = 2x + 1
     f(0) = 2(0) + 1 = 1
     f(3) = 2(3) + 1 = 7
     f(-4) = 2(-4) + 1= -7

17. $g(u) = u^2 + u$

    $g(-2) = (-2)^2 + (-2) = 4 - 2 = 2$

    $g(2v) = (2v)^2 + (2v) = 4v^2 + 2v$

    $g(-x^2) = (-x^2)^2 + (-x^2) = x^4 - x^2$

21. $g(x) = \dfrac{x - 5}{x^2 + 4}$

    $g(5) = \dfrac{5 - 5}{5^2 + 4} = 0;$ $g(3x) = \dfrac{3x - 5}{(3x)^2 + 4} = \dfrac{3x - 5}{9x^2 + 4}$

    $g(x + h) = \dfrac{(x + h) - 5}{(x + h)^2 + 4} = \dfrac{x + h - 5}{x^2 + 2xh + h^2 + 4}$

25. $f(x) = 4x - 5$

    (a) $f(x + h) = 4(x + h) - 5 = 4x + 4h - 5$

    (b) $\dfrac{f(x + h) - f(x)}{h} = \dfrac{(4x + 4h - 5) - (4x - 5)}{h} = \dfrac{4h}{h} = 4$

29. $y - 3x - 4 = 0$. The equivalent form $y = 3x + 4$ shows that for each input x there is exactly one output, $3x - 4$. Thus y is a function of x. Solving for x gives $x = \dfrac{y - 4}{3}$. This shows that for each input y there is exactly one output, $\dfrac{y - 4}{3}$. Thus x is a function of y.

33. Yes, because corresponding to each input r there is exactly one output, πr^2.

37. Yes. For each input q there corresponds exactly one output, 1.25q, so P is a function of q. The dependent variable is P and the independent variable is q.

41. (a) Domain: 3000, 2900, 2300, 2000.

    f(2900) = 12,   f(3000) = 10

    (b) Domain: 10, 12, 17, 20.

    g(10) = 3000,   g(17) = 2300

EXERCISE 3.2

1. all real numbers

5. (a) 3,   (b) 7

9. f(x) = 8

    f(2) = 8,   f(t + 8) = 8, $f(-\sqrt{17}) = 8$

13. G(8) = 8, G(3) = 3, G(-1) = 2-(-1) = 3, G(1) = 2-1 = 1

17. (4 - 2)! = 2! = 2·1 = 2

21. (a) C = 850 + 3q
    (b) 1600 = 850 + 3q, 750 = 3q, q = 250

25. (a) all T such that $30 \leqq T \leqq 39$

    (b) $f(30) = \frac{1}{24}(30) + \frac{11}{4} = \frac{5}{4} + \frac{11}{4} = \frac{16}{4} = 4$

    $f(36) = \frac{1}{24}(36) + \frac{11}{4} = \frac{6}{4} + \frac{11}{4} = \frac{17}{4}$

    $f(39) = \frac{4}{3}(39) - \frac{175}{4} = 52 - \frac{175}{4} = \frac{33}{4}$

EXERCISE 3.3

1. $f(x) = x + 3$, $g(x) = x + 5$

   (a) $(f + g)(x) = f(x) + g(x) = (x + 3) + (x + 5) = 2x + 8$

   (b) $(f + g)(0) = 2(0) + 8 = 8$

   (c) $(f - g)(x) = f(x) - g(x) = (x + 3) - (x + 5) = -2$

   (d) $(fg)(x) = f(x)g(x) = (x + 3)(x + 5) = x^2 + 8x + 15$

   (e) $(fg)(-2) = (-2)^2 + 8(-2) + 15 = 3$

   (f) $\frac{f}{g}(x) = \frac{f(x)}{g(x)} = \frac{x + 3}{x + 5}$

   (g) $(f \circ g)(x) = f(g(x)) = f(x + 5) = (x + 5) + 3 = x + 8$

   (h) $(f \circ g)(3) = 3 + 8 = 11$

   (i) $(g \circ f)(x) = g(f(x)) = g(x + 3) = (x + 3) + 5 = x + 8$

5. $f(g(2)) = f(4 - 4) = f(0) = 0 + 6 = 6$

   $g(f(2)) = g(12 + 6) = g(18) = 4 - 36 = -32$

9. $(f \circ g)(v) = f(g(v)) = f(\sqrt{v + 2}) = \dfrac{2}{(\sqrt{v + 2})^2 + 1}$

$$= \frac{1}{v + 2 + 1} = \frac{1}{v + 3}$$

   $(g \circ f)(w) = g(f(w)) = g\left(\dfrac{1}{w^2 + 1}\right) = \sqrt{\dfrac{1}{w^2 + 1} + 2}$

$$= \sqrt{\frac{1 + 2(w^2 + 1)}{w^2 + 1}} = \sqrt{\frac{2w^2 + 3}{w^2 + 1}}$$

13. Let $g(x) = x^2 - 2$ and $f(x) = \frac{1}{x}$. Then

$$h(x) = \frac{1}{x^2 - 2} = \frac{1}{g(x)} = f(g(x))$$

17. $(g \circ f)(m) = g(f(m)) = g\left(\dfrac{40m - m^2}{4}\right) = 40\left(\dfrac{40m - m^2}{4}\right)$

$$= 10(40m - m^2) = 400m - 10m^2.$$

This represents the total revenue received when the
total output of m employees is sold.

EXERCISE 3.4

1.

5. (a) $f(0) = 0$, $f(1) = -1$, $f(-1) = -1$

   (b) Domain: all real numbers

   (c) Range: all nonpositive reals

9. $y = 3x-5$. If $y = 0$, then $0 = 3x-5$, $x = \frac{5}{3}$. If $x = 0$,

   then $y = -5$. Int.: $\left(\frac{5}{3}, 0\right)$, $(0,-5)$. y is a function of x.

   Domain: all real numbers. Range: all real numbers.

   See graph on next page.

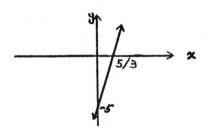

13. x = 0. If y = 0, then x = 0. If x = 0, then y can be
    any real number. Int.: every point on y-axis.
    y is not a function of x.

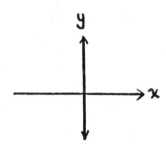

17. x = $-3y^2$. If y = 0, then x = 0. If x = 0, then
    0 = $-3y^2$, y = 0. Int.: (0,0). y is not a function of x.

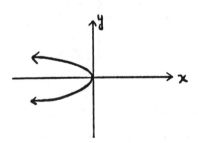

21. s = f(t) = 4-t². If s = 0, then 0 = 4-t²,
     0 = (2+t)(2-t), t = ±2. If t = 0, then s = 4.
     Int.: (2,0), (-2,0), (0,4). Domain: all real numbers.
     Range: all reals ≤ 4.

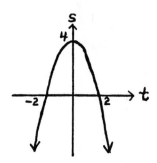

25. y = h(x) = x²-4x+1. If y = 0, then 0 = x²-4x+1, and by

     the quadratic formula, x = $\frac{4 \pm \sqrt{12}}{2}$ = 2 ± $\sqrt{3}$. If x = 0,

     then, y = 1.   Int.: (2±$\sqrt{3}$,0), (0,1).   Domain: all real
     numbers.   Range: all reals ≥ -3.

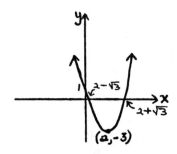

29. s = F(r) = $\sqrt{r-5}$. Note that for $\sqrt{r-5}$ to be a real

     number, r-5 ≥ 0, or r ≥ 5.   If s = 0, then 0 = $\sqrt{r-5}$,
     0 = r-5, or r = 5.   Because r ≥ 5, then r ≠ 0, so no
     s-intercept exists.   Int.: (5,0).   Domain: all reals ≥ 5.
     Range: all reals ≥ 0.   See graph on next page.

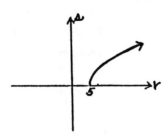

33. $F(t) = \frac{16}{t^2}$. If $F(t) = 0$, then $0 = \frac{16}{t^2}$, which has no

   solution. Because $t \neq 0$, there is no vertical-axis
   intercept. Int.: none. Domain: all nonzero reals.
   Range: all positive reals.

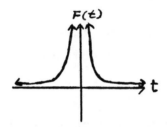

37. Domain: all real numbers; range: all reals ≥ 0

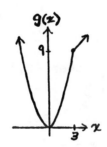

41.

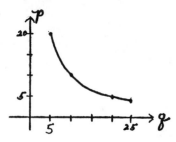

As price decreases, quantity
increases; p is a function of q.

EXERCISE 3.5

1. $y = 5x$. Intercepts: If $y = 0$, then $5x = 0$, or $x = 0$;
   if $x = 0$, then $y = 5 \cdot 0 = 0$. Testing for symmetry about
   (a) x-axis, (b) y-axis, and (c) origin gives:
   a. $-y = 5x$, $y = -5x$;   b. $y = 5(-x) = -5x$;
   c. $-y = 5(-x)$, $y = 5x$.
   Since equivalent equation is obtained in case (c) only,
   the graph only has symmetry about the origin.
   Ans. $(0,0)$; sym. about origin

5. $4x^2 - 9y^2 = 36$. Intercepts: If $y = 0$, then $4x^2 = 36$,
   $x^2 = 9$, $x = \pm 3$; if $x = 0$, then $-9y^2 = 36$, $y^2 = -4$, which
   has no real root. Testing for symmetry gives:
   a. $4x^2 - 9(-y)^2 = 36$, $4x^2 - 9y^2 = 36$;
   b. $4(-x)^2 - 9y^2 = 36$, $4x^2 - 9y^2 = 36$.
   Since equivalent equations are obtained in (a) and (b),
   the graph has symmetry about x- and y-axes. Thus there
   is also symmetry about origin.
   Ans. $(\pm 3, 0)$; sym. about x-axis, y-axis, origin

9. $x = -y^{-4}$. Intercepts: Because $y \neq 0$, there is no x-intercept; if $x = 0$, then $0 = -1/y^4$, which has no solution. Symmetry: a. $x = -(-y)^{-4}$, $x = -y^{-4}$; b. $-x = -y^{-4}$, $x = y^{-4}$; c. $-x = -(-y)^{-4}$, $x = y^{-4}$.

Ans. no intercepts; sym. about x-axis

13. $y = f(x) = \dfrac{x^3}{x^2+5}$. Intercepts: If $y = 0$, then $\dfrac{x^3}{x^2+5} = 0$, $x = 0$; if $x = 0$, then $y = 0$. Symmetry: a. because f is not the zero function, there is no x-axis symmetry;

b. $-y = \dfrac{x^3}{x^2+5}$, $y = -\dfrac{x^3}{x^2+5}$; c. $-y = \dfrac{(-x)^3}{(-x)^2+5}$, $y = \dfrac{x^3}{x^2+5}$

Ans. $(0,0)$; sym. about origin

17. $2x+y^2 = 4$. Intercepts: If $y = 0$, then $2x = 4$, $x = 2$; if $x = 0$, then $y^2 = 4$, $y = \pm 2$. Symmetry: a. $2x+(-y)^2 = 4$, $2x+y^2 = 4$; b. $2(-x)+y^2 = 4$, $-2x+y^2 = 4$; c. $2(-x)+(-y)^2 = 4$, $-2x+y^2 = 4$.

Ans. $(2,0)$, $(0,\pm 2)$; sym. about x-axis

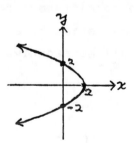

21. $|x|-|y| = 0$.   Intercepts: If $y = 0$, then $|x| = 0$, $x = 0$, if $x = 0$, then $-|y| = 0$, $y = 0$.   Symmetry: a. $|x|-|-y| = 0$, $|x|-|y| = 0$; b. $|-x|-|y| = 0$, $|x|-|y| = 0$; c. from (a) and (b) there is symmetry about x- and y-axes, so symmetry about origin exists.

  Ans. $(0,0)$; sym. about x-axis, y-axis, origin

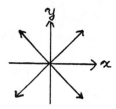

CHAPTER 3 - REVIEW PROBLEMS

1. Denominator is 0 when $x^2 - 3x + 2 = 0$, $(x - 1)(x - 2) = 0$, $x = 1, 2$.   Domain: all real numbers except 1 and 2.

5. For $\sqrt{x}$ to be real, x must be nonnegative.   For the denominator $x - 1$ to be different from 0, x cannot be 1. Both conditions are satisfied by all nonnegative numbers except 1.   Domain: all nonnegative reals except 1.

9. $G(1) = \sqrt{0} = 0$

   $G(10) = \sqrt{9} = 3$

   $G(t + 1) = \sqrt{(t + 1) - 1} = \sqrt{t}$

   $G(x^2) = \sqrt{x^2 - 1}$

13. $f(4) = 8 - 4^2 = 8 - 16 = -8$

$f(-2) = 4$

$f(0) = 4$

$f(10) = 8 - 10^2 = 8 - 100 = -92$

17. $f(x) = 3x - 1$, $g(x) = 2x + 3$

(a) $(f + g)(x) = f(x) + g(x) = (3x-1)+(2x+3) = 5x + 2$

(b) $(f + g)(4) = 5(4) + 2 = 22$

(c) $(f - g)(x) = f(x) - g(x) = (3x-1)-(2x+3) = x - 4$

(d) $(fg)(x) = f(x)g(x) = (3x-1)(2x+3) = 6x^2 + 7x - 3$

(e) $(fg)(1) = 6(1)^2 + 7(1) - 3 = 10$

(f) $\frac{f}{g}(x) = \frac{f(x)}{g(x)} = \frac{3x - 1}{2x + 3}$

(g) $(f \circ g)(x) = f(g(x)) = f(2x+3) = 3(2x+3)-1 = 6x + 8$

(h) $(f \circ g)(5) = 6(5) + 8 = 38$

(i) $(g \circ f)(x) = g(f(x)) = g(3x-1) = 2(3x-1)+3 = 6x + 1$

21. $f(x) = x + 2$, $g(x) = x^3$

$(f \circ g)(x) = f(g(x)) = f(x^3) = x^3 + 2$

$(g \circ f)(x) = g(f(x)) = g(x + 2) = (x + 2)^3$

25. $y = 9-x^2$. Intercepts: If $y = 0$, then $0 = 9-x^2 = (3+x)(3-x)$, or $x = \pm3$; if $x = 0$, then $y = 9$. Testing for symmetry about (a) x-axis, (b) y-axis, and (c) origin gives:

a. $-y = 9-x^2$, $y = -9+x^2$, which is not orig. eq.;

b. $y = 9-(-x)^2$, $y = 9-x^2$, which is orig. eq.;

c. from (b) there is y-axis sym. and from (a) there is

no x-axis sym. So there can be no sym. about origin.

Ans. (0,9), (±3,0); sym. about y-axis

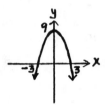

29. y = g(t) = $\frac{2}{t-4}$. Intercepts: If y = 0, then 0 = $\frac{2}{t-4}$,
which has no solution; if t = 0, then y = 2/(-4) = -1/2.
Domain: all real numbers t such that t ≠ 4. Range: all
reals ≠ 0.

Ans. (0, $-\frac{1}{2}$); all t ≠ 4; all nonzero real numbers

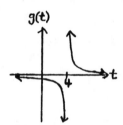

33. From the vertical-line test, the graphs that represent
functions of x are (a) and (c).

CHAPTER 3 -- MATHEMATICAL SNAPSHOT

1. f(100,000) = 16,264.50 + 0.33(100,000 - 71,900)

              = 16,264.50 + 0.33(28,100)

              = 16,264.50 + 9273 = 25,537.50.

Ans. $25,537.50

4

Lines, Parabolas and Systems

1. $m = (10-1)/(7-4) = 9/3 = 3$

5. The difference in the x-coordinates is $5-5 = 0$, so the slope is undefined.

9. $y-8 = 6(x-2)$, $y-8 = 6x-12$, or $6x-y-4 = 0$. See graph on next page.

13. $m = (4-1)/[1-(-6)] = 3/7$, so $y-4 = \frac{3}{7}(x-1)$,

$7(y-4) = 3(x-1)$, $7y-28 = 3x-3$, or $3x-7y+25 = 0$.
See graph on next page.

9.

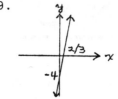

13.

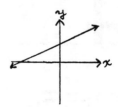

17. y = 2x+4, or 2x-y+4 = 0.   See graph below.

21. A horizontal line has the form y = b.   Thus y = -2, or
    y+2 = 0.   See graph below.

17.

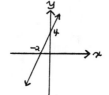

21.

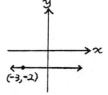

25. y = 2x-1 has the form y = mx+b, where m = 2 and b = -1.
    See graph below.

29. x = -5 is a vertical line.   Thus the slope is undefined.
    There is no y-intercept.   See graph below.

25.

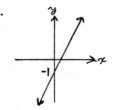

29.

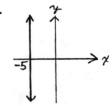

33. y = 1, y = 0x+1. m = 0, b = 1.

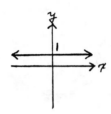

37. 4x+9y-5 = 0 is a general form. 9y = -4x+5, or

    y = - $\frac{4}{9}$x + $\frac{5}{9}$ (slope-intercept form).

41. (1,2), (-3,8). m = (8-2)/(-3-1) = 6/(-4) = -3/2.

    Point-slope form: y-2 = - $\frac{3}{2}$(x-1). If first coordinate is

    5, then x = 5 and y-2 = - $\frac{3}{2}$(5-1), y-2 = - $\frac{3}{2}$(4), y-2 = -6,

    or y = -4. Thus the point is (5,-4).

EXERCISE 4.2

1. y = f(x) = -4x = -4x+0 has the form f(x) = ax+b where

   a = -4 and b = 0. Thus slope = -4 and vertical-axis

   intercept is 0.

   <u>Ans.</u> -4; 0;

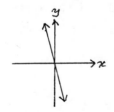

5. $h(q) = \frac{7-q}{2} = \frac{7}{2} - \frac{1}{2}q$ has the form $h(q) = aq+b$ where

   $a = -1/2$ and $b = 7/2$.

   <u>Ans.</u> $-1/2$; $7/2$;

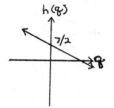

9. Let $y = f(x)$. The points $(1,2)$ and $(-2,8)$ lie on the

   graph of f. $m = (8-2)/(-2-1) = -2$. Thus $y-2 = -2(x-1)$

   or $y = -2x+4$.   <u>Ans.</u> $f(x) = -2x+4$

13. Let $y = f(x)$. The points $(-2,-1)$ and $(-4,-3)$ lie on the

   graph of f. $m = (-3+1)/(-4+2) = 1$. Thus $y+1 = 1(x+2)$ or

   $y = x+1$.   <u>Ans.</u> $f(x) = x+1$

17. The line passing through $(10,40)$ and $(20,70)$ has slope

   $(70-40)/(20-10) = 3$ and an equation for the line is

   $c-40 = 3(q-10)$ or $c = 3q+10$. If $q = 35$, then $c =$

   $3(35)+10 = 105+10 = 115$.   <u>Ans.</u> $c = 3q+10$; \$115

21. At \$200/ton, x tons cost 200x, and at \$2000/acre, y acres

   cost 2000y. Hence the required equation is $200x+2000y =$

   $20,000$, which can be written as $x+10y = 100$.

   <u>Ans.</u> $x+10y = 100$

25. $p = f(t) = at+b$, $f(5) = 0.32$, a = slope = 0.059.

    (a) $p = f(t) = 0.059t+b$. Since $f(5) = 0.32$,

       $0.32 = 0.059(5)+b$, $0.32 = 0.295+b$, or $b = 0.025$.

       Thus $p = 0.059t + 0.025$.

    (b) When $t = 9$, then $p = 0.059(9) + 0.025 = 0.556$.

    <u>Ans.</u> (a) $p = 0.059t + 0.025$; (b) 0.556

EXERCISE 4.3

1. $f(x) = 5x^2$ has the form $f(x) = ax^2+bx+c$ where $a = 5$,

   $b = 0$, and $c = 0$.   <u>Ans.</u> quadratic

5. $h(q) = (q+4)^2 = q^2+8q+16$ has the form $h(q) = aq^2+bq+c$

   where $a = 1$, $b = 8$, and $c = 16$.   <u>Ans.</u> quadratic

9. $y = f(x) = -4x^2+8x+7$. $a = -4$, $b = 8$, $c = 7$.

    (a) Vertex occurs when $x = -b/(2a) = -8/[2(-4)] = 1$.

       When $x = 1$, then $y = f(1) = -4(1)^2+8(1)+7 = 11$.

       Vertex: $(1,11)$.

    (b) $a = -4 < 0$. Thus vertex corresponds to highest

       point.

13. $y = f(x) = x^2-6x+5$. $a = 1$, $b = -6$, $c = 5$.

    Vertex: $-b/(2a) = -(-6)/(2 \cdot 1) = 3$.

         $f(3) = 3^2-6(3)+5 = -4$. Vertex $= (3,-4)$.

    y-intercept: $c = 5$.

    x-intercepts: $x^2-6x+5 = (x-1)(x-5) = 0$, so $x = 1, 5$.

    Range: all $y \geqq -4$. See next page for graph.

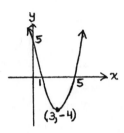

17. $s = h(t) = t^2+2t+1.$ $a = 1, b = 2, c = 1.$

    Vertex: $-b/(2a) = -2/(2 \cdot 1) = -1.$

           $h(-1) = (-1)^2+2(-1)+1 = 0.$ Vertex $= (-1,0).$

    s-intercept: $c = 1.$

    t-intercepts: $t^2+2t+1 = (t+1)^2 = 0,$ so $t = -1.$

    Range: all $s \geqq 0.$

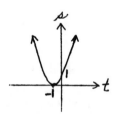

21. $t = f(s) = s^2-8s+13.$ $a = 1, b = -8, c = 13.$

    Vertex: $-b/(2a) = -(-8)/(2 \cdot 1) = 4.$

           $f(4) = 4^2-8(4)+13 = -3.$ Vertex $= (4,-3).$

    t-intercept: $c = 13.$

    s-intercepts: Solving $s^2-8s+13 = 0$ by the quadratic form-

         ula gives $s = \dfrac{-(-8) \pm \sqrt{(-8)^2 - 4(1)(13)}}{2(1)} =$

     $\dfrac{8 \pm \sqrt{12}}{2} = \dfrac{8 \pm 2\sqrt{3}}{2} = 4 \pm \sqrt{3}.$

    Range: all $t \geqq -3.$ See next page for graph.

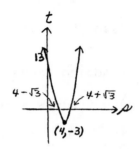

25. $f(x) = 4x - 50 - 0.1x^2$. Because $a = -0.1 < 0$, parabola
    opens downward and $f(x)$ has a maximum value. $-b/(2a) =$
    $-4/[2(-0.1)] = 20$. $f(20) = 4(20) - 50 - 0.1(20)^2 = -10$.
    <u>Ans.</u> maximum; -10

29. $f(P) = (-1/50)P^2+2P+20$, $0 \leqq P \leqq 100$.   Because $a =$
    $-1/50 < 0$, $f(P)$ has a maximum value that occurs at the
    vertex. $- \dfrac{b}{2a} = - \dfrac{2}{2(-1/50)} = 50$.   The maximum value of
    $f(P)$ is $f(50) = (-1/50)(50)^2+2(50)+20 = 70$.
    <u>Ans.</u> 70 grams

EXERCISE 4.4

1. $\begin{cases} x+4y = 3, \\ 3x-2y = -5. \end{cases}$ From Eq.(1), $x = 3-4y$.   Substituting in
    Eq.(2) gives $3(3-4y)-2y = -5$, $9-12y-2y = -5$, $-14y = -14$,
    or $y = 1$. $x = 3-4y = 3-4(1) = -1$.
    <u>Ans.</u> $x = -1$, $y = 1$

5. $\begin{cases} 5v+2w = 36, \\ 8v-3w = -54. \end{cases}$ Multiplying Eq.(1) by 3 and Eq.(2) by 2

gives $\begin{cases} 15v+6w = 108, \\ 16v-6w = -108. \end{cases}$ Adding gives $31v = 0$, or $v = 0$.

From $5v+2w = 36$, we have $5(0)+2w = 36$, or $w = 18$.

<u>Ans.</u> $v = 0$, $w = 18$

9. $\begin{cases} \frac{2}{3}x + \frac{1}{2}y = 2, \\ \frac{3}{8}x + \frac{5}{6}y = -\frac{11}{2}. \end{cases}$ Clearing of fractions, we have

$\begin{cases} 4x+ 3y = 12, \\ 9x+20y = -132. \end{cases}$ Multiplying first equation by 9 and

second equation by -4 gives $\begin{cases} 36x+27y = 108, \\ -36x-80y = 528. \end{cases}$ Adding

gives $-53y = 636$, or $y = -12$. From $4x+3y = 12$, we have

$4x+3(-12) = 12$, $4x = 48$, or $x = 12$. <u>Ans.</u> $x = 12$, $y = -12$

13. $\begin{cases} 2x+ y+6z = 3, \\ x- y+4z = 1, \\ 3x+2y-2z = 2. \end{cases}$ Adding Eqs.(1) and (2), and adding 2

times Eq.(2) to Eq.(3) give $\begin{cases} 3x+10z = 4, \\ 5x+ 6z = 4. \end{cases}$ Multiplying

the first equation by 5 and the second equation by -3

give $\begin{cases} 15x+50z = 20, \\ -15x-18z = -12. \end{cases}$ By adding, we have $32z = 8$, or

$z = 1/4$. From $3x+10z = 4$, we have $3x+10(1/4) = 4$,

$3x = 3/2$, or $x = 1/2$. From $2x+y+6z = 3$, we have

$2(1/2) + y + 6(1/4) = 3$, or $y = 1/2$.

<u>Ans.</u> $x = 1/2$, $y = 1/2$, $z = 1/4$

17. Let x = number of gallons of 20% solution and y = number
    of gallons of 30% solution. Then
    $$\begin{cases} x + y = 700, \\ 0.20x + 0.30y = 0.24(700). \end{cases}$$
    From Eq.(1), y = 700-x. Substituting in Eq.(2) gives
    0.20x + 0.30(700-x) = 0.24(700), -0.10x + 210 = 168,
    -0.10x = -42, or x = 420. y = 700-x = 700 - 420 = 280.
    <u>Ans.</u> 420 gal of 20% solution and 280 gal of 30% solution

21. Let x = number of calculators produced at Exton, y =
    number of calculators produced at Whyton. The total cost
    at Exton is 7.50x + 7000 and the total cost at Whyton is
    6.00y + 8800. Thus 7.50x + 7000 = 6.00y + 8800. Also,
    x + y = 1500. This gives the system
    $$\begin{cases} x + y = 1500, \\ 7.50x + 7000 = 6.00y + 8800. \end{cases}$$
    From Eq.(1), y = 1500-x. Substituting in Eq.(2) gives
            7.50x + 7000 = 6.00(1500-x) + 8800,
    7.50x + 7000 = 9000 - 6x + 8800, 13.5x = 10,800, or
    x = 800. y = 1500 - x = 1500 - 800 = 700.
    <u>Ans.</u> 800 calculators at Exton plant, 700 calculators at
        Whyton plant

25. Let x = number of units of Argon I and y = number of
    units of Argon II that the company can make. These
    require 6x+10y doodles and 3x+8y skeeters. Thus
    $\begin{cases} 6x+10y = 760, \\ 3x+ 8y = 500. \end{cases}$ Multiplying Eq.(2) by -2 gives
    $\begin{cases} 6x+10y = 760, \\ -6x-16y = -1000. \end{cases}$ By adding, we obtain -6y = -240, or
    y = 40. From Eq.(1), 6x+10(40) = 760, 6x = 360, or

x = 60.   Ans. 60 units of Argon I, 40 units of Argon II

29. Let x = number of skilled workers employed,
    y = number of semiskilled workers employed,
    z = number of shipping clerks employed.

number of workers: x+y+z = 70,
wages: 8x+4y+5z = 370,
semiskilled: y = 2x.

From Eq.(3), y = 2x. Substituting in Eqs.(1) and (2)

gives $\begin{cases} x+(2x)+z = 70, \\ 8x+4(2x)+5z = 370, \end{cases}$ or $\begin{cases} 3x+ z = 70, \\ 16x+5z = 370. \end{cases}$

Adding -5 times first equation to second equation gives

x = 20. From y = 2x, y = 2(20) = 40. From x+y+z = 70,

20+40+z = 70, or z = 10.   Ans. 40 semiskilled workers,

20 skilled workers, 10 shipping clerks

EXERCISE 4.5

1. From Eq.(2), y = -3x. Substituting in Eq.(1) gives

   $-3x = 4-x^2$, $x^2-3x-4 = 0$, $(x-4)(x+1) = 0$. Thus x = 4, -1.
   From y = -3x, if x = 4, then y = -3(4) = -12; if x = -1,
   then y = -3(-1) = 3.   Ans. x = 4, y = -12; x = -1, y = 3

5. Substituting $y = x^2$ into $x = y^2$ gives $x = x^4$, $x^4-x = 0$,

   $x(x^3-1) = 0$. Thus x = 0, 1. From $y = x^2$, if x = 0, then

   $y = 0^2 = 0$; if x = 1, then $y = 1^2 = 1$.

   Ans. x = 0, y = 0; x = 1, y = 1

9. Substituting $p = \sqrt{q}$ in Eq.(2) gives $\sqrt{q} = q^2$. By squaring both sides, we have $q = q^4$, $q^4 - q = 0$, $q(q^3 - 1) = 0$.
Thus $q = 0$, 1. From $p = \sqrt{q}$, if $q = 0$, then $p = \sqrt{0} = 0$;
if $q = 1$, then $p = \sqrt{1} = 1$.
<u>Ans.</u> $p = 0$, $q = 0$; $p = 1$, $q = 1$

13. Substituting $x = y+6$ in Eq.(2) gives $y = 3\sqrt{(y+6)+4} =$
$3\sqrt{y+10}$. Squaring gives $y^2 = 9(y+10)$, $y^2 - 9y - 90 = 0$,
$(y-15)(y+6) = 0$. Thus $y = 15$, -6. But $y = -6$ does not
satify Eq.(2) [a negative number does not equal a non-
negative number]. If $y = 15$, then $x = y+6 = 15+6 = 21$.
These values of x and y satisfy the system.
<u>Ans.</u> $x = 21$, $y = 15$

<u>EXERCISE 4.6</u>

1. Equating p-values gives $\frac{3}{100}q + 2 = -\frac{7}{100}q + 12$,
$\frac{1}{10}q = 10$, or $q = 100$. When $q = 100$, then $p = \frac{3}{100}q + 2 =$
$\frac{3}{100}(100) + 2 = 5$.
<u>Ans.</u> (100, 5);

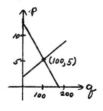

5. Equating p-values gives $2q+20 = 200-2q^2$, $2q^2+2q-180 = 0$, $q^2+q-90 = 0$, $(q+10)(q-9) = 0$. Thus q = -10, 9. Since q $\geqq$ 0, choose q = 9. Then p = 2q+20 = 2(9)+20 = 38. <u>Ans.</u> (9, 38)

9. Letting $y_{TR} = y_{TC}$ gives 3q = 2q+4500, or q = 4500. <u>Ans.</u> 4500 units;

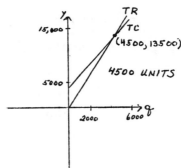

13. Letting $y_{TR} = y_{TC}$ gives $100 - \dfrac{1000}{q+10} = q+40$. Multiplying both sides by q+10 gives $100(q+10)-1000 = (q+10)(q+40)$, $q^2-50q+400 = 0$, $(q-10)(q-40) = 0$. Thus q =10, 40. <u>Ans.</u> 10 units or 40 units

17. Since profit = tot. rev. - tot. cost, then
4600 = 8.35q-(2116+7.20q). Solving gives
4600 = 1.15q-2116, 1.15q = 6716, q = 6716/1.15 = 5840.
For a loss (negative profit) of $1150 we solve -1150 = 8.35q-(2116+7.20q). Thus -1150 = 1.15q-2116, 1.15q = 966, or q = 840. To break even, we have $y_{TR} = y_{TC}$, which gives 8.35q = 2116+7.20q, 1.15q = 2167, or q = 1840. <u>Ans.</u> 5840 units; 840 units; 1840 units

21. $y_{TC} = 2q+1050$; $y_{TR} = 50\sqrt{q}$. Letting $y_{TR} = y_{TC}$ gives

$50\sqrt{q} = 2q+1050$, or $25\sqrt{q} = q+525$. Squaring gives

$625q = q^2+1050q+(525)^2$, or $q^2+425q+(525)^2 = 0$. By the

quadratic formula, $q = \dfrac{-425 \pm \sqrt{(425)^2 - 4(1)(525)^2}}{2}$,

which is not real. <u>Ans.</u> total cost always exceeds

total revenue - no break-even point.

25. Equating q_A-values gives $8-p_A+p_B = -2+5p_A-p_B$,

$10 = 6p_A-2p_B$, or $5 = 3p_A-p_B$. Equating q_B-values gives

$26+p_A-p_B = -4-p_A+3p_B$, $30 = -2p_A+4p_B$, or $15 = -p_A+2p_B$.

Now we solve $\begin{cases} 3p_A- p_B = 5, \\ -p_A+2p_B = 15. \end{cases}$ Adding 2 times the first

equation to the second gives $5p_A = 25$, or $p_A = 5$. From

$3p_A-p_B = 5$, $3(5)-p_B = 5$, or $p_B = 10$.

<u>Ans.</u> $p_A = 5$, $p_B = 10$

CHAPTER 4 - REVIEW PROBLEMS

1. Solving $\dfrac{k-5}{3-2} = 4$ gives $k-5 = 4$, $k = 9$.

5. $y-4 = \frac{1}{2}(x-10)$, $y-4 = \frac{1}{2}x - 5$.

Slope-intercept form: $y = \frac{1}{2}x - 1$.

$2y = 2\left(\frac{1}{2}x - 1\right)$, $2y = x-2$. General form: $x-2y-2 = 0$.

9. $3x-2y = 4$, $-2y = -3x+4$, or $y = \frac{3}{2}x - 2$. $m = 3/2$

   Ans. $y = \frac{3}{2}x - 2$; $\frac{3}{2}$;

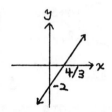

13. $y = f(x) = 4-2x$ has the linear form $f(x) = ax+b$ where
    $a = -2$, $b = 4$.

    Ans. -2; $(0,4)$;

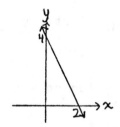

17. $y = h(t) = t^2-4t-5$ has the quadratic form $h(t) = at^2+bt+c$
    where $a = 1$, $b = -4$, $c = -5$.
    Vertex: $-b/(2a) = -(-4)/(2 \cdot 1) = 2$.

    $\qquad h(2) = 2^2-4(2)-5 = -9$.   Vertex $= (2,-9)$.
    y-intercept: $c = -5$.

    t-intercepts: $t^2-4t-5 = (t-5)(t+1) = 0$, so $t = 5$, -1.

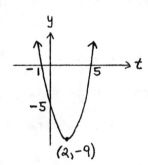

21. $y = F(x) = -(x^2+2x+3) = -x^2-2x-3$ has the quadratic form

$F(x) = ax^2+bx+c$ where $a = -1$, $b = -2$, $c = -3$.

Vertex: $-b/(2a) = -(-2)/[2(-1)] = -1$.

$F(-1) = -[(-1)^2+2(-1)+3] = -2$.   Vertex $= (-1,-2)$.

y-intercept: $c = -3$.

x-intercepts: Because parabola opens downward ($a < 0$) and

vertex is below x-axis, there is no

x-intercept.

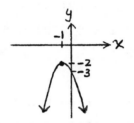

25. $\begin{cases} 4x+5y = 3, \\ 3x+4y = 2. \end{cases}$ Multiplying Eq.(1) by 3 and Eq.(2) by -4

gives $\begin{cases} 12x+15y = 9, \\ -12x-16y = -8. \end{cases}$ Adding gives $-y = 1$, or $y = -1$.

From Eq.(1), $4x+5(-1) = 3$, $4x = 8$, or $x = 2$.

Ans. $x = 2$, $y = -1$

29. $\begin{cases} 3x-2y+z = -2, \\ 2x+ y+z = 1, \\ x+3y-z = 3. \end{cases}$ Subtracting Eq.(2) from Eq.(1), and

adding Eq.(2) to Eq.(3) give $\begin{cases} x-3y = -3, \\ 3x+4y = 4. \end{cases}$ Adding -3

times the first equation to the second equation gives

$13y = 13$, or $y = 1$.   From $x-3y = -3$, $x-3(1) = -3$, or

$x = 0$.   From $3x-2y+z = -2$, $3(0)-2(1)+z = -2$, or $z = 0$.

Ans. $x = 0$, $y = 1$, $z = 0$

33. a = 1 when b = 2; a = 2 when b = 1. $m = \dfrac{a_2-a_1}{b_2-b_1} = \dfrac{2-1}{1-2} =$
$\dfrac{1}{-1}$ = -1. An equation is a-1 = -1(b-2), or a = -b+3 or
a+b-3 = 0. When b = 3, then a = -b+3 = -(3)+3 = 0.
<u>Ans.</u> a+b-3 = 0; 0

37. r = pq = (200-2q)q = $200q-2q^2$, which is a quadratic
function with a = -2, b = 200, c = 0. Since a < 0, r has
a maximum value when q = -b/(2a) = -200/(-4) = 50. If
q = 50, then r = [200-2(50)](50) = 5000.
<u>Ans.</u> 50 units; $5000

41. (a) R = aL+b. If L = 0, then R = 1310. Thus
1310 = 0L+b, or b = 1310. So R = aL+1310. Since
R = 1460 when L = 2, 1460 = a(2)+1310, 150 = 2a, or
a = 75. Thus R = 75L+1310.   <u>Ans.</u> R = 75L+1310

(b) If L = 1, then R = 75(1)+1310 = 1385.
<u>Ans.</u> 1385 milliseconds

(c) Since R = 75L+1310, the slope is 75. The slope gives
the change in R for each 1-unit increase in L.
<u>Ans.</u> The slope is 75. The time necessary to travel
from one level to the next level is 75 milli-
seconds.

CHAPTER 4 - MATHEMATICAL SNAPSHOT

1. $m = 16$, $h = 1$, $t = 45$, $c = 4$.

(a) $z = \left[\dfrac{(m-c)(60h+t)}{30c} + 1.5\right] = \left[\dfrac{(16-4)(60 \cdot 1+45)}{30 \cdot 4} + 1.5\right]$

$= \left[\dfrac{12(105)}{120} + 1.5\right] = [10.5 + 1.5] = [12] = 12$

(b) $F(x) = \begin{cases} \left[\frac{12}{11}c + 0.5\right], & \text{if } x = 2, \\ \left[\frac{16}{11}c + 0.5\right], & \text{if } x = 3, \\ \left[\frac{m-c}{z-1}(x-1) + c + 0.5\right], & \text{otherwise} \end{cases}$

$= \begin{cases} \left[\frac{12}{11}(4) + 0.5\right], & \text{if } x = 2, \\ \left[\frac{16}{11}(4) + 0.5\right], & \text{if } x = 3, \\ \left[\frac{16-4}{12-1}(x-1) + 4 + 0.5\right], & \text{otherwise} \end{cases}$

$= \begin{cases} [4.864], & \text{if } x = 2, \\ [6.318], & \text{if } x = 3, \\ \left[\frac{12}{11}(x-1) + 4.5\right], & \text{otherwise} \end{cases}$

$= \begin{cases} 4, & \text{if } x = 2, \\ 6, & \text{if } x = 3, \\ \left[\frac{12}{11}(x-1) + 4.5\right], & \text{otherwise} \end{cases}$

(c) $F(1) = [0 + 4.5] = [4.5] = 4$,

$F(2) = 4$,

$F(3) = 6$,

$F(4) = \left[\frac{12}{11}(3) + 4.5\right] = [7.773] = 7$,

$F(5) = \left[\frac{12}{11}(4) + 4.5\right] = [8.864] = 8$,

$F(6) = \left[\frac{12}{11}(5) + 4.5\right] = [9.955] = 9$,

$$F(7) = \left[\frac{12}{11}(6) + 4.5\right] = [11.045] = 11,$$

$$F(8) = \left[\frac{12}{11}(7) + 4.5\right] = [12.136] = 12,$$

$$F(9) = \left[\frac{12}{11}(8) + 4.5\right] = [13.227] = 13,$$

$$F(10) = \left[\frac{12}{11}(9) + 4.5\right] = [14.318] = 14,$$

$$F(11) = \left[\frac{12}{11}(10) + 4.5\right] = [15.409] = 15,$$

$$F(12) = \left[\frac{12}{11}(11) + 4.5\right] = [16.5] = 16.$$

5

Exponential and Logarithmic Functions

1.

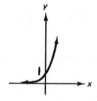

5.

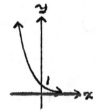

9.

13. (a) $700(1.035)^{30} \approx 700(2.806794) \approx \$1964.76$

   (b) $1964.76 - 700 = \$1264.76$

17. (a) $5000(1.0075)^{30} \approx 5000(1.251272) = \$6256.36$

    (b) $6256.36 - 5000 = \$1256.36$

21. $8000\left(1 + \frac{0.0625}{365}\right)^{3(365)} \approx \$9649.69$

25. 4.4817

29. For 2010 we have t = 20, so

    $P = 125,000(1.12)^{20/20} = 125,000(1.12)^1 = 140,000$

33. $f(0) = 0.399e^0 = 0.399(1) = 0.399$

    $f(-1) = f(1) = (0.399)e^{-0.5} \approx (0.399)(0.60653) \approx 0.242$

37. After one half-life, $\frac{1}{2}$ gram remains. After two half-

    lives, $\frac{1}{2} \cdot \frac{1}{2} = \left(\frac{1}{2}\right)^2 = \frac{1}{4}$ gram remains. Continuing in this

    manner, after n half-lives, $\left(\frac{1}{2}\right)^n$ gram remains. Because

    $\frac{1}{16} = \left(\frac{1}{2}\right)^4$, after 4 half-lives, $\frac{1}{16}$ gram remains. This

    corresponds to $4 \cdot 8 = 32$ years.   <u>Ans.</u> 32 years

<u>EXERCISE 5.2</u>

1. $\log 10,000 = 4$

5. $\ln 7.3891 = 2$

9.

13. Because $3^3 = 27$, $\log_3 27 = 3$

17. Because $10^{-2} = 0.01$, $\log 0.01 = -2$

21. Because $2^{-3} = \frac{1}{8}$, $\log_2 \frac{1}{8} = -3$

25. $5^3 = x$, $x = 125$

29. $e^2 = x$

33. $x^{-1} = \frac{1}{6}$, $x = 6$

37. $x^2 = 6 - x$, $x^2 + x - 6 = 0$, $(x + 3)(x - 2) = 0$. The roots of this equation are -3 and 2. But since $x > 0$, we choose $x = 2$.

41. $e^{3x} = 2$. In logarithmic form, $3x = \ln 2$, $x = \frac{\ln 2}{3}$

45. 1.60944

49. $c = (12 \ln 6) + 20 \approx 12(1.79176) + 20 \approx 41.50$

53. $u_0 = A \ln(x_1) + \dfrac{x_2^2}{2}, \quad u_0 - \dfrac{x_2^2}{2} = A \ln(x_1),$

$\ln(x_1) = \dfrac{u_0 - \dfrac{x_2^2}{2}}{A}, \quad x_1 = e^{[u_0-(x_2^2/2)]/A}$

EXERCISE 5.3

1. $\log 15 = \log(5 \cdot 3) = \log 5 + \log 3 = 0.6990 + 0.4771$
$$= 1.1761$$

5. $\log 36 = \log 6^2 = 2 \log 6 = 2(0.7782) = 1.5564$

9. $\log_7 7^{48} = 48$

13. $\log_2 3 = \dfrac{\log 3}{\log 2} = \dfrac{0.4771}{0.3010} = 1.5850$

17. $\log 10 + \ln e^3 = \log_{10} 10 + \log_e e^3 = 1 + 3 = 4$

21. $\ln \dfrac{x^2}{(x + 1)^3} = \ln x^2 - \ln(x + 1)^3 = 2 \ln x - 3 \ln(x + 1)$

25. $\ln \dfrac{x}{(x + 1)(x + 2)} = \ln x - \ln[(x + 1)(x + 2)]$
$$= \ln x - [\ln(x + 1) + \ln (x + 2)]$$
$$= \ln x - \ln(x + 1) - \ln(x + 2)$$

29. $\ln\left[\dfrac{1}{x+2}\sqrt[5]{\dfrac{x^2}{x+1}}\right] = \ln\left[\dfrac{1}{x+2}\left(\dfrac{x^2}{x+1}\right)^{1/5}\right]$

$\qquad\qquad\qquad = \ln\dfrac{x^{2/5}}{(x+2)(x+1)^{1/5}}$

$\qquad\qquad\qquad = \ln x^{2/5} - \ln[(x+2)(x+1)^{1/5}]$

$\qquad\qquad\qquad = \dfrac{2}{5}\ln x - [\ln(x+2) + \ln(x+1)^{1/5}]$

$\qquad\qquad\qquad = \dfrac{2}{5}\ln x - \ln(x+2) - \dfrac{1}{5}\ln(x+1)$

33. $\log_2 \dfrac{2x}{x+1}$

37. $2 + 10\log(1.05) = \log 100 + \log(1.05)^{10}$

$\qquad\qquad\qquad\quad = \log[100(1.05)^{10}]$

41. $10^{\log x^2} = 4, \quad x^2 = 4, \quad x = \pm 2$

45. From the change of base formula with $b = 3$, $m = x^2 + 1$,
and $a = e$, we have

$$\log_3(x^2 + 1) = \dfrac{\log_e(x^2 + 1)}{\log_e 3} = \dfrac{\ln(x^2 + 1)}{\ln 3}.$$

49. $M = \log(A) + 3$

   (a) $M = \log(1) + 3 = 0 + 3 = 3$

   (b) Given $M_1 = \log(A_1) + 3$, let

$\qquad\qquad M = \log(100A_1) + 3$

$\qquad\qquad M = \log 100 + \log(A_1) + 3$

$\qquad\qquad M = 2 + [\log(A_1) + 3]$

$\qquad\qquad M = 2 + M_1$

EXERCISE 5.4

1. $\log(2x + 1) = \log(x + 6)$, $2x + 1 = x + 6$, $x = 5.000$

5. $e^{2x}e^{5x} = e^{14}$, $e^{7x} = e^{14}$, $7x = 14$, $x = 2.000$

9. $e^{2x} = 5$, $2x = \ln 5$, $x = \dfrac{\ln 5}{2} \approx \dfrac{1.60944}{2} \approx 0.805$

13. $10^{4/x} = 6$, $\dfrac{4}{x} = \log 6$, $x = \dfrac{4}{\log 6} \approx \dfrac{4}{0.7782} \approx 5.140$

17. $2^x = 5$, $\ln 2^x = \ln 5$, $x \ln 2 = \ln 5$,

   $x = \dfrac{\ln 5}{\ln 2} \approx \dfrac{1.60944}{0.69315} \approx 2.322$

21. $2^{-2x/3} = \dfrac{4}{5}$, $\ln 2^{-2x/3} = \ln \dfrac{4}{5}$, $-\dfrac{2x}{3} \ln 2 = \ln \dfrac{4}{5}$,

   $-\dfrac{2x}{3} = \dfrac{\ln \frac{4}{5}}{\ln 2} = \dfrac{\ln 4 - \ln 5}{\ln 2}$,

   $x = -\dfrac{3}{2}\left(\dfrac{\ln 4 - \ln 5}{\ln 2}\right) \approx -\dfrac{3}{2}\left(\dfrac{1.38629 - 1.60944}{0.69315}\right) \approx 0.483$

25. $\log(x-3) = 3$, $10^3 = x - 3$, $x = 10^3 + 3 = 1003.000$

29. $\log(3x-1) - \log(x-3) = 2$, $\log \dfrac{3x-1}{x-3} = 2$, $10^2 = \dfrac{3x-1}{x-3}$,

   $100(x - 3) = 3x - 1$, $97x = 301$, $x = \dfrac{299}{97} \approx 3.082$

33. $\log_2\left(\dfrac{2}{x}\right) = 3 + \log_2 x$, $\log_2\left(\dfrac{2}{x}\right) - \log_2 x = 3$, $\log_2 \dfrac{2/x}{x} = 3$,

   $\log_2 \dfrac{2}{x^2} = 3$, $2^3 = \dfrac{2}{x^2}$, $x^2 = \dfrac{1}{4}$, $x = \pm\dfrac{1}{2}$. However, $x = \dfrac{1}{2}$ is

   the only value that satisfies the original equation.

   Ans. 0.500

37. (a) When t = 0, $Q = 100e^{-0.035(0)} = 100e^0 = 100 \cdot 1 = 100$

   (b) If Q = 20, then $20 = 100e^{-0.035t}$. Solving for t gives

   $$\frac{20}{100} = e^{-0.035t}$$

   $$\frac{1}{5} = e^{-0.035t}$$

   $$\ln \frac{1}{5} = -0.035t$$

   $$-\ln 5 = -0.035t$$

   $$t = \frac{\ln 5}{0.035} \approx \frac{1.60944}{0.035} \approx 46$$

41. If P = 1,500,000, then $1,500,000 = 1,000,000(1.02)^t$.
   Solving for t gives

   $$\frac{1,500,000}{1,000,000} = (1.02)^t$$

   $$1.5 = (1.02)^t$$

   $$\ln 1.5 = \ln(1.02)^t$$

   $$\ln 1.5 = t \ln 1.02$$

   $$t = \frac{\ln 1.5}{\ln 1.02} \approx \frac{0.40547}{0.01980} \approx 20.48$$

45. Let I be the original intensity. The intensity of light
   passing through 1 sheet is 0.9I. The intensity of light
   passing through 2 sheets is $0.9[(0.9)I[= (0.9)^2 I$. Continuing in this manner, the light passing through n sheets
   is $(0.9)^n I$. The equation to solve is $(0.9)^n I = 0.5I$ or,
   more simply, $(0.9)^n = 0.5$. Solving gives

   $$\ln(0.9)^n = \ln 0.5$$

   $$n \ln 0.9 = \ln 0.5$$

   $$n = \frac{\ln 0.5}{\ln 0.9} \approx \frac{\ln(1/2)}{\ln(9/10)} = \frac{-\ln 2}{\ln 9 - \ln 10}$$

   $$n \approx \frac{-0.69315}{2.19722 - 2.30259} \approx 7$$

CHAPTER 5 - REVIEW PROBLEMS

1. $\log_3 243 = 5$

5. $\ln 54.598 = 4$

9. Because $2^{-4} = \frac{1}{16}$, $\log_2 \frac{1}{16} = -4$

13. $5^x = 125$, $x = 3$

17. $x^2 = 2x + 3$, $x^2 - 2x - 3 = 0$, $(x - 3)(x + 1) = 0$.
    Because $x > 0$, we choose $x = 3$.

21. $2 \log 5 - 3 \log 3 = \log 5^2 - \log 3^3 = \log \frac{5^2}{3^3} = \log \frac{25}{27}$

25. $\frac{1}{2} \log_2 x + 2 \log_2 x^2 - 3 \log_2(x + 1) - 4 \log_2(x + 2)$

    $= \log_2 x^{1/2} + \log_2(x^2)^2 - [\log_2(x + 1)^3 + \log_2(x + 2)^4]$

    $= \log_2(x^{1/2}x^4) - \log_2[(x + 1)^3(x + 2)^4]$

    $= \log_2 \frac{x^{9/2}}{(x + 1)^3(x + 2)^4}$

29. $\ln \sqrt[3]{xyz} = \ln(xyz)^{1/3} = \frac{1}{3} \ln(xyz) = \frac{1}{3}(\ln x + \ln y + \ln z)$

33. $\log_3(x + 5) = \frac{\log_e(x + 5)}{\log_e 3} = \frac{\ln(x + 5)}{\ln 3}$

37. $\log(16\sqrt{3}) = \log 4^2 + \log\sqrt{3} = 2 \log 4 + \frac{1}{2} \log 3 = 2y + \frac{1}{2}x$

41. In exponential form, $y = e^{x^2+2}$.

45. $3^{4x} 9^{x+1}$, $3^{4x} = (3^2)^{x+1}$, $3^{4x} = 3^{2(x+1)}$, $4x = 2(x + 1)$,

   $4x = 2x + 2$, $2x = 2$, $x = 1$

49. $e^{3x} = 2$, $3x = \ln 2$, $x = \dfrac{\ln 2}{3} \approx \dfrac{0.69315}{3} \approx 0.231$

53. $4^{x+3} = 7$, $\ln 4^{x+3} = \ln 7$, $(x + 3)\ln 4 = \ln 7$,

   $x + 3 = \dfrac{\ln 7}{\ln 4}$, $x = \dfrac{\ln 7}{\ln 4} - 3$, $x \approx \dfrac{1.94591}{1.38629} - 3 \approx -1.596$

57. $4000\left(1 + \dfrac{0.11}{12}\right)^{60} \approx \$6915.66$

61. $R = 10e^{-t/40}$

   (a) If $t = 20$,

   $R = 10e^{-20/40} = 10e^{-1/2} \approx 10(0.60653) \approx 6$

   (b) $5 = 10e^{-t/40}$, $\dfrac{1}{2} = e^{-t/40}$. Thus

   $-\dfrac{t}{40} = \ln \dfrac{1}{2} = -\ln 2$,

   so $t = 40 \ln 2 \approx 40(0.69315) \approx 28$

CHAPTER 5 — MATHEMATICAL SNAPSHOT

1. $T = \dfrac{P(1 - e^{-dkI})}{e^{kI} - 1}$.

   (a) $T(e^{kI} - 1) = P(1 - e^{-dkI})$, $\dfrac{T(e^{kI} - 1)}{1 - e^{-dkI}} = P$ or

   $P = \dfrac{T(e^{kI} - 1)}{1 - e^{-dkI}}$

(b) $T(e^{kI} - 1) = P - Pe^{-dkI}$, $Pe^{-dkI} = P - T(e^{kI} - 1)$,

$$e^{-dkI} = \frac{P - T(e^{kI} - 1)}{P}, \quad -dkI = \ln\left[\frac{P - T(e^{kI} - 1)}{P}\right],$$

$$d = -\frac{1}{kI} \ln\left[\frac{P - T(e^{kI} - 1)}{P}\right],$$

$$d = \frac{1}{kI} \ln\left[\frac{P}{P - T(e^{kI} - 1)}\right]$$

6

Mathematics of Finance

1. (a) $6000(1.08)^8 \approx 6000(1.850930) \approx \$11,105.58$

   (b) $11,105.58 - 6000 = \$5105.58$

5. $\left(1 + \frac{0.08}{365}\right)^{365} - 1 \approx 0.0832776$ or 8.32776%

9. $6000(1.08)^7 \approx 6000(1.713824) \approx \$10,282.94$

13. (a) $(0.015)(12) = 0.18$ or 18%

    (b) $(1.015)^{12} - 1 \approx 0.195618$ or 19.56%

17. 7.8% compounded semiannually is equivalent to an effective rate of $(1.039)^2 - 1 = 0.079521$ or 7.9521%. Thus 8% compounded annually, which is the effective rate, is the better rate.

21. Let r = effective rate.

    $300,000 = 100,000(1 + r)^{10}$, $(1 + r)^{10} = 3$, $1 + r = 3^{1/10}$,

    $r = 3^{1/10} - 1 \approx 0.1161$ or 11.61%

EXERCISE 6.2

1. $6000(1.05)^{-20} \approx 6000(0.376889) \approx 2261.33

5. $2000(1.0075)^{-30} \approx 2000(0.799187) \approx 1598.37

9. $8000\left(1 + \frac{0.10}{12}\right)^{-60} \approx 4862.31

13. $27,000(1.03)^{-22} \approx 27,000(0.521893) \approx $14,091.11$

17. Let x be the payment at the end of 6 years. The equation
    of value at year 6 is

    $2000(1.07)^4 + 4000(1.07)^2 + x = 5000(1.07) + 5000(1.07)^{-4}$
    Thus

    $x = 5000(1.07)+5000(1.07)^{-4}-2000(1.07)^4-4000(1.07)^2$

    $\approx 5000(1.07)+5000(0.762895)-2000(1.310796)-4000(1.144900)$

    $\approx $1963.28.$

21. We consider the value of each investment at the end of
    eight years. The savings account has a value of

    $10,000(1.03)^{16} \approx 1000(1.604706) = $16,047.06.$

    The business investment has a value of $16,000. Thus the
    better choice is the savings account.

25. $4700 = 10,000\left(1 + \frac{r}{4}\right)^{-32}$, $\quad 4700 = \dfrac{10,000}{\left(1 + \frac{r}{4}\right)^{32}}$,

$\left(1 + \frac{r}{4}\right)^{32} = \dfrac{10,000}{4700} = \dfrac{100}{47}$, $\quad 1 + \frac{r}{4} = \sqrt[32]{\dfrac{100}{47}}$,

$r = 4\left[\sqrt[32]{\dfrac{100}{47}} - 1\right] \approx 0.0955$ or 9.55%

EXERCISE 6.3

1. 64, $64\left(\frac{1}{2}\right) = 32$, $64\left(\frac{1}{2}\right)^2 = 16$, $64\left(\frac{1}{2}\right)^3 = 8$, $64\left(\frac{1}{2}\right)^4 = 4$

5. $s = \dfrac{\frac{2}{3}\left[1 - \left(\frac{2}{3}\right)^5\right]}{1 - \frac{2}{3}} = \dfrac{\frac{2}{3}\left[\frac{211}{243}\right]}{\frac{1}{3}} = \dfrac{422}{243}$

9. $a_{\overline{35}|.04} \approx 18.664613$

13. $500a_{\overline{5}|.07} \approx 500(4.100197) \approx \$2050.10$

17. $800 + 800a_{\overline{11}|.035} \approx 800 + 800(9.001551) \approx \$8001.24$

21. $5000s_{\overline{20}|.07} \approx 5000(40.995492) = \$204{,}977.46$

25. $75a_{\overline{30}|.005} - 25a_{\overline{6}|.005} \approx 75(27.794054) - 25(5.896384)$

$\approx \$1937.14$

29. (a) $\left(50s_{\overline{48}|.005}\right)(1.005)^{24} \approx 50(54.097832)(1.127160)$

$\approx \$3048.85$

(b) $3048.85 - 48(50) = \$648.85$

33. The original annual payment is $25,000/s_{\overline{10}|.06}$. After

    six years the value of the fund is

    $$\frac{25,000}{s_{\overline{10}|.06}} s_{\overline{6}|.06}.$$

    This accumulates to

    $$\left[\frac{25,000}{s_{\overline{10}|.06}} s_{\overline{6}|.06}\right](1.07)^4.$$

    Let x be the amount of the new payment.

    $$x s_{\overline{4}|.07} = 25,000 - \left[\frac{25,000}{s_{\overline{10}|.06}} s_{\overline{6}|.06}(1.07)^4\right]$$

    $$x = \frac{25,000 - \left[\frac{25,000}{s_{\overline{10}|.06}} s_{\overline{6}|.06}(1.07)^4\right]}{s_{\overline{4}|.07}}$$

    $$x \approx \frac{25,000 - \left[\frac{25,000}{13.180795}(6.975319)(1.310796)\right]}{4.439943}$$

    $$x \approx \$1725$$

37. $700 a_{\overline{360}|.0125} = 700\left[\frac{1 - (1.0125)^{-360}}{0.0125}\right] \approx 55,360.30$

41. $50,000 + 50,000 a_{\overline{19}|.12}$

    $= 50,000 + 50,000\left[\frac{1 - (1.12)^{-19}}{0.12}\right]$

    $\approx \$418,288.84$

EXERCISE 6.4

1. $R = \frac{2000}{a_{\overline{36}|.0125}} \approx \frac{2000}{28.847267} \approx \$69.33$

5. (a) $R = \dfrac{7500}{a_{\overline{36}|}.01} \approx \dfrac{7500}{30.107505} \approx \$249.11$

   (b) $7500(.01) = \$75$ (c) $249.11 - 75 = \$174.11$

9. $R = \dfrac{900}{a_{\overline{5}|}.025} \approx \dfrac{900}{4.645828} \approx \$193.72$

   The interest for period 1 is $(0.025)(900) = \$22.50$,
   so the principal repaid at the end of that period is
   $193.72 - 22.50 = \$171.22$. The principal outstanding at
   the beginning of period 2 is $900 - 171.22 = \$728.78$. The
   interest for that period is $(0.025)(728.78) = \$18.22$,
   so the principal repaid at the end of that period is
   $193.72 - 18.22 = \$175.50$. The principal outstanding at
   the beginning of period 3 is $728.78 - 175.50 = \$553.28$.
   Continuing in this manner, we obtain the following
   amortization schedule.

Period	Prin. Outs. at beginning	Int. for period	Pmt. at end	Prin. repaid at end
1	900.00	22.50	193.72	171.22
2	728.78	18.22	193.72	175.50
3	553.28	13.83	193.72	179.89
4	373.39	9.33	193.72	184.39
5	189.00	4.73	193.72	188.99
		68.61	968.60	899.99

13. Each of the original payments is $\dfrac{10,000}{a_{\overline{10}|}.04}$. After two

    years the value of the remaining payments is

    $\left(\dfrac{10,000}{a_{\overline{10}|}.04}\right)a_{\overline{6}|}.04$. Thus the new annual payment is

    $\dfrac{10,000a_{\overline{6}|}.04}{a_{\overline{10}|}.04} \cdot \dfrac{1}{a_{\overline{6}|}.05} \approx \dfrac{10,000(5.242137)}{8.110896} \cdot \dfrac{1}{5.075692} \approx \$1273.$

17. $n = \dfrac{\ln\left[\dfrac{100}{100 - 2000(0.015)}\right]}{\ln 1.015} \approx 23.956.$ Thus the number of

full payments is 23.

21. $\dfrac{25,000}{a_{\overline{60}|}.0125} - \dfrac{25,000}{a_{\overline{60}|}.01}$

$= 25,000\left[\dfrac{1}{a_{\overline{60}|}.0125} - \dfrac{1}{a_{\overline{60}|}.01}\right]$

$= 25,000\left[\dfrac{0.0125}{1 - (1.0125)^{-60}} - \dfrac{0.01}{1 - (1.01)^{-60}}\right]$

$\approx \$38.64$

CHAPTER 6 – REVIEW PROBLEMS

1. $s = 2 + 1 + \dfrac{1}{2} + \ldots + 2\left(\dfrac{1}{2}\right)^5 = \dfrac{2\left[1 - \left(\dfrac{1}{2}\right)^6\right]}{1 - \dfrac{1}{2}} = \dfrac{2\left[\dfrac{63}{64}\right]}{\dfrac{1}{2}} = \dfrac{63}{16}$

5. Let x be the payment at the end of 2 years. The equation
of value at the end of year 2 is

$$1000(1.04)^4 + x = 1200(1.04)^{-4} + 1000(1.04)^{-8}.$$

Thus

$x = 1200(1.04)^{-4} + 1000(1.04)^{-8} - 1000(1.04)^4$

$\approx 1200(0.854804) + 1000(0.730690) - 1000(1.169859)$

$\approx \$586.60$

9. $100s_{\overline{9}|}.035 \approx 100(10.368496) \approx \$1036.85$

13. Let x be the first payment. An equation of value now is

$$x + 2x(1.07)^{-3} = 500(1.05)^{-3} + 500(1.03)^{-8}$$

$$x[1 + 2(1.07)^{-3}] = 500(1.05)^{-3} + 500(1.03)^{-8}$$

$$x = \frac{500(1.05)^{-3} + 500(1.03)^{-8}}{1 + 2(1.07)^{-3}}$$

$$x \approx \frac{500(0.863838) + 500(0.789409)}{1 + 2(0.816298)}$$

$$\approx \$314.00$$

17. Monthly payment is

$$\frac{11,000}{a_{\overline{48}|.01125}} = 11,000\left[\frac{0.01125}{1 - (1.01125)^{-48}}\right] \approx \$297.84$$

Finance charge is $48(297.84) - 11,000 = \$3296.32$

MATHEMATICAL SNAPSHOT - CHAPTER 6

1. $\dfrac{12 + 11 + 10 + 9}{78} \cdot 150 = \$80.77$

7

Introduction to Probability and Statistics

1.

	Assembly Line	Finishing Line	Production Route
		D	AD
	A	E	AE
		D	BD
Start	B	E	BE
		D	CD
	C	E	CE

5. $P_{6,6} = \dfrac{6!}{(6-6)!} = \dfrac{6!}{0!} = \dfrac{6 \cdot 5 \cdot 4 \cdot 3 \cdot 2 \cdot 1}{1} = 720$

9. $C_{100,100} = \dfrac{100!}{100!(100-100)!} = \dfrac{1}{0!} = \dfrac{1}{1} = 1$

13. There are 5 science courses and 4 humanities. By the basic counting principle, the number of selections is $5 \cdot 4 = 20$.   Ans. 20

17. For each of the 10 questions, there are 2 choices. By the basic counting principle, the number of ways to answer the examination is $2 \cdot 2 \cdot \ldots \cdot 2 = 2^{10} = 1024$.
<u>Ans.</u> 1024

21. On each roll of a die, there are 6 possible outcomes. By the basic counting principle, on 3 rolls the number of possible results is $6 \cdot 6 \cdot 6 = 6^3 = 216$.   <u>Ans.</u> 216

25. The number of ways of selecting 10 of 12 questions (without regard to order) is $C_{12,10} = \dfrac{12!}{10!(12-10)!} = \dfrac{12!}{10! \cdot 2!} = \dfrac{12 \cdot 11 \cdot 10!}{10! \cdot 2 \cdot 1} = 66$.   <u>Ans.</u> 66

29. To score 80, 90, or 100, exactly 8, 9, or 10 questions must be correct, respectively. The number of ways in which 8 of 10 questions are correct is $C_{10,8} = \dfrac{10!}{8!(10-8)!} = \dfrac{10!}{8! \cdot 2!} = \dfrac{10 \cdot 9 \cdot 8!}{8! \cdot 2 \cdot 1} = 45$. For 9 of 10 questions, the number of ways is $C_{10,9} = \dfrac{10!}{9!(10-9)!} = \dfrac{10!}{9! \cdot 1!} = \dfrac{10 \cdot 9!}{9! \cdot 1} = 10$, and for 10 of 10 questions, it is $C_{10,10} = \dfrac{10!}{10!(10-10)!} = \dfrac{10!}{10! \cdot 0!} = 1$. Thus the number of ways to score 80 or better is $45+10+1 = 56$.   <u>Ans.</u> 56

33. To fill the four offices by different people, 4 of 12 members must be selected, and order is important. This can be done in $P_{12,4} = 12 \cdot 11 \cdot 10 \cdot 9 = 11,880$ ways. If the president and vice president must be different members, then there are 12 choices for president, 11 for vice

president, 12 for secretary, and 12 for treasurer. By
the basic counting principle, the offices can be filled
in $12 \cdot 11 \cdot 12 \cdot 12 = 19{,}008$ ways.   <u>Ans.</u> 11,880; 19,008

37. Since there are 26 letters, there are 26 choices for the
first symbol. For the second symbol, there are 9 choices
(the numbers 1 through 9). For each of the third,
fourth, and fifth symbols, there are 10 choices (the numbers 0 through 9). By the basic counting principle, the
number of codes is $26 \cdot 9 \cdot 10 \cdot 10 \cdot 10 = 234{,}000$.
<u>Ans.</u> 234,000

EXERCISE 7.2

1. $\{9D, 9H, 9C, 9S\}$

5. $\{lo, lv, le, ov, oe, ve, ol, vl, el, vo, eo, ev\}$

9. There are 52 ways to draw a card and 6 ways for a die to
turn up. By the basic counting principle, the number of
sample points is $52 \cdot 6 = 312$.   <u>Ans.</u> 312

13. The sample points that are either in E_1, or in E_2, or in
both E_1 and E_2 are 1, 3, 5, 7, and 9. Thus $E_1 \cup E_2 =$
$\{1, 3, 5, 7, 9\}$.   <u>Ans.</u> $\{1, 3, 5, 7, 9\}$

17. The sample points in S that are not in E_2 are 1, 2, 4, 6,
8, and 10. Thus $E_2' = \{1, 2, 4, 6, 8, 10\}$.
<u>Ans.</u> $\{1, 2, 4, 6, 8, 10\}$

21. $E_1 \cap E_2 \neq \emptyset$; $E_1 \cap E_3 \neq \emptyset$; $E_1 \cap E_4 = \emptyset$; $E_2 \cap E_3 = \emptyset$;

   $E_2 \cap E_4 \neq \emptyset$; $E_3 \cap E_4 = \emptyset$. Thus E_1 and E_4, E_2 and E_3,

   and E_3 and E_4 are mutually exclusive.

   <u>Ans.</u> E_1 and E_4, E_2 and E_3, E_3 and E_4

25. (a) {HHH,HHT,HTH,HTT,THH,THT,TTH,TTT};

   (b) {HHH,HHT,HTH,HTT,THH,THT,TTH};

   (c) {HHT,HTH,HTT,THH,THT,TTH,TTT};

   (d) $E_1 \cup E_2$ = {HHH,HHT,HTH,HTT,THH,THT,TTH,TTT} = S;

   (e) {HHT,HTH,HTT,THH,THT,TTH};

   (f) $(E_1 \cup E_2)'$ = S' = $\emptyset$;

   (g) $(E_1 \cap E_2)'$ = {HHT,HTH,HTT,THH,THT,TTH}' = {HHH,TTT}

<u>EXERCISE 7.3</u>

1. (a) E_8 = {(2,6),(3,5),(4,4),(5,3),(6,2)}.

   $$P(E_8) = \frac{n(E_8)}{n(S)} = \frac{5}{36}.$$

   (b) E_{2or3} = {(1,1),(1,2),(2,1)}.

   $$P(E_{2or3}) = \frac{n(E_{2or3})}{n(S)} = \frac{3}{36} = \frac{1}{12}.$$

   (c) $E_{3,4,or5}$ = $\begin{Bmatrix} (1,2),(2,1),(1,3),(2,2), \\ (3,1),(1,4),(2,3),(3,2),(4,1) \end{Bmatrix}$.

   $$P(E_{3,4,or5}) = \frac{n(E_{3,4,or5})}{n(S)} = \frac{9}{36} = \frac{1}{4}.$$

   (d) E_{12or13} = E_{12}, since E_{13} is an impossible event.

   E_{12} = {(6,6)}. $P(E_{12or13}) = \frac{n(E_{12or13})}{n(S)} = \frac{1}{36}.$

(e) $E_2 = \{(1,1)\}$, $\quad E_4 = \{(1,3),(2,2),(3,1)\}$,

$\quad E_6 = \{(1,5),(2,4),(3,3),(4,2),(5,1)\}$,

$\quad E_8 = \{(2,6),(3,5),(4,4),(5,3),(6,2)\}$,

$\quad E_{10} = \{(4,6),(5,5),(6,4)\}$, $\quad E_{12} = \{(6,6)\}$.

$\quad P(E_{even}) = P(E_2)+P(E_4)+P(E_6)+P(E_8)+P(E_{10})+P(E_{12})$

$$= \frac{1}{36} + \frac{3}{36} + \frac{5}{36} + \frac{5}{36} + \frac{3}{36} + \frac{1}{36} = \frac{18}{36} = \frac{1}{2}.$$

(f) $P(E_{odd}) = 1 - P(E_{even}) = 1 - \frac{1}{2} = \frac{1}{2}$.

(g) $E'_{less\ than\ 10} = E_{10} \cup E_{11} \cup E_{12} =$

$\quad \{(4,6),(5,5),(6,4)\} \cup \{(5,6),(6,5)\} \cup \{(6,6)\} =$

$\quad \{(4,6),(5,5),(6,4),(5,6),(6,5),(6,6)\}$.

$\quad P(E_{less\ than\ 10}) = 1 - P(E'_{less\ than\ 10}) = 1 - \frac{6}{36} = \frac{5}{6}$.

5. $n(S) = 2 \cdot 6 \cdot 52 = 624$.

(a) $P(tail,3,queen\ of\ hearts) = \frac{n(E_{T,3,QH})}{n(S)} = \frac{1 \cdot 1 \cdot 1}{624} = \frac{1}{624}$

(b) $P(tail,3,queen) = \frac{n(E_{T,3,Q})}{n(S)} = \frac{1 \cdot 1 \cdot 4}{624} = \frac{1}{156}$

(c) $P(head,2or3,queen) = \frac{n(E_{H,2or3,Q})}{n(S)} = \frac{1 \cdot 2 \cdot 4}{624} = \frac{1}{78}$

(d) $P(head,even,diamond) = \frac{n(E_{H,E,D})}{n(S)} = \frac{1 \cdot 3 \cdot 13}{624} = \frac{1}{16}$

9. $n(S) = 2 \cdot 2 \cdot 2 = 8$.

(a) $E_{3\ girls} = \{GGG\}$. $P(3\ girls) = \frac{n(E_{3\ girls})}{n(S)} = \frac{1}{8}$.

(b) $E_{1\ boy} = \{BGG,GBG,GGB\}$. $P(1\ boy) = \frac{n(E_{1\ boy})}{n(S)} = \frac{3}{8}$.

(c) $E_{no\ girl} = \{BBB\}$. $P(no\ girl) = \frac{n(E_{no\ girl})}{n(S)} = \frac{1}{8}$.

(d) $P(at\ least\ 1\ girl) = 1 - P(no\ girl) = 1 - \frac{1}{8} = \frac{7}{8}$.

13. The sample space consists of 60 stocks. Thus $n(S) = 60$.

(a) $P(10\% \text{ or more}) = \dfrac{n(E_{10\% \text{ or more}})}{n(S)} = \dfrac{48}{60} = \dfrac{4}{5}$

(b) $P(\text{less than } 10\%) = 1 - P(10\% \text{ or more}) = 1 - \dfrac{4}{5} = \dfrac{1}{5}$

17. The sample space consists of combinations of 2 people selected from 5. Thus $n(S) = C_{5,2} = \dfrac{5!}{2! \cdot 3!} = \dfrac{5 \cdot 4}{2} = 10$. Because there are only 2 women in the group, the number of possible 2 women committees is 1. Thus $P(2 \text{ women}) = \dfrac{n(E_{2 \text{ women}})}{n(S)} = \dfrac{1}{10}$.

21. A poker hand is a 5 card deal from 52 cards. Thus $n(S) = C_{52,5}$. In 52 cards, there are 4 cards with a particular face value. Thus, for a full house, the number of ways of selecting 3 of 4 cards with a particular face value is $C_{4,3}$. Since there are 13 face values, 3 cards with the same face value can be dealt in $13 \cdot C_{4,3}$ ways.

For the two remaining cards in the full house, there are 12 face values that are possible, and for each face value there are $C_{4,2}$ ways of dealing a pair. Thus

$$P(\text{full house}) = \frac{n(E_{\text{full house}})}{n(S)} = \frac{13 \cdot C_{4,3} \cdot 12 \cdot C_{4,2}}{C_{52,5}}.$$

EXERCISE 7.4

1. $\mu = \underset{X}{\Sigma}xf(x) = 0(0.1)+1(0.4)+2(0.2)+3(0.3) = 0 + 0.4 +$

   $0.4 + 0.9 = 1.7.$ $Var(X) = \underset{X}{\Sigma}x^2f(x) - \mu^2 =$

   $[0^2(0.1)+1^2(0.4)+2^2(0.2)+3^2(0.3)] - (1.7)^2 =$
   $[0 + 0.4 + 0.8 + 2.7] - 2.89 = 3.9 - 2.89 = 1.01.$

   $\sigma = \sqrt{Var(X)} = \sqrt{1.01} = 1.00.$

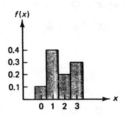

5. Dist. of X: $f(0) = \frac{1}{8}$, $f(1) = \frac{3}{8}$, $f(2) = \frac{3}{8}$, $f(3) = \frac{1}{8}$.

   $E(X) = \underset{X}{\Sigma}xf(x) = 0\left(\frac{1}{8}\right)+1\left(\frac{3}{8}\right)+2\left(\frac{3}{8}\right)+3\left(\frac{1}{8}\right) = \frac{12}{8} = \frac{3}{2} = 1.5;$

   $\sigma^2 = Var(X) = \underset{X}{\Sigma}x^2f(x) - [E(x)]^2 =$

   $\left[0^2\left(\frac{1}{8}\right)+1^2\left(\frac{3}{8}\right)+2^2\left(\frac{3}{8}\right)+3^2\left(\frac{1}{8}\right)\right] - \left(\frac{3}{2}\right)^2 = \frac{24}{8} - \frac{9}{4} = \frac{6}{8} = \frac{3}{4} = 0.75;$

   $\sigma = \sqrt{\frac{3}{4}} = \frac{\sqrt{3}}{2} = 0.87$

9. Let X = daily earnings (in dollars).
   Dist. of X: $f(200) = 4/7$, $f(-30) = 3/7$.

   $E(X) = \underset{X}{\Sigma}xf(x) = 200\left(\frac{4}{7}\right) + (-30)\left(\frac{3}{7}\right) = \frac{710}{7} = 101.43.$

   Ans. $101.43

13. Let p = annual premium (in dollars). If X = gain (in dollars) to company from a policy, then X = p or X = -(80,000-p). Thus

$$E(X) = -(80,000-p)(0.0002) + p(0.9998) = 50.$$

Hence -16 + 0.0002p + 0.9998p = 50,   -16+p = 50, or

p = 66.   <u>Ans.</u> $66

<u>EXERCISE 7.5</u>

1. $f(0) = C_{2,0}\left(\frac{1}{4}\right)^0\left(\frac{3}{4}\right)^2 = \frac{2!}{0! \cdot 2!} \cdot 1 \cdot \frac{9}{16} = 1 \cdot 1 \cdot \frac{9}{16} = \frac{9}{16};$

$f(1) = C_{2,1}\left(\frac{1}{4}\right)^1\left(\frac{3}{4}\right)^1 = \frac{2!}{1! \cdot 1!} \cdot \frac{1}{4} \cdot \frac{3}{4} = 2 \cdot \frac{1}{4} \cdot \frac{3}{4} = \frac{3}{8};$

$f(2) = C_{2,2}\left(\frac{1}{4}\right)^2\left(\frac{3}{4}\right)^0 = \frac{2!}{2! \cdot 0!} \cdot \frac{1}{16} \cdot 1 = 1 \cdot \frac{1}{16} \cdot 1 = \frac{1}{16}.$

$\mu = np = 2 \cdot \frac{1}{4} = \frac{1}{2};$ $\sigma = \sqrt{npq} = \sqrt{2 \cdot \frac{1}{4} \cdot \frac{3}{4}} = \sqrt{\frac{6}{16}} = \frac{\sqrt{6}}{4}.$

5. Let X = number of heads that occurs.

   (a) $P(X=2) = C_{3,2}\left(\frac{1}{4}\right)^2\left(\frac{3}{4}\right)^1 = 3 \cdot \frac{1}{16} \cdot \frac{3}{4} = \frac{9}{64}.$

   (b) $P(X=3) = C_{3,3}\left(\frac{1}{4}\right)^3\left(\frac{3}{4}\right)^0 = 1 \cdot \frac{1}{64} \cdot 1 = \frac{1}{64}.$ Thus

   $$P(X=2) + P(X=3) = \frac{9}{64} + \frac{1}{64} = \frac{10}{64} = \frac{5}{32}.$$

<u>Ans.</u> (a) 9/64;   (b) 5/32

9. Let X = number of green marbles drawn. The probability of selecting a green marble on any draw is $p = \frac{6}{10} = \frac{3}{5}.$

$P(X=1) = C_{4,1}\left(\frac{3}{5}\right)^1\left(\frac{2}{5}\right)^3 = \frac{4!}{1! \cdot 3!} \cdot \frac{3}{5} \cdot \frac{8}{125} = 4 \cdot \frac{3}{5} \cdot \frac{8}{125} = \frac{96}{625} =$

0.1536.   <u>Ans.</u> 0.1536

CHAPTER 7 - REVIEW PROBLEMS

1. $P_{8,3} = 8 \cdot 7 \cdot 6 = 336$

5. For each of the first two symbols there are 26 choices, for the third there are 9 choices, and for each of the last two symbols there are 10 choices. By the basic counting principle, the number of license plates that are possible is $26 \cdot 26 \cdot 9 \cdot 10 \cdot 10 = 608,400$.   <u>Ans.</u> 608,400

9. A possibility for first, second, and third place is a selection of three of the seven teams so that order is important. Thus the number of ways the season can end is $P_{7,3} = 7 \cdot 6 \cdot 5 = 210$.   <u>Ans.</u> 210

13. (a) Three bulbs are selected from 24, and the order of selection is not important. Thus the number of possible selections is $C_{24,3} = \dfrac{24!}{3!(24-3)!} = \dfrac{24!}{3! \cdot 21!} = \dfrac{24 \cdot 23 \cdot 22 \cdot 21!}{3 \cdot 2 \cdot 1 \cdot 21!} = \dfrac{24 \cdot 23 \cdot 22}{3 \cdot 2 \cdot 1} = 2024$.

    (b) Only one bulb is defective and that bulb must be included in the selection. The other two bulbs must be selected from the 23 remaining bulbs and there are $C_{23,2}$ such selections that are possible. Thus the number of ways of selecting three bulbs such that one is defective is $1 \cdot C_{23,2} = C_{23,2} = \dfrac{23!}{2!(23-2)!} = \dfrac{23!}{2! \cdot 21!} = \dfrac{23 \cdot 22 \cdot 21!}{2 \cdot 1 \cdot 21!} = \dfrac{23 \cdot 22}{2 \cdot 1} = 253$.

<u>Ans.</u> (a) 2024; (b) 253

17. (a) $\left\{\begin{array}{l} R_1R_2R_3, \ R_1R_2G_3, \ R_1G_2R_3, \ R_1G_2G_3, \\ G_1R_2R_3, \ G_1R_2G_3, \ G_1G_2R_3, \ G_1G_2G_3 \end{array}\right\}$;

(b) $\{R_1R_2G_3, \ R_1G_2R_3, \ G_1R_2R_3\}$;

(c) $\{R_1R_2R_3, \ G_1G_2G_3\}$

21. (a) There are 10 marbles in the urn. $n(S) = 10 \cdot 10 = 100$.

$n(E_{both\ red}) = 4 \cdot 4 = 16$. Thus $P(E_{both\ red}) =$

$\dfrac{n(E_{both\ red})}{n(S)} = \dfrac{16}{100} = \dfrac{4}{25}$.

(b) $n(S) = 10 \cdot 9 = 90$. $n(E_{both\ red}) = 4 \cdot 3 = 12$. Thus

$P(E_{both\ red}) = \dfrac{12}{90} = \dfrac{2}{15}$.

Ans. (a) 4/25; (b) 2/15

25. $\mu = \underset{x}{\Sigma} xf(x) = 1 \cdot f(1) + 2 \cdot f(2) + 3 \cdot f(3)$

$= 1(0.7)\ 2(0.1) + 3(0.2) = 0.7 + 0.2 + 0.6 = 1.5$.

$Var(X) = \underset{x}{\Sigma} x^2 f(x) - \mu^2$

$= [1^2(0.7) + 2^2(0.1) + 3^2(0.2)] - (1.5)^2$

$= [0.7 + 0.4 + 1.8] - 2.25 = 2.9 - 2.25 = 0.65$.

$\sigma = \sqrt{Var(X)} = \sqrt{0.65} = 0.81$.

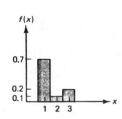

29. Let X = gain (in dollars) on a play. If no 10 appears, then $X = 0 - (1/4) = -1/4$; if exactly one 10 appears, then $X = 1 - (1/4) = 3/4$; if two 10's appear, then $X = 2 - (1/4) =$

7/4. $n(S) = 52 \cdot 52$. In a deck, there are 4 10's and 48 non-10's. Thus $n(E_{no\ 10}) = 48 \cdot 48$. The event $E_{one\ 10}$ occurs if the first card is a 10 and the second is a non-10, or vice versa. Thus $n(E_{one\ 10}) = 4 \cdot 48 + 48 \cdot 4 = 2 \cdot 4 \cdot 48$. $n(E_{two\ 10's}) = 4 \cdot 4$.

Dist. of X: $f\left(-\frac{1}{4}\right) = \frac{48 \cdot 48}{52 \cdot 52} = \frac{144}{169}$, $f\left(\frac{3}{4}\right) = \frac{2 \cdot 4 \cdot 48}{52 \cdot 52} = \frac{24}{169}$,

$$f\left(\frac{7}{4}\right) = \frac{4 \cdot 4}{52 \cdot 52} = \frac{1}{169}.$$

$E(X) = -\frac{1}{4} \cdot \frac{144}{169} + \frac{3}{4} \cdot \frac{24}{169} + \frac{7}{4} \cdot \frac{1}{169} = \frac{-144+72+7}{4 \cdot 169} = -\frac{65}{676} =$

$-\frac{5}{52} = -0.10$.   <u>Ans.</u> loss of $0.10 per play

33. Let X = number of heads that occur. Then X is binomial.

$P(X=0) = C_{4,0}\left(\frac{1}{3}\right)^0\left(\frac{2}{3}\right)^4 = \frac{4!}{0! \cdot 4!}(1)\left(\frac{16}{81}\right) = 1(1)\left(\frac{16}{81}\right) = \frac{16}{81}$,

$P(X=1) = C_{4,1}\left(\frac{1}{3}\right)^1\left(\frac{2}{3}\right)^3 = \frac{4!}{1! \cdot 3!}\left(\frac{1}{3}\right)\left(\frac{8}{27}\right) = 4\left(\frac{1}{3}\right)\left(\frac{8}{27}\right) = \frac{32}{81}$.

$P(X \geq 2) = 1 - [P(X=0) + P(X=1)] = 1 - \left[\frac{16}{81} + \frac{32}{81}\right] =$

$1 - \frac{48}{81} = \frac{33}{81}$.   <u>Ans.</u> 33/81

CHAPTER 7 - MATHEMATICAL SNAPSHOT

1. If X = number of correct predictions on first part of game, then X has a binomial distribution with n = 3 and p = 1/2. Thus $E(X) = np = 3 \cdot \frac{1}{2} = \frac{3}{2}$. If P(B) is the probability of selecting the shell with the ball under it, then $P(B) = \frac{\text{avg. no. of correct predictions}}{\text{no. of shells}} = \frac{3/2}{4} = \frac{3}{8}$.   <u>Ans.</u> $\frac{3}{8}$

8

Matrix Algebra

1. (a) The order is the number of rows by the number of columns. Thus A is 2 × 3, B is 3 × 3, C is 3 × 2, D is 2 × 2, E is 4 × 4, F is 1 × 2, G is 3 × 1, H is 3 × 3, J is 1 × 1.

   (b) A square matrix has the same number of rows as number of columns. Thus the square matrices are B, D, E, H, and J.

   (c) An upper triangular matrix is a square matrix with all entries below the main diagonal zeros. Thus H and J are upper triangular. A lower triangular matrix is a square matrix with all entries above the main diagonal zeros. Thus D and J are lower triangular.

   (d) A row matrix has only one row. Thus F and J are row matrices.

(e) A column matrix has only one column. Thus G and J are column matrices.

5. a_{32} = entry in 3rd row and 2nd column = 4

9. The main diagonal entries are the entries on the diagonal extending from the upper left corner to the lower right corner. Thus the main diagonal entries are 7, 2, 1, 0.

13. $12 \cdot 10 = 120$. Thus A has 120 entries. Since 3 = 3, a_{33} = 1. Since $5 \neq 2$, a_{52} = 0. Since 10 = 10, $a_{10,10}$ = 1. Since $12 \neq 10$, $a_{12,10}$ = 0.

17. Equating corresponding entries gives 6 = 6, 2 = 2, x = 6, 7 = 7, 3y = 2, 2z = 7.   Ans. x = 6, y = 2/3, z = 7/2

21. (a) From J, the entry in row 3 (super-duper) and column 2 (white) is 7. Thus in January, 7 white super-duper models were sold.

    (b) From F, the entry in row 2 (deluxe) and column 3 (blue) is 3. Thus in February, 3 blue deluxe models were sold.

    (c) The entries in row 1 (regular) and column 4 (purple) give the number of purple regular models sold. For J the entry is 2 and for F the entry is 4. Thus more purple regular models were sold in February.

    (d) In both January and February, the deluxe blue models (row 2, column 3) sold the same number of units (3).

    (e) In January a total of 0 + 1 + 3 + 5 = 9 deluxe models were sold. In February a total of 2 + 3 + 3 + 2 = 10 deluxe models were sold. Thus more deluxe models were sold in February.

(f) In January a total of 2 + 0 + 2 = 4 red widgets were sold, while in February a total of 0 + 2 + 4 = 6 red widgets were sold. Thus more red widgets were sold in February.

(g) Adding all entries in matrix J yields that a total of 35 widgets were sold in January.

EXERCISE 8.2

1. $\begin{bmatrix} 2 & 0 & -3 \\ -1 & 4 & 0 \\ 1 & -6 & 5 \end{bmatrix} + \begin{bmatrix} 2 & -3 & 4 \\ -1 & 6 & 5 \\ 9 & 11 & -2 \end{bmatrix} = \begin{bmatrix} 2+2 & 0+(-3) & -3+4 \\ -1+(-1) & 4+6 & 0+5 \\ 1+9 & -6+(11) & 5+(-2) \end{bmatrix}$

$= \begin{bmatrix} 4 & -3 & 1 \\ -2 & 10 & 5 \\ 10 & 5 & 3 \end{bmatrix}$

5. $3[1 \quad -3 \quad 2 \quad 1] + 2[-6 \quad 1 \quad 0 \quad 4] - 0[-2 \quad 7 \quad 6 \quad 4] =$

$[3 \quad -9 \quad 6 \quad 3] + [-12 \quad 2 \quad 0 \quad 8] - [0 \quad 0 \quad 0 \quad 0] =$

$[3-12-0 \quad -9+2-0 \quad 6+0-0 \quad 3+8-0] = [-9 \quad -7 \quad 6 \quad 11]$

9. $-6\begin{bmatrix} 2 & -6 & 7 & 1 \\ 7 & 1 & 6 & -2 \end{bmatrix} = \begin{bmatrix} -6 \cdot 2 & -6(-6) & -6 \cdot 7 & -6 \cdot 1 \\ -6 \cdot 7 & -6 \cdot 1 & -6 \cdot 6 & -6(-2) \end{bmatrix}$

$= \begin{bmatrix} -12 & 36 & -42 & -6 \\ -42 & -6 & -36 & 12 \end{bmatrix}$

13. $-\begin{bmatrix} -6 & -5 \\ 2 & -3 \end{bmatrix} = (-1)\begin{bmatrix} -6 & -5 \\ 2 & -3 \end{bmatrix} = \begin{bmatrix} -1(-6) & -1(-5) \\ -1(2) & -1(-3) \end{bmatrix} = \begin{bmatrix} 6 & 5 \\ -2 & 3 \end{bmatrix}$

17. $2(A - 2B) = 2\left\{\begin{bmatrix} 2 & 1 \\ 3 & -3 \end{bmatrix} - \begin{bmatrix} -12 & -10 \\ 4 & -6 \end{bmatrix}\right\} = 2\begin{bmatrix} 14 & 11 \\ -1 & 3 \end{bmatrix} = \begin{bmatrix} 28 & 22 \\ -2 & 6 \end{bmatrix}$

21. $2B - 3A + 2C = \begin{bmatrix} 2(-6)-3(2)+2(-2) & 2(-5)-3(1)+2(-1) \\ 2(2)-3(3)+2(-3) & 2(-3)-3(-3)+2(3) \end{bmatrix}$

$$= \begin{bmatrix} -22 & -15 \\ -11 & 9 \end{bmatrix}$$

25. $3(A + B) = 3\begin{bmatrix} -4 & -4 \\ 5 & -6 \end{bmatrix} = \begin{bmatrix} -12 & -12 \\ 15 & -18 \end{bmatrix}$.

$3A + 3B = \begin{bmatrix} 6 & 3 \\ 9 & -9 \end{bmatrix} + \begin{bmatrix} -18 & -15 \\ 6 & -9 \end{bmatrix} = \begin{bmatrix} -12 & -12 \\ 15 & -18 \end{bmatrix}$.

Thus $3(A + B) = 3A + 3B$.

29. $x\begin{bmatrix} 2 \\ 1 \end{bmatrix} - y\begin{bmatrix} -3 \\ 5 \end{bmatrix} = \begin{bmatrix} 2x \\ x \end{bmatrix} - \begin{bmatrix} -3y \\ 5y \end{bmatrix} = \begin{bmatrix} 2x + 3y \\ x - 5y \end{bmatrix} = \begin{bmatrix} 16 \\ 22 \end{bmatrix}$.

Equating corresponding entries gives $\begin{cases} 2x + 3y = 16, \\ x - 5y = 22. \end{cases}$

From second equation, $x = 22+5y$. Substituting in first
equation gives $2(22+5y)+3y = 16$, $13y = -28$, or $y = -28/13$.
$x = 22+5y = 22 + 5(-28/13) = 146/13$.
<u>Ans.</u> $x = 146/13$, $y = -28/13$

33. $\begin{bmatrix} 2 \\ 4 \\ 6 \end{bmatrix} + 2\begin{bmatrix} x \\ y \\ 4z \end{bmatrix} = \begin{bmatrix} -10 \\ -24 \\ 14 \end{bmatrix}$, $\begin{bmatrix} 2 + 2x \\ 4 + 2y \\ 6 + 8z \end{bmatrix} = \begin{bmatrix} -10 \\ -24 \\ 14 \end{bmatrix}$.

$2+2x = -10$, $2x = -12$, or $x = -6$. $4+2y = -24$, $2y = -28$, or
$y = -14$. $6+8z = 14$, $8z = 8$, or $z = 1$.
<u>Ans.</u> $x = -6$, $y = -14$, $z = 1$

EXERCISE 8.3

1. $c_{11} = 1(0) + 3(-2) + (-2)(3) = -12$

5. $c_{22} = -2(-2) + 1(4) + (-1)(1) = 7$

9. E is 3 × 2 and C is 2 × 5, so EC is 3 × 5; 3·5 = 15.
   Ans. 3 × 5; 15

13. E is 3 × 2 and A is 2 × 3, so EA is 3 × 3; 3·3 = 9.
    Ans. 3 × 3; 9

17. An identity matrix is a square   Ans. $\begin{bmatrix} 1 & 0 & 0 & 0 \\ 0 & 1 & 0 & 0 \\ 0 & 0 & 1 & 0 \\ 0 & 0 & 0 & 1 \end{bmatrix}$
    matrix (in this case 4 × 4) with
    1's on the main diagonal and all
    other entries 0's.

21. $\begin{bmatrix} 2 & 0 & 3 \\ -1 & 4 & 5 \end{bmatrix} \begin{bmatrix} 1 \\ 4 \\ 7 \end{bmatrix} = \begin{bmatrix} 2(1)+0(4)+3(7) \\ -1(1)+4(4)+5(7) \end{bmatrix} = \begin{bmatrix} 23 \\ 50 \end{bmatrix}$

25. $[-1 \quad 2 \quad 3] \begin{bmatrix} 3 & 1 & -1 & 2 \\ 0 & 4 & 3 & 1 \\ -1 & 3 & 1 & -2 \end{bmatrix} =$

    $[-3+0-3 \quad -1+8+9 \quad 1+6+3 \quad -2+2-6] = [-6 \quad 16 \quad 10 \quad -6]$

29. $3\left\{ \begin{bmatrix} -2 & 0 & 2 \\ 3 & -1 & 1 \end{bmatrix} + 2 \begin{bmatrix} -1 & 0 & 2 \\ 1 & 1 & -2 \end{bmatrix} \right\} \begin{bmatrix} 1 & 2 \\ 3 & 4 \\ 5 & 6 \end{bmatrix} =$

    $3\left\{ \begin{bmatrix} -2 & 0 & 2 \\ 3 & -1 & 1 \end{bmatrix} + \begin{bmatrix} -2 & 0 & 4 \\ 2 & 2 & -4 \end{bmatrix} \right\} \begin{bmatrix} 1 & 2 \\ 3 & 4 \\ 5 & 6 \end{bmatrix} =$

$$3\left\{\begin{bmatrix} -4 & 0 & 6 \\ 5 & 1 & -3 \end{bmatrix}\right\}\begin{bmatrix} 1 & 2 \\ 3 & 4 \\ 5 & 6 \end{bmatrix} = \begin{bmatrix} -12 & 0 & 18 \\ 15 & 3 & -9 \end{bmatrix}\begin{bmatrix} 1 & 2 \\ 3 & 4 \\ 5 & 6 \end{bmatrix} =$$

$$\begin{bmatrix} -12(1)+0(3)+18(5) & -12(2)+0(4)+18(6) \\ 15(1)+3(3)+(-9)(5) & 15(2)+3(4)+(-9)(6) \end{bmatrix} = \begin{bmatrix} 78 & 84 \\ -21 & -12 \end{bmatrix}$$

33. $$\begin{bmatrix} 1 & 0 & 0 \\ 0 & 1 & 0 \\ 0 & 0 & 1 \end{bmatrix}\begin{bmatrix} x \\ y \\ z \end{bmatrix} = I\begin{bmatrix} x \\ y \\ z \end{bmatrix} = \begin{bmatrix} x \\ y \\ z \end{bmatrix}$$

37. $$AB = \begin{bmatrix} -2-2 & 3+8 & 0-2 \\ 0+3 & 0-12 & 0+3 \end{bmatrix} = \begin{bmatrix} -4 & 11 & -2 \\ 3 & -12 & 3 \end{bmatrix}$$

41. $$DG = \begin{bmatrix} 3+0+0 & 0+0+0 & 0+0+0 \\ 0+0+0 & 0+6+0 & 0+0+3 \\ 3+0+0 & 0+12+0 & 0+0+3 \end{bmatrix} = \begin{bmatrix} 3 & 0 & 0 \\ 0 & 6 & 3 \\ 3 & 12 & 3 \end{bmatrix}$$

45. $$DI - \tfrac{1}{3}G = D - \tfrac{1}{3}G = \begin{bmatrix} 1 & 0 & 0 \\ 0 & 1 & 1 \\ 1 & 2 & 1 \end{bmatrix} - \begin{bmatrix} 1 & 0 & 0 \\ 0 & 2 & 0 \\ 0 & 0 & 1 \end{bmatrix} = \begin{bmatrix} 0 & 0 & 0 \\ 0 & -1 & 1 \\ 1 & 2 & 0 \end{bmatrix}$$

49. $$2I - \tfrac{1}{2}GH = 2I - \begin{bmatrix} \tfrac{3}{2} & 0 & 0 \\ 0 & 3 & 0 \\ 0 & 0 & \tfrac{3}{2} \end{bmatrix}H = 2I - \begin{bmatrix} \tfrac{3}{2} & 0 & 0 \\ 0 & 2 & 0 \\ 0 & 0 & \tfrac{3}{2} \end{bmatrix}\begin{bmatrix} \tfrac{1}{3} & 0 & 0 \\ 0 & \tfrac{1}{6} & 0 \\ 0 & 0 & \tfrac{1}{3} \end{bmatrix}$$

$$= 2I - \begin{bmatrix} \tfrac{1}{2}+0+0 & 0+0+0 & 0+0+0 \\ 0+0+0 & 0+\tfrac{1}{2}+0 & 0+0+0 \\ 0+0+0 & 0+0+0 & 0+0+\tfrac{1}{2} \end{bmatrix}$$

$$= \begin{bmatrix} 2 & 0 & 0 \\ 0 & 2 & 0 \\ 0 & 0 & 2 \end{bmatrix} - \begin{bmatrix} \tfrac{1}{2} & 0 & 0 \\ 0 & \tfrac{1}{2} & 0 \\ 0 & 0 & \tfrac{3}{2} \end{bmatrix} = \begin{bmatrix} \tfrac{3}{2} & 0 & 0 \\ 0 & \tfrac{3}{2} & 0 \\ 0 & 0 & \tfrac{3}{2} \end{bmatrix}$$

53. AX = C. A = $\begin{bmatrix} 3 & 1 \\ 7 & -2 \end{bmatrix}$, X = $\begin{bmatrix} x \\ y \end{bmatrix}$, C = $\begin{bmatrix} 6 \\ 5 \end{bmatrix}$.

<u>Ans.</u> $\begin{bmatrix} 3 & 1 \\ 7 & -2 \end{bmatrix}\begin{bmatrix} x \\ y \end{bmatrix} = \begin{bmatrix} 6 \\ 5 \end{bmatrix}$

57. Q = [7 3 5], R = $\begin{bmatrix} 5 & 20 & 16 & 7 & 17 \\ 7 & 18 & 12 & 9 & 21 \\ 6 & 25 & 8 & 5 & 13 \end{bmatrix}$, C = $\begin{bmatrix} 1500 \\ 800 \\ 500 \\ 100 \\ 1000 \end{bmatrix}$. QRC =

$$Q(RC) = Q\begin{bmatrix} 5 \cdot 1500 + 20 \cdot 800 + 16 \cdot 500 + 7 \cdot 100 + 17 \cdot 1000 \\ 7 \cdot 1500 + 18 \cdot 800 + 12 \cdot 500 + 9 \cdot 100 + 21 \cdot 1000 \\ 6 \cdot 1500 + 25 \cdot 800 + 8 \cdot 500 + 5 \cdot 100 + 13 \cdot 1000 \end{bmatrix} =$$

$$[7 \quad 3 \quad 5]\begin{bmatrix} 49,200 \\ 52,800 \\ 46,500 \end{bmatrix} = [7 \cdot 49,200 + 3 \cdot 52,800 + 5 \cdot 46,500] =$$

[735,300].

<u>Ans.</u> $735,300

EXERCISE 8.4

1. The first nonzero entry in row 2 is not to the right of the first nonzero entry in row 1.   <u>Ans.</u> not reduced

5. The first row consists entirely of zeros and is not below each row containing a nonzero entry.   <u>Ans.</u> not reduced

9.
$$\begin{bmatrix} 2 & 4 & 6 \\ 1 & 2 & 3 \\ 1 & 2 & 3 \end{bmatrix} \sim \begin{bmatrix} 1 & 2 & 3 \\ 1 & 2 & 3 \\ 2 & 4 & 6 \end{bmatrix} \sim \begin{bmatrix} 1 & 2 & 3 \\ 0 & 0 & 0 \\ 2 & 4 & 6 \end{bmatrix} \sim \begin{bmatrix} 1 & 2 & 3 \\ 0 & 0 & 0 \\ 0 & 0 & 0 \end{bmatrix}$$

13.
$$\begin{bmatrix} 2 & 3 & | & 5 \\ 1 & -2 & | & -1 \end{bmatrix} \sim \begin{bmatrix} 1 & -2 & | & -1 \\ 2 & 3 & | & 5 \end{bmatrix} \sim \begin{bmatrix} 1 & -2 & | & -1 \\ 0 & 7 & | & 7 \end{bmatrix} \sim \begin{bmatrix} 1 & -2 & | & -1 \\ 0 & 1 & | & 1 \end{bmatrix} \sim$$

$$\begin{bmatrix} 1 & 0 & | & 1 \\ 0 & 1 & | & 1 \end{bmatrix}. \qquad \underline{\text{Ans.}} \quad x = 1, \ y = 1$$

17.
$$\begin{bmatrix} 1 & 2 & 1 & | & 4 \\ 3 & 0 & 2 & | & 5 \end{bmatrix} \sim \begin{bmatrix} 1 & 2 & 1 & | & 4 \\ 0 & -6 & -1 & | & -7 \end{bmatrix} \sim \begin{bmatrix} 1 & 2 & 1 & | & 4 \\ 0 & 1 & 1/6 & | & 7/6 \end{bmatrix} \sim$$

$$\begin{bmatrix} 1 & 0 & 2/3 & | & 5/3 \\ 0 & 1 & 1/6 & | & 7/6 \end{bmatrix}. \qquad \begin{cases} x + \frac{2}{3}z = \frac{5}{3}, \\ y + \frac{1}{6}z = \frac{7}{6}. \end{cases}$$

$$\underline{\text{Ans.}} \quad x = -\frac{2}{3}z + \frac{5}{3}, \ y = -\frac{1}{6}z + \frac{7}{6}, \ z = z$$

21.
$$\begin{bmatrix} 1 & -1 & -3 & | & -4 \\ 2 & -1 & -4 & | & -7 \\ 1 & 1 & -1 & | & -2 \end{bmatrix} \sim \begin{bmatrix} 1 & -1 & -3 & | & -4 \\ 0 & 1 & 2 & | & 1 \\ 0 & 2 & 2 & | & 2 \end{bmatrix} \sim \begin{bmatrix} 1 & 0 & -1 & | & -3 \\ 0 & 1 & 2 & | & 1 \\ 0 & 0 & -2 & | & 0 \end{bmatrix} \sim$$

$$\begin{bmatrix} 1 & 0 & -1 & | & -3 \\ 0 & 1 & 2 & | & 1 \\ 0 & 0 & 1 & | & 0 \end{bmatrix} \sim \begin{bmatrix} 1 & 0 & 0 & | & -3 \\ 0 & 1 & 0 & | & 1 \\ 0 & 0 & 1 & | & 0 \end{bmatrix}.$$

$$\underline{\text{Ans.}} \quad x = -3, \ y = 1, \ z = 0$$

25.
$$\begin{bmatrix} 1 & 1 & -1 & 1 & 1 & | & 0 \\ 1 & 1 & 1 & -1 & 1 & | & 0 \\ 1 & -1 & -1 & 1 & -1 & | & 0 \\ 1 & 1 & -1 & -1 & -1 & | & 0 \end{bmatrix} \sim \begin{bmatrix} 1 & 1 & -1 & 1 & 1 & | & 0 \\ 0 & 0 & 2 & -2 & 0 & | & 0 \\ 0 & -2 & 0 & 0 & -2 & | & 0 \\ 0 & 0 & 0 & -2 & -2 & | & 0 \end{bmatrix} \sim$$

$$\begin{bmatrix} 1 & 1 & -1 & 1 & 1 & | & 0 \\ 0 & -2 & 0 & 0 & -2 & | & 0 \\ 0 & 0 & 2 & -2 & 0 & | & 0 \\ 0 & 0 & 0 & -2 & -2 & | & 0 \end{bmatrix} \sim \begin{bmatrix} 1 & 1 & -1 & 1 & 1 & | & 0 \\ 0 & 1 & 0 & 0 & 1 & | & 0 \\ 0 & 0 & 1 & -1 & 0 & | & 0 \\ 0 & 0 & 0 & 1 & 1 & | & 0 \end{bmatrix} \sim$$

$$\begin{bmatrix} 1 & 0 & -1 & 1 & 0 & | & 0 \\ 0 & 1 & 0 & 0 & 1 & | & 0 \\ 0 & 0 & 1 & -1 & 0 & | & 0 \\ 0 & 0 & 0 & 1 & 1 & | & 0 \end{bmatrix} \sim \begin{bmatrix} 1 & 0 & 0 & 0 & 0 & | & 0 \\ 0 & 1 & 0 & 0 & 1 & | & 0 \\ 0 & 0 & 1 & -1 & 0 & | & 0 \\ 0 & 0 & 0 & 1 & 1 & | & 0 \end{bmatrix} \sim$$

$$\begin{bmatrix} 1 & 0 & 0 & 0 & 0 & | & 0 \\ 0 & 1 & 0 & 0 & 1 & | & 0 \\ 0 & 0 & 1 & 0 & 1 & | & 0 \\ 0 & 0 & 0 & 1 & 1 & | & 0 \end{bmatrix}.$$

<u>Ans.</u> $x_1 = 0$, $x_2 = -x_5$, $x_3 = -x_5$, $x_4 = -x_5$, $x_5 = x_5$

29. Let x = number of units of A produced, y = number of units of B produced, and z = number of units of C produced. Then

        no. of units: x + y + z = 11,000,
        total cost: 4x + 5y + 7z + 17,000 = 80,000,
        total profit: x + 2y + 3z = 25,000.

Equivalently,

$$\begin{cases} x + y + z = 11,000, \\ 4x + 5y + 7z = 63,000, \\ x + 2y + 3z = 25,000. \end{cases}$$

$$\begin{bmatrix} 1 & 1 & 1 & | & 11,000 \\ 4 & 5 & 7 & | & 63,000 \\ 1 & 2 & 3 & | & 25,000 \end{bmatrix} \sim \begin{bmatrix} 1 & 1 & 1 & | & 11,000 \\ 0 & 1 & 3 & | & 19,000 \\ 0 & 1 & 2 & | & 14,000 \end{bmatrix} \sim$$

$$\begin{bmatrix} 1 & 0 & -2 & | & -8,000 \\ 0 & 1 & 3 & | & 19,000 \\ 0 & 0 & -1 & | & -5,000 \end{bmatrix} \sim \begin{bmatrix} 1 & 0 & -2 & | & -8,000 \\ 0 & 1 & 3 & | & 19,000 \\ 0 & 0 & 1 & | & 5,000 \end{bmatrix} \sim$$

$$\begin{bmatrix} 1 & 0 & 0 & | & 2000 \\ 0 & 1 & 0 & | & 4000 \\ 0 & 0 & 1 & | & 5000 \end{bmatrix}.$$ x = 2000, y = 4000, and z = 5000.

<u>Ans.</u> 2000 units of A, 4000 units of B, 5000 units of C

EXERCISE 8.5

1. $\begin{bmatrix} 1 & -1 & -1 & 4 & | & 5 \\ 2 & -3 & -4 & 9 & | & 13 \\ 2 & 1 & 4 & 5 & | & 1 \end{bmatrix} \sim \begin{bmatrix} 1 & -1 & -1 & 4 & | & 5 \\ 0 & -1 & -2 & 1 & | & 3 \\ 0 & 3 & 6 & -3 & | & -9 \end{bmatrix} \sim$

$\begin{bmatrix} 1 & -1 & -1 & 4 & | & 5 \\ 0 & 1 & 2 & -1 & | & -3 \\ 0 & 3 & 6 & -3 & | & -9 \end{bmatrix} \sim \begin{bmatrix} 1 & 0 & 1 & 3 & | & 2 \\ 0 & 1 & 2 & -1 & | & -3 \\ 0 & 0 & 0 & 0 & | & 0 \end{bmatrix}.$

Ans. $w = -y-3z+2$, $x = -2y+z-3$, $y = y$, $z = z$

5. $\begin{bmatrix} 1 & 1 & 3 & -1 & | & 2 \\ 2 & 1 & 5 & -2 & | & 0 \\ 2 & -1 & 3 & -2 & | & -8 \\ 3 & 2 & 8 & -3 & | & 2 \\ 1 & 0 & 2 & -1 & | & -2 \end{bmatrix} \sim \begin{bmatrix} 1 & 1 & 3 & -1 & | & 2 \\ 0 & -1 & -1 & 0 & | & -4 \\ 0 & -3 & -3 & 0 & | & -12 \\ 0 & -1 & -1 & 0 & | & -4 \\ 0 & -1 & -1 & 0 & | & -4 \end{bmatrix} \sim$

$\begin{bmatrix} 1 & 1 & 3 & -1 & | & 2 \\ 0 & 1 & 1 & 0 & | & 4 \\ 0 & -3 & -3 & 0 & | & -12 \\ 0 & -1 & -1 & 0 & | & -4 \\ 0 & -1 & -1 & 0 & | & -4 \end{bmatrix} \sim \begin{bmatrix} 1 & 0 & 2 & -1 & | & -2 \\ 0 & 1 & 1 & 0 & | & 4 \\ 0 & 0 & 0 & 0 & | & 0 \\ 0 & 0 & 0 & 0 & | & 0 \\ 0 & 0 & 0 & 0 & | & 0 \end{bmatrix}.$

Ans. $w = -2y+z-2$, $x = -y+4$, $y = y$, $z = z$

9. System is homogeneous with fewer equations than unknowns
   $(2 < 3)$.   Ans. infinite

13. $\begin{bmatrix} 1 & 1 & 1 \\ 1 & 0 & -1 \\ 1 & -2 & -5 \end{bmatrix} \sim \begin{bmatrix} 1 & 1 & 1 \\ 0 & -1 & -2 \\ 0 & -3 & -6 \end{bmatrix} \sim \begin{bmatrix} 1 & 1 & 1 \\ 0 & 1 & 2 \\ 0 & -3 & -6 \end{bmatrix} \sim \begin{bmatrix} 1 & 0 & -1 \\ 0 & 1 & 2 \\ 0 & 0 & 0 \end{bmatrix} = A.$

A has $k = 2$ nonzero rows. Number of unknowns is $n = 3$.
Thus $k < n$.   Ans. infinite

17. $\begin{bmatrix} 1 & 6 & -2 \\ 2 & -3 & 4 \end{bmatrix} \sim \begin{bmatrix} 1 & 6 & -2 \\ 0 & -15 & 8 \end{bmatrix} \sim \begin{bmatrix} 1 & 6 & -2 \\ 0 & 1 & -8/15 \end{bmatrix} \sim$

$\begin{bmatrix} 1 & 0 & 6/5 \\ 0 & 1 & -8/15 \end{bmatrix}.$

Ans. $x = (-6/5)z, \quad y = (8/15)z, \quad z = z$

21. $\begin{bmatrix} 1 & 1 & 1 \\ 5 & -2 & -9 \\ 3 & 1 & -1 \\ 3 & -2 & -7 \end{bmatrix} \sim \begin{bmatrix} 1 & 1 & 1 \\ 0 & -7 & -14 \\ 0 & -2 & -4 \\ 0 & -5 & -10 \end{bmatrix} \sim \begin{bmatrix} 1 & 1 & 1 \\ 0 & 1 & 2 \\ 0 & -2 & -4 \\ 0 & -5 & -10 \end{bmatrix} \sim \begin{bmatrix} 1 & 0 & -1 \\ 0 & 1 & 2 \\ 0 & 0 & 0 \\ 0 & 0 & 0 \end{bmatrix}.$

Ans. $x = z, \quad y = -2z, \quad z = z$

EXERCISE 8.6

1. $\begin{bmatrix} 6 & 1 & | & 1 & 0 \\ 5 & 1 & | & 0 & 1 \end{bmatrix} \sim \begin{bmatrix} 1 & 1/6 & | & 1/6 & 0 \\ 5 & 1 & | & 0 & 1 \end{bmatrix} \sim \begin{bmatrix} 1 & 1/6 & | & 1/6 & 0 \\ 0 & 1/6 & | & -5/6 & 1 \end{bmatrix} \sim$

$\begin{bmatrix} 1 & 0 & | & 1 & -1 \\ 0 & 1/6 & | & -5/6 & 1 \end{bmatrix} \sim \begin{bmatrix} 1 & 0 & | & 1 & -1 \\ 0 & 1 & | & -5 & 6 \end{bmatrix}.$

Ans. $\begin{bmatrix} 1 & -1 \\ -5 & 6 \end{bmatrix}$

5. $\begin{bmatrix} 1 & 0 & 0 & | & 1 & 0 & 0 \\ 0 & -3 & 0 & | & 0 & 1 & 0 \\ 0 & 0 & 4 & | & 0 & 0 & 1 \end{bmatrix} \sim \begin{bmatrix} 1 & 0 & 0 & | & 1 & 0 & 0 \\ 0 & 1 & 0 & | & 0 & -1/3 & 0 \\ 0 & 0 & 1 & | & 0 & 0 & 1/4 \end{bmatrix}.$

Ans. $\begin{bmatrix} 1 & 0 & 0 \\ 0 & -1/3 & 0 \\ 0 & 0 & 1/4 \end{bmatrix}$

9. Matrix is not square.   Ans. not invertible

13. $\begin{bmatrix} 7 & 0 & -2 & | & 1 & 0 & 0 \\ 0 & 1 & 0 & | & 0 & 1 & 0 \\ -3 & 0 & 1 & | & 0 & 0 & 1 \end{bmatrix} \sim \begin{bmatrix} 1 & 0 & -2/7 & | & 1/7 & 0 & 0 \\ 0 & 1 & 0 & | & 0 & 1 & 0 \\ -3 & 0 & 1 & | & 0 & 0 & 1 \end{bmatrix} \sim$

$\begin{bmatrix} 1 & 0 & -2/7 & | & 1/7 & 0 & 0 \\ 0 & 1 & 0 & | & 0 & 1 & 0 \\ 0 & 0 & 1/7 & | & 3/7 & 0 & 1 \end{bmatrix} \sim \begin{bmatrix} 1 & 0 & 0 & | & 1 & 0 & 2 \\ 0 & 1 & 0 & | & 0 & 1 & 0 \\ 0 & 0 & 1/7 & | & 3/7 & 0 & 1 \end{bmatrix} \sim$

$\begin{bmatrix} 1 & 0 & 0 & | & 1 & 0 & 2 \\ 0 & 1 & 0 & | & 0 & 1 & 0 \\ 0 & 0 & 1 & | & 3 & 0 & 7 \end{bmatrix}$.   Ans. $\begin{bmatrix} 1 & 0 & 2 \\ 0 & 1 & 0 \\ 3 & 0 & 7 \end{bmatrix}$

17. $\begin{bmatrix} 1 & 2 & 3 & | & 1 & 0 & 0 \\ 1 & 3 & 5 & | & 0 & 1 & 0 \\ 1 & 5 & 12 & | & 0 & 0 & 1 \end{bmatrix} \sim \begin{bmatrix} 1 & 2 & 3 & | & 1 & 0 & 0 \\ 0 & 1 & 2 & | & -1 & 1 & 0 \\ 0 & 3 & 9 & | & -1 & 0 & 1 \end{bmatrix} \sim$

$\begin{bmatrix} 1 & 0 & -1 & | & 3 & -2 & 0 \\ 0 & 1 & 2 & | & -1 & 1 & 0 \\ 0 & 0 & 3 & | & 2 & -3 & 1 \end{bmatrix} \sim \begin{bmatrix} 1 & 0 & -1 & | & 3 & -2 & 0 \\ 0 & 1 & 2 & | & -1 & 1 & 0 \\ 0 & 0 & 1 & | & 2/3 & -1 & 1/3 \end{bmatrix} \sim$

$\begin{bmatrix} 1 & 0 & 0 & | & 11/3 & -3 & 1/3 \\ 0 & 1 & 0 & | & -7/3 & 3 & -2/3 \\ 0 & 0 & 1 & | & 2/3 & -1 & 1/3 \end{bmatrix}$.   Ans. $\begin{bmatrix} 11/3 & -3 & 1/3 \\ -7/3 & 3 & -2/3 \\ 2/3 & -1 & 1/3 \end{bmatrix}$

21. $\begin{bmatrix} 2 & 1 & | & 1 & 0 \\ 3 & -1 & | & 0 & 1 \end{bmatrix} \sim \begin{bmatrix} 1 & 1/2 & | & 1/2 & 0 \\ 3 & -1 & | & 0 & 1 \end{bmatrix} \sim \begin{bmatrix} 1 & 1/2 & | & 1/2 & 0 \\ 0 & -5/2 & | & -3/2 & 1 \end{bmatrix} \sim$

$\begin{bmatrix} 1 & 1/2 & | & 1/2 & 0 \\ 0 & 1 & | & 3/5 & -2/5 \end{bmatrix} \sim \begin{bmatrix} 1 & 0 & | & 1/5 & 1/5 \\ 0 & 1 & | & 3/5 & -2/5 \end{bmatrix}$.

$\begin{bmatrix} x \\ y \end{bmatrix} = A^{-1}C = \begin{bmatrix} 1/5 & 1/5 \\ 3/5 & -2/5 \end{bmatrix}\begin{bmatrix} 5 \\ 0 \end{bmatrix} = \begin{bmatrix} 1 \\ 3 \end{bmatrix}$.

Ans.   x = 1,   y = 3

25. $\begin{bmatrix} 1 & 2 & 1 & | & 1 & 0 & 0 \\ 3 & 0 & 1 & | & 0 & 1 & 0 \\ 1 & -1 & 1 & | & 0 & 0 & 1 \end{bmatrix} \sim \begin{bmatrix} 1 & 2 & 1 & | & 1 & 0 & 0 \\ 0 & -6 & -2 & | & -3 & 1 & 0 \\ 0 & -3 & 0 & | & -1 & 0 & 1 \end{bmatrix} \sim$

$\begin{bmatrix} 1 & 2 & 1 & | & 1 & 0 & 0 \\ 0 & 1 & 1/3 & | & 1/2 & -1/6 & 0 \\ 0 & -3 & 0 & | & -1 & 0 & 1 \end{bmatrix} \sim \begin{bmatrix} 1 & 0 & 1/3 & | & 0 & 1/3 & 0 \\ 0 & 1 & 1/3 & | & 1/2 & -1/6 & 0 \\ 0 & 0 & 1 & | & 1/2 & -1/2 & 1 \end{bmatrix} \sim$

$\begin{bmatrix} 1 & 0 & 0 & | & -1/6 & 1/2 & -1/3 \\ 0 & 1 & 0 & | & 1/3 & 0 & -1/3 \\ 0 & 0 & 1 & | & 1/2 & -1/2 & 1 \end{bmatrix}.$

$\begin{bmatrix} x \\ y \\ z \end{bmatrix} = A^{-1}C = \begin{bmatrix} -1/6 & 1/2 & -1/3 \\ 1/3 & 0 & -1/3 \\ 1/2 & -1/2 & 1 \end{bmatrix} \begin{bmatrix} 4 \\ 2 \\ 1 \end{bmatrix} = \begin{bmatrix} 0 \\ 1 \\ 2 \end{bmatrix}.$

<u>Ans.</u> $x = 0$, $y = 1$, $z = 2$

29. Coefficient matrix is not invertible. Method of reduction yields

$\begin{bmatrix} 1 & 3 & 3 & | & 7 \\ 2 & 1 & 1 & | & 4 \\ 1 & 1 & 1 & | & 4 \end{bmatrix} \sim \begin{bmatrix} 1 & 3 & 3 & | & 7 \\ 0 & -5 & -5 & | & -10 \\ 0 & -2 & -2 & | & -3 \end{bmatrix} \sim \begin{bmatrix} 1 & 3 & 3 & | & 7 \\ 0 & 1 & 1 & | & 2 \\ 0 & -2 & -2 & | & -3 \end{bmatrix} \sim$

$\begin{bmatrix} 1 & 0 & 0 & | & 1 \\ 0 & 1 & 1 & | & 2 \\ 0 & 0 & 0 & | & 1 \end{bmatrix}.$ The third row indicates that $0 = 1$, which is never true.

<u>Ans.</u> no solution

33. $I - A = \begin{bmatrix} 1 & 0 \\ 0 & 1 \end{bmatrix} - \begin{bmatrix} 2 & -1 \\ 1 & 3 \end{bmatrix} = \begin{bmatrix} -1 & 1 \\ -1 & -2 \end{bmatrix}.$

$\begin{bmatrix} -1 & 1 & | & 1 & 0 \\ -1 & -2 & | & 0 & 1 \end{bmatrix} \sim \begin{bmatrix} 1 & -1 & | & -1 & 0 \\ -1 & -2 & | & 0 & 1 \end{bmatrix} \sim \begin{bmatrix} 1 & -1 & | & -1 & 0 \\ 0 & -3 & | & -1 & 1 \end{bmatrix} \sim$

$\begin{bmatrix} 1 & -1 & | & -1 & 0 \\ 0 & 1 & | & 1/3 & -1/3 \end{bmatrix} \sim \begin{bmatrix} 1 & 0 & | & -2/3 & -1/3 \\ 0 & 1 & | & 1/3 & -1/3 \end{bmatrix}.$

<u>Ans.</u> $(I - A)^{-1} = \begin{bmatrix} -2/3 & -1/3 \\ 1/3 & -1/3 \end{bmatrix}$

EXERCISE 8.7

1. $2(2) - 1(3) = 4 - 3 = 1$

5. $1(y) - x(0) = y$

9. $2(k) - 3(4) = 2k - 12 = 12$, $2k = 24$, $k = 12$.   <u>Ans.</u>   12

13. $(-1)^{3+2} \begin{vmatrix} 1 & 3 \\ 4 & 6 \end{vmatrix} = -[1(6) - 3(4)] = -[-6] = 6$

17. $(-1)^{1+3} \begin{vmatrix} a_{21} & a_{22} & a_{24} \\ a_{31} & a_{32} & a_{34} \\ a_{41} & a_{42} & a_{44} \end{vmatrix} = 1^4 \cdot \begin{vmatrix} a_{21} & a_{22} & a_{24} \\ a_{31} & a_{32} & a_{34} \\ a_{41} & a_{42} & a_{44} \end{vmatrix}$

$$= \begin{vmatrix} a_{21} & a_{22} & a_{24} \\ a_{31} & a_{32} & a_{34} \\ a_{41} & a_{42} & a_{44} \end{vmatrix}$$

21. Expanding along row 1 gives

$1(-1)^2 \begin{vmatrix} 5 & 4 \\ -2 & 1 \end{vmatrix} + 2(-1)^3 \begin{vmatrix} 4 & 4 \\ 3 & 1 \end{vmatrix} - 3(-1)^4 \begin{vmatrix} 4 & 5 \\ 3 & -2 \end{vmatrix} =$

$1(1)[5 - (-8)] + 2(-1)[4 - 12] - 3(1)[-8 - 15] =$

$13 + 16 + 69 = 98$.

25. Expanding along row 1 gives

$2(-1)^2 \begin{vmatrix} 1 & -1 \\ 2 & -3 \end{vmatrix} - 1(-1)^3 \begin{vmatrix} 1 & -1 \\ 1 & -3 \end{vmatrix} + 3(-1)^4 \begin{vmatrix} 1 & 1 \\ 1 & 2 \end{vmatrix} =$

$2(1)[-3 - (-2)] - 1(-1)[-3 - (-1)] + 3(1)[2 - 1] =$

$-2 - 2 + 3 = -1$.

29. Expanding along column 3 gives

$$3(-1)^4 \begin{vmatrix} 4 & -1 & 1 \\ 2 & 1 & 3 \\ -1 & 2 & -1 \end{vmatrix} + 0 + 0 + 3(-1)^7 \begin{vmatrix} 1 & 0 & 2 \\ 4 & -1 & 1 \\ 2 & 1 & 3 \end{vmatrix} =$$

$$3\left\{ 4(-1)^2 \begin{vmatrix} 1 & 3 \\ 2 & -1 \end{vmatrix} - 1(-1)^3 \begin{vmatrix} 2 & 3 \\ -1 & -1 \end{vmatrix} + 1(-1)^4 \begin{vmatrix} 2 & 1 \\ -1 & 2 \end{vmatrix} \right\} -$$

$$3\left\{ 1(-1)^2 \begin{vmatrix} -1 & 1 \\ 1 & 3 \end{vmatrix} + 0 + 2(-1)^4 \begin{vmatrix} 4 & -1 \\ 2 & 1 \end{vmatrix} \right\} =$$

$$3\{4(1)[-1-6] - 1(-1)[-2-(-3)] + 1(1)[4-(-1)]\} -$$
$$-3\{1(1)[-3-1] + 2(1)[4-(-2)]\} =$$
$$3\{-28 + 1 + 5\} - 3\{-4 + 12\} = -66 - 24 = -90.$$

33. Since all entries below (as well as above) main diagonal
    are zeros, the determinant is (1)(-2)(4)(-3) = 24.
    Ans. 24

37. Multiplying each entry of A by 2 gives 2A. But 2A is the
    result of multiplying each of the four rows of A by 2. Thus
    $|2A| = 2\cdot2\cdot2\cdot2|A| = 2^4|A| = 16\cdot12 = 192.$ Ans.   192

EXERCISE 8.8

1. $\Delta = \begin{vmatrix} 2 & -1 \\ 3 & 1 \end{vmatrix} = 5, \quad \Delta_x = \begin{vmatrix} 4 & -1 \\ 5 & 1 \end{vmatrix} = 9, \quad \Delta_y = \begin{vmatrix} 2 & 4 \\ 3 & 5 \end{vmatrix} = -2.$

   $x = \Delta_x/\Delta = 9/5, \quad y = \Delta_y/\Delta = -2/5.$

   Ans. $x = 9/5, y = -2/5$

5. $\begin{cases} 3(x+2) = 5 \\ 6(x+y) = -8 \end{cases}$ is equivalent to $\begin{cases} 3x \quad\quad = -1 \\ 6x + 6y = -8. \end{cases}$

$\Delta = \begin{vmatrix} 3 & 0 \\ 6 & 6 \end{vmatrix} = 18, \quad \Delta_x = \begin{vmatrix} -1 & 0 \\ -8 & 6 \end{vmatrix} = -6, \quad \Delta_y = \begin{vmatrix} 3 & -1 \\ 6 & -8 \end{vmatrix} = -18.$

$x = \Delta_x/\Delta = -6/18 = -1/3, \quad y = \Delta_y/\Delta = -18/18 = -1.$

<u>Ans.</u> $x = -1/3, \ y = -1$

9. $\Delta = \begin{vmatrix} 1 & 1 & 1 \\ 1 & -1 & 1 \\ 2 & -1 & 3 \end{vmatrix} = -2, \quad \Delta_x = \begin{vmatrix} 6 & 1 & 1 \\ 2 & -1 & 1 \\ 6 & -1 & 3 \end{vmatrix} = -8,$

$\Delta_y = \begin{vmatrix} 1 & 6 & 1 \\ 1 & 2 & 1 \\ 2 & 6 & 3 \end{vmatrix} = -4, \quad \Delta_z = \begin{vmatrix} 1 & 1 & 6 \\ 1 & -1 & 2 \\ 2 & -1 & 6 \end{vmatrix} = 0.$

$x = \Delta_x/\Delta = -8/(-2) = 4, \quad y = \Delta_y/\Delta = -4/(-2) = 2,$

$z = \Delta_z/\Delta = 0/(-2) = 0.$ \quad\quad <u>Ans.</u> $x = 4, \ y = 2, \ z = 0$

13. $\Delta = \begin{vmatrix} 1 & -2 & 1 \\ 2 & 1 & 2 \\ 1 & 8 & 1 \end{vmatrix} = 0,$ so Cramer's rule does not apply. We

solve the system by matrix reduction.

$\begin{bmatrix} 1 & -2 & 1 & | & 3 \\ 2 & 1 & 2 & | & 6 \\ 1 & 8 & 1 & | & 3 \end{bmatrix} \sim \begin{bmatrix} 1 & -2 & 1 & | & 3 \\ 0 & 5 & 0 & | & 0 \\ 0 & 10 & 0 & | & 0 \end{bmatrix} \sim \begin{bmatrix} 1 & -2 & 1 & | & 3 \\ 0 & 1 & 0 & | & 0 \\ 0 & 0 & 0 & | & 0 \end{bmatrix} \sim$

$\begin{bmatrix} 1 & 0 & 1 & | & 3 \\ 0 & 1 & 0 & | & 0 \\ 0 & 0 & 0 & | & 0 \end{bmatrix}.$ \quad\quad <u>Ans.</u> $x = -z+3, \ y = 0, \ z = z$

17. $\Delta = \begin{vmatrix} 1 & -1 & 3 & 1 \\ 1 & 2 & 0 & -3 \\ 2 & 3 & 6 & 1 \\ 1 & 1 & 1 & 1 \end{vmatrix} =$

$1(-1)^3 \begin{vmatrix} -1 & 3 & 1 \\ 3 & 6 & 1 \\ 1 & 1 & 1 \end{vmatrix} + 2(-1)^4 \begin{vmatrix} 1 & 3 & 1 \\ 2 & 6 & 1 \\ 1 & 1 & 1 \end{vmatrix} + 0 - 3(-1)^6 \begin{vmatrix} 1 & -1 & 3 \\ 2 & 3 & 6 \\ 1 & 1 & 1 \end{vmatrix} =$

$1(-1)(-14) + 2(1)(-2) - 3(1)(-10) = 14 - 4 + 30 = 40.$

$\Delta_y = \begin{vmatrix} 1 & -14 & 3 & 1 \\ 1 & 12 & 0 & -3 \\ 2 & 1 & 6 & 1 \\ 1 & 6 & 1 & 1 \end{vmatrix} =$

$3(-1)^4 \begin{vmatrix} 1 & 12 & -3 \\ 2 & 1 & 1 \\ 1 & 6 & 1 \end{vmatrix} + 0 + 6(-1)^6 \begin{vmatrix} 1 & -14 & 1 \\ 1 & 12 & -3 \\ 1 & 6 & 1 \end{vmatrix} + 1(-1)^7 \begin{vmatrix} 1 & -14 & 1 \\ 1 & 12 & -3 \\ 2 & 1 & 1 \end{vmatrix} =$

$3(1)(-50) + 6(1)(80) + 1(-1)(90) = -150 + 480 - 90 = 240.$

$\Delta_w = \begin{vmatrix} 1 & -1 & 3 & -14 \\ 1 & 2 & 0 & 12 \\ 2 & 3 & 6 & 1 \\ 1 & 1 & 1 & 6 \end{vmatrix} =$

$1(-1)^3 \begin{vmatrix} -1 & 3 & -14 \\ 3 & 6 & 1 \\ 1 & 1 & 6 \end{vmatrix} + 2(-1)^4 \begin{vmatrix} 1 & 3 & -14 \\ 2 & 6 & 1 \\ 1 & 1 & 6 \end{vmatrix} + 0 + 12(-1)^6 \begin{vmatrix} 1 & -1 & 3 \\ 2 & 3 & 6 \\ 1 & 1 & 1 \end{vmatrix} =$

$1(-1)(-44) + 2(1)(58) + 12(1)(-10) = 44 + 116 - 120 = 40.$

$y = \Delta_y/\Delta = 240/40 = 6, \quad w = \Delta_w/\Delta = 40/40 = 1.$

<u>Ans.</u> $y = 6, w = 1$

EXERCISE 8.9

1. $[c_{ij}] = \begin{bmatrix} 2 & -1 \\ 2 & 3 \end{bmatrix}$. $\text{adj } A = [c_{ij}]^T = \begin{bmatrix} 2 & 2 \\ -1 & 3 \end{bmatrix}$. $|A| = 8$.

     $A^{-1} = \frac{1}{|A|} \text{ adj } A = \frac{1}{8}\begin{bmatrix} 2 & 2 \\ -1 & 3 \end{bmatrix} = \begin{bmatrix} 1/4 & 1/4 \\ -1/8 & 3/8 \end{bmatrix}$.

5. $[c_{ij}] = \begin{bmatrix} 7 & -4 & 1 \\ -8 & 5 & -1 \\ 5 & -3 & 1 \end{bmatrix}$. $\text{adj } A = [c_{ij}]^T = \begin{bmatrix} 7 & -8 & 5 \\ -4 & 5 & -3 \\ 1 & -1 & 1 \end{bmatrix}$.

     $|A| = 1$. $A^{-1} = \frac{1}{|A|} \text{ adj } A = 1\begin{bmatrix} 7 & -8 & 5 \\ -4 & 5 & -3 \\ 1 & -1 & 1 \end{bmatrix} = \begin{bmatrix} 7 & -8 & 5 \\ -4 & 5 & -3 \\ 1 & -1 & 1 \end{bmatrix}$.

9. $[c_{ij}] = \begin{bmatrix} -1/4 & 0 & -1/4 \\ 1/8 & -1/4 & -1/8 \\ -3/8 & 0 & -1/8 \end{bmatrix}$.

     $\text{adj } A = [c_{ij}]^T = \begin{bmatrix} -1/4 & 1/8 & -3/8 \\ 0 & -1/4 & 0 \\ -1/4 & -1/8 & -1/8 \end{bmatrix}$. $|A| = -\frac{1}{8}$.

     $A^{-1} = \frac{1}{|A|} \text{ adj } A = -8\begin{bmatrix} -1/4 & 1/8 & -3/8 \\ 0 & -1/4 & 0 \\ -1/4 & -1/8 & -1/8 \end{bmatrix} = \begin{bmatrix} 2 & -1 & 3 \\ 0 & 2 & 0 \\ 2 & 1 & 1 \end{bmatrix}$.

13. $A = \begin{bmatrix} a & b \\ c & d \end{bmatrix}$. $[c_{ij}] = \begin{bmatrix} (-1)^{1+1}d & (-1)^{1+2}c \\ (-1)^{2+1}b & (-1)^{2+2}a \end{bmatrix} = \begin{bmatrix} d & -c \\ -b & a \end{bmatrix}$.

     $\text{adj } A = [c_{ij}]^T = \begin{bmatrix} d & -b \\ -c & a \end{bmatrix}$.

EXERCISE 8.10

1. $A = \begin{bmatrix} \dfrac{200}{1200} & \dfrac{500}{1500} \\ \dfrac{400}{1200} & \dfrac{200}{1500} \end{bmatrix} = \begin{bmatrix} \dfrac{1}{6} & \dfrac{1}{3} \\ \dfrac{1}{3} & \dfrac{2}{15} \end{bmatrix}.$

$I - A = \begin{bmatrix} 1 & 0 \\ 0 & 1 \end{bmatrix} - \begin{bmatrix} 1/6 & 1/3 \\ 1/3 & 2/15 \end{bmatrix} = \begin{bmatrix} 5/6 & -1/3 \\ -1/3 & 13/15 \end{bmatrix}.$

$(I - A)^{-1} = \begin{bmatrix} 78/55 & 6/11 \\ 6/11 & 15/11 \end{bmatrix}.$

$X = (I - A)^{-1}C = \begin{bmatrix} 78/55 & 6/11 \\ 6/11 & 15/11 \end{bmatrix}\begin{bmatrix} 600 \\ 805 \end{bmatrix} = \begin{bmatrix} 1290 \\ 1425 \end{bmatrix}.$

The total value of other production costs is

$P_A + P_B = \dfrac{600}{1200}(1290) + \dfrac{800}{1500}(1425) = 645 + 760 = 1405.$

<u>Ans.</u> $\begin{bmatrix} 1290 \\ 1425 \end{bmatrix}$; 1405

CHAPTER 8 - REVIEW PROBLEMS

1. $\begin{bmatrix} 3 & 4 \\ -5 & 1 \end{bmatrix} - 2\begin{bmatrix} 1 & 0 \\ 2 & 4 \end{bmatrix} = \begin{bmatrix} 9 & 12 \\ -15 & 3 \end{bmatrix} - \begin{bmatrix} 2 & 0 \\ 4 & 8 \end{bmatrix} = \begin{bmatrix} 7 & 12 \\ -19 & -5 \end{bmatrix}$

5. $\begin{bmatrix} 1 & 0 \\ -1 & 4 \end{bmatrix}\left\{\begin{bmatrix} 1 & 4 \\ 6 & 5 \end{bmatrix} - \begin{bmatrix} 2 & 6 \\ 5 & 0 \end{bmatrix}\right\} = \begin{bmatrix} 1 & 0 \\ -1 & 4 \end{bmatrix}\begin{bmatrix} -1 & -2 \\ 1 & 5 \end{bmatrix} =$

$\begin{bmatrix} -1+0 & -2+0 \\ 1+4 & 2+20 \end{bmatrix} = \begin{bmatrix} -1 & -2 \\ 5 & 22 \end{bmatrix}$

9. $\begin{bmatrix} 1 & 4 \\ 5 & 8 \end{bmatrix} \sim \begin{bmatrix} 1 & 4 \\ 0 & -12 \end{bmatrix} \sim \begin{bmatrix} 1 & 4 \\ 0 & 1 \end{bmatrix} \sim \begin{bmatrix} 1 & 0 \\ 0 & 1 \end{bmatrix}$

13. $\begin{bmatrix} 2 & -5 \\ 4 & 3 \end{bmatrix} \sim \begin{bmatrix} 2 & -5 \\ 0 & 13 \end{bmatrix} \sim \begin{bmatrix} 1 & -1/5 \\ 0 & 1 \end{bmatrix} \sim \begin{bmatrix} 1 & 0 \\ 0 & 1 \end{bmatrix}$

<u>Ans.</u> x = 0, y = 0

17. $\begin{bmatrix} 1 & 5 & | & 1 & 0 \\ 3 & 9 & | & 0 & 1 \end{bmatrix} \sim \begin{bmatrix} 1 & 5 & | & 1 & 0 \\ 0 & -6 & | & -3 & 1 \end{bmatrix} \sim \begin{bmatrix} 1 & 5 & | & 1 & 0 \\ 0 & 1 & | & 1/2 & -1/6 \end{bmatrix} \sim$

$\begin{bmatrix} 1 & 0 & | & -3/2 & 5/6 \\ 0 & 1 & | & 1/2 & -1/6 \end{bmatrix}.$ $\qquad$ <u>Ans.</u> $\begin{bmatrix} -3/2 & 5/6 \\ 1/2 & -1/6 \end{bmatrix}$

21. $\begin{bmatrix} 3 & 1 & 4 & | & 1 & 0 & 0 \\ 1 & 0 & 1 & | & 0 & 1 & 0 \\ 0 & 2 & 1 & | & 0 & 0 & 1 \end{bmatrix} \sim \begin{bmatrix} 1 & 0 & 1 & | & 0 & 1 & 0 \\ 3 & 1 & 4 & | & 1 & 0 & 0 \\ 0 & 2 & 1 & | & 0 & 0 & 1 \end{bmatrix} \sim$

$\begin{bmatrix} 1 & 0 & 1 & | & 0 & 1 & 0 \\ 0 & 1 & 1 & | & 1 & -3 & 0 \\ 0 & 2 & 1 & | & 0 & 0 & 1 \end{bmatrix} \sim \begin{bmatrix} 1 & 0 & 1 & | & 0 & 1 & 0 \\ 0 & 1 & 1 & | & 1 & -3 & 0 \\ 0 & 0 & -1 & | & -2 & 6 & 1 \end{bmatrix} \sim$

$\begin{bmatrix} 1 & 0 & 1 & | & 0 & 1 & 0 \\ 0 & 1 & 1 & | & 1 & -3 & 0 \\ 0 & 0 & 1 & | & 2 & -6 & -1 \end{bmatrix} \sim \begin{bmatrix} 1 & 0 & 0 & | & -2 & 7 & 1 \\ 0 & 1 & 0 & | & -1 & 3 & 1 \\ 0 & 0 & 1 & | & 2 & -6 & -1 \end{bmatrix}.$

$\begin{bmatrix} x \\ y \\ z \end{bmatrix} = A^{-1}C = \begin{bmatrix} -2 & 7 & 1 \\ -1 & 3 & 1 \\ 2 & -6 & -1 \end{bmatrix} \begin{bmatrix} 1 \\ 0 \\ 2 \end{bmatrix} = \begin{bmatrix} 0 \\ 1 \\ 0 \end{bmatrix}.$

<u>Ans.</u> x = 0, y = 1, z = 0

25. Expanding along row 2 gives

$0 + 1(-1)^4 \begin{vmatrix} 1 & -1 \\ 1 & 2 \end{vmatrix} + 4(-1)^5 \begin{vmatrix} 1 & 2 \\ 1 & 2 \end{vmatrix} =$

$1(1)[2 - (-1)] + 4(-1)[2 - 2] = 3 + 0 = 3.$ $\qquad$ <u>Ans.</u> 3

29. $\Delta = \begin{vmatrix} 3 & -1 \\ 2 & 3 \end{vmatrix} = 11$, $\Delta_x = \begin{vmatrix} 1 & -1 \\ 8 & 3 \end{vmatrix} = 11$, $\Delta_y = \begin{vmatrix} 3 & 1 \\ 2 & 8 \end{vmatrix} = 22$.

$x = \Delta_x/\Delta = 11/11 = 1$, $y = \Delta_y/\Delta = 22/11 = 2$.

<u>Ans.</u> $x = 1$, $y = 2$

33. $A = \begin{bmatrix} 0/3 & 2/4 \\ 1/3 & 0/4 \end{bmatrix} = \begin{bmatrix} 0 & 1/2 \\ 1/3 & 0 \end{bmatrix}$.

$I - A = \begin{bmatrix} 1 & 0 \\ 0 & 1 \end{bmatrix} - \begin{bmatrix} 0 & 1/2 \\ 1/3 & 0 \end{bmatrix} = \begin{bmatrix} 1 & -1/2 \\ -1/3 & 1 \end{bmatrix}$.

$(I - A)^{-1} = \begin{bmatrix} 6/5 & 3/5 \\ 2/5 & 6/5 \end{bmatrix}$.

$X = (I - A)^{-1}C = \begin{bmatrix} 6/5 & 3/5 \\ 2/5 & 6/5 \end{bmatrix} \begin{bmatrix} 2 \\ 2 \end{bmatrix} = \begin{bmatrix} 3.6 \\ 3.2 \end{bmatrix}$. <u>Ans.</u> $\begin{bmatrix} 3.6 \\ 3.2 \end{bmatrix}$

CHAPTER 8 — MATHEMATICAL SNAPSHOT

1. $A = \begin{bmatrix} 20 & 40 & 30 & 10 \\ 30 & 0 & 10 & 10 \\ 10 & 0 & 30 & 50 \end{bmatrix}$, $T = \begin{bmatrix} 7 \\ 10 \\ 7 \\ 5 \end{bmatrix}$, $C = \begin{bmatrix} 9 \\ 8 \\ 10 \end{bmatrix}$.

$C^T(AT) = C^T \left\{ \begin{bmatrix} 20 & 40 & 30 & 10 \\ 30 & 0 & 10 & 10 \\ 10 & 0 & 30 & 50 \end{bmatrix} \begin{bmatrix} 7 \\ 10 \\ 7 \\ 5 \end{bmatrix} \right\} = C^T \begin{bmatrix} 800 \\ 330 \\ 530 \end{bmatrix}$

$= \begin{bmatrix} 9 & 8 & 10 \end{bmatrix} \begin{bmatrix} 800 \\ 330 \\ 530 \end{bmatrix} = [15,140]$. <u>Ans.</u> $151.40

9

Linear
Programming

1.

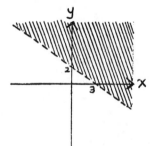

5.

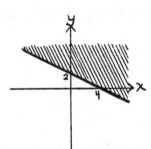

9.

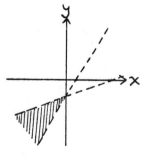

13.

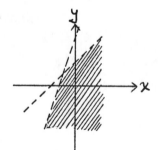

17.

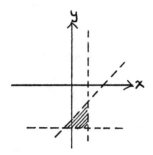

21.

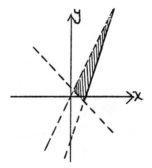

25.

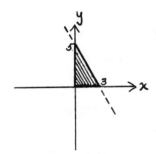

EXERCISE 9.2

1. Feasible region appears on next page. The corner points
   are (0,0), (60,0), and (40,20). P is maximized at (40,20)
   where its value is 640.
   <u>Ans.</u> P = 640 when x = 40, y = 20

5. Feasible region (see next page) is empty.
   <u>Ans.</u> no optimum solution

1.

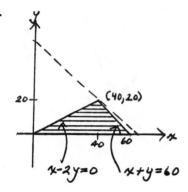

5.

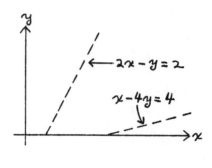

9. Feasible region (see next page) is unbounded. C is minimized at the corner point (3/5,6/5) where its value is
   2.4.   <u>Ans.</u> C = 2.4 when x = 3/5, y = 6/5

13. Let x and y be the numbers of widgets and wadgits made per
    week, respsctively. Then we are to maximize P = 4x + 6y
    where

$$\begin{cases} x \geqq 0, \\ y \geqq 0, \\ 2x + y \leqq 70 \quad \text{(for machine A),} \\ x + y \leqq 40 \quad \text{(for machine B),} \\ x + 3y \leqq 90 \quad \text{(for finishing).} \end{cases}$$

Feasible region appears on **next page**. The corner points
are (0,0), (0,30), (15,25), (30,10), and (35,0). P is
maximized at (15,25) where its value is 210.
<u>Ans.</u> 15 widgets, 25 wadgits; $210

9.

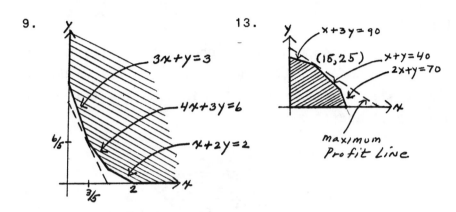

13.

17. Let x and y be the numbers of tons of ores I and II, respectively, that are processed. Then we are to minimize C = 50x + 60y where

$$\begin{cases} x \geqq 0, \\ y \geqq 0, \\ 100x + 200y \geqq 3000 \quad \text{(for mineral A)}, \\ 200x + 50y \geqq 2500 \quad \text{(for mineral B)}, \end{cases}$$

The feasible region (see below) is unbounded. C is mini-mized at the corner point (10,10) where C = 1100.

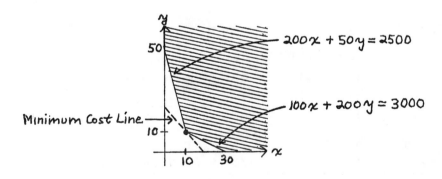

Ans.   10 tons of ore I, 10 tons of ore II; $1100

EXERCISE 9.3

1. Feasible region (see below) is unbounded. Z is minimized
   at the corner points (2,3) and (5,2) where its value is
   33. Z is also minimized at all points on the line segment
   joining (2,3) and (5,2).

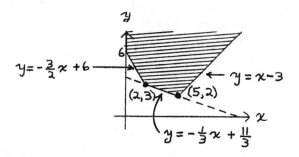

Ans. Z = 33 when x = (1-t)(2)+5t = 2+3t,

      y = (1-t)(3)+2t = 3-t, and 0 ≤ t ≤ 1

EXERCISE 9.4

	x_1	x_2	s_1	s_2	Z		
1. s_1	2	1	1	0	0	8	8
s_2	2	③	0	1	0	12	4
Z	-1	-2	0	0	1	0	

	x_1	x_2	s_1	s_2	Z	
s_1	4/3	0	1	-1/3	0	4
x_2	2/3	1	0	1/3	0	4
Z	1/3	0	0	2/3	1	8

Ans. Z = 8 when x_1 = 0, x_2 = 4

5.

	x_1	x_2	s_1	s_2	s_3	Z		
s_1	[1]	-1	1	0	0	0	1	1
s_2	1	2	0	1	0	0	8	8
s_3	1	1	0	0	1	0	5	5
Z	-8	-2	0	0	0	1	0	

	x_1	x_2	s_1	s_2	s_3	Z		
x_1	1	-1	1	0	0	0	1	
s_2	0	3	-1	1	0	0	7	7/3
s_3	0	[2]	-1	0	1	0	4	2
Z	0	-10	8	0	0	1	8	

	x_1	x_2	s_1	s_2	s_3	Z	
x_1	1	0	1/2	0	1/2	0	3
s_2	0	0	1/2	1	-3/2	0	1
x_2	0	1	-1/2	0	1/2	0	2
Z	0	0	3	0	5	1	28

<u>Ans.</u> $Z = 28$ when $x_1 = 3$, $x_2 = 2$

9. To obtain a standard linear programming problem, we write the second constraint as $-x_1 + 2x_2 + x_3 \leqq 2$.

	x_1	x_2	x_3	s_1	s_2	Z		
s_1	[1]	1	0	1	0	0	1	1
s_2	-1	2	1	0	1	0	2	
Z	-2	-1	1	0	0	1	0	

	x_1	x_2	x_3	s_1	s_2	Z	
x_1	1	1	0	1	0	0	1
s_2	0	3	1	1	1	0	3
Z	0	1	1	2	0	1	2

<u>Ans.</u> $Z = 2$ when $x_1 = 1$, $x_2 = 0$, $x_3 = 0$

13. To obtain a standard linear programming problem, we write the second constraint as $x_1 - x_2 + x_3 \leq 2$ and the third constraint as $x_1 - x_2 - x_3 \leq 1$.

	x_1	x_2	x_3	s_1	s_2	s_3	W		
s_1	4	3	-1	1	0	0	0 |	1	
s_2	-1	-1	☐1	0	1	0	0 |	2	2
s_3	1	-1	-1	0	0	1	0 |	1	
W	-1	12	-4	0	0	0	1 |	0	

	x_1	x_2	x_3	s_1	s_2	s_3	W		
s_1	☐3	2	0	1	1	0	0 |	3	1
x_3	-1	-1	1	0	1	0	0 |	2	
s_3	0	-2	0	0	1	1	0 |	3	
W	-5	8	0	0	4	0	1 |	8	

	x_1	x_2	x_3	s_1	s_2	s_3	W	
x_1	1	2/3	0	1/3	1/3	0	0 |	1
x_3	0	-1/3	1	1/3	4/3	0	0 |	3
s_3	0	-2	0	0	1	1	0 |	3
W	0	34/3	0	5/3	17/3	0	1 |	13

<u>Ans.</u> $W = 13$ when $x_1 = 1$, $x_2 = 0$, $x_3 = 3$

17. Let x_1 and x_2 denote the numbers of boxes transported from A and B, respectively. The revenue received is $R = 0.75x_1 + 0.50x_2$. We want to maximize R subject to

$$2x_1 + x_2 \leq 2400 \quad \text{(volume)},$$
$$3x_1 + 5x_2 \leq 9200 \quad \text{(weight)},$$
$$x_1, x_2 \geq 0.$$

	x_1	x_2	s_1	s_2	R		
s_1	☐2	1	1	0	0 |	2400	1200
s_2	3	5	0	1	0 |	9200	$3066\frac{2}{3}$
R	-3/4	-1/2	0	0	1 |	0	

	x_1	x_2	s_1	s_2	R		
x_1	1	1/2	1/2	0	0	1200	2400
s_2	0	⌷7/2⌷	-3/2	1	0	5600	1600
R	0	-1/8	3/8	0	1	900	

	x_1	x_2	s_1	s_2	R	
x_1	1	0	5/7	-1/7	0	400
x_2	0	1	-3/7	2/7	0	1600
R	0	0	9/28	1/28	1	1100

<u>Ans.</u> 400 from A, 1600 from B; $1100

EXERCISE 9.5

1. Yes; for the tableau, x_2 is the entering variable and the
quotients 6/2 and 3/1 tie for being the smallest.

	x_1	x_2	s_1	s_2	s_3	Z		
5. s_1	⌷1⌷	-1	1	0	0	0	4	4
s_2	-1	1	0	1	0	0	4	
s_3	1	1	0	0	1	0	6	6
Z	-3	3	0	0	0	1	0	

	x_1	x_2	s_1	s_2	s_3	Z		
x_1	1	-1	1	0	0	0	4	
s_2	0	0	1	1	0	0	8	
s_3	0	⌷2⌷	-1	0	1	0	2	1
Z	0	0	3	0	0	1	12	

The maximum value of Z is 12, when $x_1 = 4$, $x_2 = 0$. Since
x_2 is nonbasic for the last tableau and its indicator is
0, there may be multiple optimum solutions. Treating x_2
as an entering variable and continuing, we have

	x_1	x_2	s_1	s_2	s_3	Z	
x_1	1	0	1/2	0	1/2	0	5
s_2	0	0	1	1	0	0	8
x_2	0	1	-1/2	0	1/2	0	1
Z	0	0	3	0	0	1	12

Here $Z = 12$ when $x_1 = 5$, $x_2 = 1$. Thus multiple optimum

solutions exist. Hence Z is maximum when

$$x_1 = (1-t)(4) + 5t = 4 + t,$$

$$x_2 = (1-t)(0) + (1)t = t,$$

and $0 \leq t \leq 1$. For the last tableau, s_3 is nonbasic and

its indicator is 0. If we continue the process for

determining other optimum solutions, we return to the

second tableau.

Ans. $Z = 12$ when $x_1 = (1-t)(4) + 5t = 4 + t,$

$x_2 = (1-t)(0) + (1)t = t$, and $0 \leq t \leq 1$

9. To obtain a standard linear programming problem, we write

the second constraint as $4x_1 + x_2 \leq 6$.

	x_1	x_2	x_3	s_1	s_2	Z		
s_1	2	1	1	1	0	0	7	7/2
s_2	[4]	1	0	0	1	0	6	3/2
Z	-6	-2	-1	0	0	1	0	
s_1	0	1/2	[1]	1	-1/2	0	4	4
x_1	1	1/4	0	0	1/4	0	3/2	
Z	0	-1/2	-1	0	3/2	1	9	
x_3	0	1/2	1	1	-1/2	0	4	8
x_1	1	[1/4]	0	0	1/4	0	3/2	6
Z	0	0	0	1	1	1	13	

Z has a maximum value of 13 when $x_1 = 3/2$, $x_2 = 0$, $x_3 = 4$. Since x_2 is nonbasic for the last tableau and its indicator is 0, there may be multiple optimum solutions. Treating x_2 as an entering variable, we have

	x_1	x_2	x_3	s_1	s_2	Z	
x_3	-2	0	1	1	-1	0	1
x_2	4	1	0	0	1	0	6
Z	0	0	0	1	1	1	13

Here $Z = 13$ when $x_1 = 0$, $x_2 = 6$, $x_3 = 1$. Thus multiple optimum solutions exist. Hence Z is maximum when

$$x_1 = (1-t)(3/2) + 0t = (3/2) - (3/2)t,$$

$$x_2 = (1-t)(0) + 6t = 6t,$$

$$x_3 = (1-t)(4) + (1)t = 4 - 3t,$$

and $0 \leq t \leq 1$. For the last tableau, x_1 is nonbasic and its indicator is 0. If we continue the process for determining other optimum solutions, we return to the third tableau.

<u>Ans.</u> $Z = 13$ when $x_1 = (1-t)(3/2) + 0t = (3/2) - (3/2)t$, $x_2 = (1-t)(0) + 6t = 6t$, $x_3 = (1-t)(4) + (1)t = 4 - 3t$, and $0 \leq t \leq 1$

EXERCISE 9.6

	x_1	x_2	s_1	s_2	t_2	W	

1.

$$
\begin{bmatrix}
1 & 1 & 1 & 0 & 0 & 0 & | & 6 \\
-1 & 1 & 0 & -1 & 1 & 0 & | & 4 \\
\hline
-2 & -1 & 0 & 0 & M & 1 & | & 0
\end{bmatrix}
$$

$$
\begin{array}{c}
s_1 \\ t_2 \\ W
\end{array}
\begin{bmatrix}
1 & 1 & 1 & 0 & 0 & 0 & | & 6 \\ 6
-1 & \boxed{1} & 0 & -1 & 1 & 0 & | & 4 \\ 4
\hline
-2+M & -1-M & 0 & M & 0 & 1 & | & -4M
\end{bmatrix}
$$

$$
\begin{array}{c}
s_1 \\ x_2 \\ W
\end{array}
\begin{bmatrix}
\boxed{2} & 0 & 1 & 1 & -1 & 0 & | & 2 \\ 1
-1 & 1 & 0 & -1 & 1 & 0 & | & 4 \\
\hline
-3 & 0 & 0 & -1 & M+1 & 1 & | & 4
\end{bmatrix}
$$

	x_1	x_2	s_1	s_2	Z	

$$
\begin{array}{c}
x_1 \\ x_2 \\ Z
\end{array}
\begin{bmatrix}
1 & 0 & 1/2 & 1/2 & 0 & | & 1 \\
0 & 1 & 1/2 & -1/2 & 0 & | & 5 \\
\hline
0 & 0 & 3/2 & 1/2 & 1 & | & 7
\end{bmatrix}
$$

<u>Ans.</u> Z = 7 when $x_1 = 1$, $x_2 = 5$

	x_1	x_2	x_3	s_1	t_2	W	

5.

$$
\begin{bmatrix}
2 & 1 & 3 & 1 & 0 & 0 & | & 10 \\
1 & -1 & 1 & 0 & 1 & 0 & | & 4 \\
\hline
-4 & -1 & -2 & 0 & M & 1 & | & 0
\end{bmatrix}
$$

$$
\begin{array}{c}
s_1 \\ t_2 \\ W
\end{array}
\begin{bmatrix}
2 & 1 & 3 & 1 & 0 & 0 & | & 10 \\ 5
\boxed{1} & -1 & 1 & 0 & 1 & 0 & | & 4 \\ 4
\hline
-4-M & -1+M & -2-M & 0 & 0 & 1 & | & -4M
\end{bmatrix}
$$

$$
\begin{array}{c}
s_1 \\ x_1 \\ W
\end{array}
\begin{bmatrix}
0 & \boxed{3} & 1 & 1 & -2 & 0 & | & 2 \\ 2/3
1 & -1 & 1 & 0 & 1 & 0 & | & 4 \\
\hline
0 & -5 & 2 & 0 & 4+M & 1 & | & 16
\end{bmatrix}
$$

$$
\begin{array}{c}
 & x_1 & x_2 & x_3 & s_1 & Z \\
x_2 & \begin{bmatrix} 0 \\ 1 \\ \hline 0 \end{bmatrix} & \begin{matrix} 1 \\ 0 \\ 0 \end{matrix} & \begin{matrix} 1/3 \\ 4/3 \\ 11/3 \end{matrix} & \begin{matrix} 1/3 \\ 1/3 \\ 5/3 \end{matrix} & \begin{matrix} 0 \mid 2/3 \\ 0 \mid 14/3 \\ 1 \mid 58/3 \end{matrix}
\end{array}
$$

Columns: x_1, x_2, x_3, s_1, Z

	x_1	x_2	x_3	s_1	Z	
x_2	0	1	1/3	1/3	0	2/3
x_1	1	0	4/3	1/3	0	14/3
Z	0	0	11/3	5/3	1	58/3

Ans. $Z = 58/3$ when $x_1 = 14/3$, $x_2 = 2/3$, $x_3 = 0$

9. We first write the third constraint as $-x_1 + x_2 + x_3 \geq 6$.

x_1	x_2	x_3	s_1	s_2	s_3	t_2	t_3	W	
1	1	1	1	0	0	0	0	0	1
1	-1	1	0	-1	0	1	0	0	2
-1	1	1	0	0	-1	0	1	0	6
-3	2	-1	0	0	0	M	M	1	0

	x_1	x_2	x_3	s_1	s_2	s_3	t_2	t_3	W		
s_1	1	1	[1]	1	0	0	0	0	0	1	1
t_2	1	-1	1	0	-1	0	1	0	0	2	2
t_3	-1	1	1	0	0	-1	0	1	0	6	6
W	-3	2	-1-2M	0	M	M	0	0	1	-8M	

	x_1	x_2	x_3	s_1	s_2	s_3	t_2	t_3	W	
x_3	1	1	1	1	0	0	0	0	0	1
t_2	0	-2	0	-1	-1	0	1	0	0	1
t_3	-2	0	0	-1	0	-1	0	1	0	5
W	-2+2M	3+2M	0	1+2M	M	M	0	0	1	1-6M

Ans. no solution (empty feasible region)

13. Let x_1 and x_2 denote the numbers of Standard and Executive bookcases produced, respectively, each week. We want to maximize the profit function $P = 10x_1 + 12x_2$ subject to

$$x_1 + 2x_2 \leq 400,$$

$$2x_1 + 3x_2 \leq 510,$$

$$2x_1 + 3x_2 \geq 240,$$

$$x_1, x_2 \geq 0.$$

The artificial objective function is $W = P - Mt_3$.

$$
\begin{array}{c}
\begin{array}{ccccccc}
x_1 & x_2 & s_1 & s_2 & s_3 & t_3 & W
\end{array} \\
\left[\begin{array}{ccccccc|c}
1 & 2 & 1 & 0 & 0 & 0 & 0 & 400 \\
2 & 3 & 0 & 1 & 0 & 0 & 0 & 510 \\
2 & 3 & 0 & 0 & -1 & 1 & 0 & 240 \\
\hline
-10 & -12 & 0 & 0 & 0 & M & 1 & 0
\end{array}\right]
\end{array}
$$

$$
\begin{array}{c}
\begin{array}{ccccccc}
 & x_1 & x_2 & s_1 & s_2 & s_3 & t_3 & W
\end{array} \\
\begin{array}{c}
s_1 \\ s_2 \\ t_3 \\ W
\end{array}
\left[\begin{array}{ccccccc|c}
1 & 2 & 1 & 0 & 0 & 0 & 0 & 400 \\
2 & 3 & 0 & 1 & 0 & 0 & 0 & 510 \\
2 & \boxed{3} & 0 & 0 & -1 & 1 & 0 & 240 \\
\hline
-10-2M & -12-3M & 0 & 0 & M & 0 & 1 & -240M
\end{array}\right]
\begin{array}{c}
200 \\ 170 \\ 80
\end{array}
\end{array}
$$

$$
\begin{array}{c}
\begin{array}{c}
s_1 \\ s_2 \\ x_2 \\ W
\end{array}
\left[\begin{array}{ccccccc|c}
-1/3 & 0 & 1 & 0 & 2/3 & -2/3 & 0 & 240 \\
0 & 0 & 0 & 1 & \boxed{1} & -1 & 0 & 270 \\
2/3 & 1 & 0 & 0 & -1/3 & 1/3 & 0 & 80 \\
\hline
-2 & 0 & 0 & 0 & -4 & 4+M & 1 & 960
\end{array}\right]
\begin{array}{c}
360 \\ 270
\end{array}
\end{array}
$$

$$
\begin{array}{c}
\begin{array}{cccccc}
x_1 & x_2 & s_1 & s_2 & s_3 & P
\end{array} \\
\begin{array}{c}
s_1 \\ s_3 \\ x_2 \\ P
\end{array}
\left[\begin{array}{cccccc|c}
-1/3 & 0 & 1 & -2/3 & 0 & 0 & 60 \\
0 & 0 & 0 & 1 & 1 & 0 & 270 \\
\boxed{2/3} & 1 & 0 & 1/3 & 0 & 0 & 170 \\
\hline
-2 & 0 & 0 & 4 & 0 & 1 & 2040
\end{array}\right]
\begin{array}{c}
255
\end{array}
\end{array}
$$

$$
\begin{array}{c}
\begin{array}{c}
s_1 \\ s_3 \\ x_1 \\ P
\end{array}
\left[\begin{array}{cccccc|c}
0 & 1/2 & 1 & -1/2 & 0 & 0 & 145 \\
0 & 0 & 0 & 1 & 1 & 0 & 270 \\
1 & 3/2 & 0 & 1/2 & 0 & 0 & 255 \\
\hline
0 & 3 & 0 & 5 & 0 & 1 & 2550
\end{array}\right]
\end{array}
$$

<u>Ans.</u> 255 Standard, 0 Executive bookcases

EXERCISE 9.7

	x_1	x_2	s_1	s_2	t_1	t_2	W	
1.	-1	1	-1	0	1	0	0	6
	1	1	0	-1	0	1	0	10
	3	6	0	0	M	M	1	0

	x_1	x_2	s_1	s_2	t_1	t_2	W		
t_1	-1	[1]	-1	0	1	0	0	6	6
t_2	1	1	0	-1	0	1	0	10	10
W	3	6-2M	M	M	0	0	1	-16M	

	x_1	x_2	s_1	s_2	t_1	t_2	W		
x_2	-1	1	-1	0	1	0	0	6	
t_2	[2]	0	1	-1	-1	1	0	4	2
W	9-2M	0	6-M	M	-6+2M	0	1	-36-4M	

	x_1	x_2	s_1	s_2	t_1	t_2	W	
x_2	0	1	-1/2	-1/2	1/2	1/2	0	8
x_1	1	0	1/2	-1/2	-1/2	1/2	0	2
W	0	0	3/2	9/2	$-\frac{3}{2}+M$	$-\frac{9}{2}+M$	1	-54

<u>Ans.</u> Z = 54 when x_1 = 2, x_2 = 8

5. We write the second constraint as $-x_1 + x_3 \geqq 4$.

	x_1	x_2	x_3	s_1	s_2	s_3	t_2	W	
	1	1	1	1	0	0	0	0	6
	-1	0	1	0	-1	0	1	0	4
	0	1	1	0	0	1	0	0	5
	2	3	1	0	0	0	M	1	0

	x_1	x_2	x_3	s_1	s_2	s_3	t_2	W		
s_1	1	1	1	1	0	0	0	0	6	6
t_2	-1	0	[1]	0	-1	0	1	0	4	4
s_3	0	1	1	0	0	1	0	0	5	5
W	2+M	3	1-M	0	M	0	0	1	-4M	

	x_1	x_2	x_3	s_1	s_2	s_3	t_2	W	
s_1	2	1	0	1	1	0	-1	0	2
x_3	-1	0	1	0	-1	0	1	0	4
s_3	1	1	0	0	1	1	-1	0	1
W	3	3	0	0	1	0	-1+M	1	-4

<u>Ans.</u> Z = 4 when x_1 = 0, x_2 = 0, x_3 = 4

	x_1	x_2	x_3	s_1	s_2	t_1	t_2	W	

9.
$$\begin{bmatrix} 1 & 1 & 1 & -1 & 0 & 1 & 0 & 0 & | & 8 \\ -1 & 2 & 1 & 0 & -1 & 0 & 1 & 0 & | & 2 \\ \hline 1 & 8 & 5 & 0 & 0 & M & M & 1 & | & 0 \end{bmatrix}$$

$$\begin{matrix} t_1 \\ t_2 \\ W \end{matrix} \begin{bmatrix} 1 & 1 & 1 & -1 & 0 & 1 & 0 & 0 & | & 8 \\ -1 & \boxed{2} & 1 & 0 & -1 & 0 & 1 & 0 & | & 2 \\ \hline 1 & 8-3M & 5-2M & M & M & 0 & 0 & 1 & | & -10M \end{bmatrix}\begin{matrix} 8 \\ 1 \\ \end{matrix}$$

$$\begin{matrix} x_2 \\ t_2 \\ W \end{matrix} \begin{bmatrix} \boxed{3/2} & 0 & 1/2 & -1 & 1/2 & 1 & -1/2 & 0 & | & 7 \\ -1/2 & 1 & 1/2 & 0 & -1/2 & 0 & 1/2 & 0 & | & 1 \\ \hline 5-\frac{3}{2}M & 0 & 1-\frac{1}{2}M & M & 4-\frac{1}{2}M & 0 & -4+\frac{3}{2}M & 1 & | & -8-7M \end{bmatrix}\begin{matrix} 14/3 \\ \\ \end{matrix}$$

$$\begin{matrix} x_1 \\ t_2 \\ W \end{matrix} \begin{bmatrix} 1 & 0 & 1/3 & -2/3 & 1/3 & 2/3 & -1/3 & 0 & | & 14/3 \\ 0 & 1 & \boxed{2/3} & -1/3 & -1/3 & 1/3 & 1/3 & 0 & | & 10/3 \\ \hline 0 & 0 & -2/3 & 10/3 & 7/3 & -\frac{10}{3}+M & -\frac{7}{3}+M & 1 & | & -94/3 \end{bmatrix}\begin{matrix} 14 \\ 5 \\ \end{matrix}$$

$$\begin{matrix} x_1 \\ x_3 \\ W \end{matrix} \begin{bmatrix} 1 & -1/2 & 0 & -1/2 & 1/2 & 1/2 & -1/2 & 0 & | & 3 \\ 0 & 3/2 & 1 & -1/2 & -1/2 & 1/2 & 1/2 & 0 & | & 5 \\ \hline 0 & 1 & 0 & 3 & 2 & -3+M & -2+M & 1 & | & -28 \end{bmatrix}$$

<u>Ans.</u> Z = 28 when $x_1 = 3$, $x_2 = 0$, $x_3 = 5$

13. Let x_A = number of refrigerators shipped from A to Exton,

x_B = number of refrigerators shipped from B to Exton,

y_A = number of refrigerators shipped from A to Whyton,

y_B = number of refrigerators shipped from B to Whyton.

We want to minimize C = $15x_A + 11x_B + 13y_A + 12y_B$

subject to
$$x_A + x_B = 30,$$
$$y_A + y_B = 30,$$
$$x_A + y_A \leq 50,$$
$$x_B + y_B \leq 20,$$
$$x_A,\ x_B,\ y_A,\ y_B \geq 0.$$

	x_A	x_B	y_A	y_B	s_3	s_4	t_1	t_2	W		
	1	1	0	0	0	0	1	0	0	30	
	0	0	1	1	0	0	0	1	0	30	
	1	0	1	0	1	0	0	0	0	50	
	0	1	0	1	0	1	0	0	0	20	
	15	11	13	12	0	0	M	M	1	0	
t_1	1	1	0	0	0	0	1	0	0	30	30
t_2	0	0	1	1	0	0	0	1	0	30	
s_3	1	0	1	0	1	0	0	0	0	50	
s_4	0	[1]	0	1	0	1	0	0	0	20	20
W	15−M	11−M	13−M	12−M	0	0	0	0	1	−60M	
t_1	1	0	0	−1	0	−1	1	0	0	10	
t_2	0	0	[1]	1	0	0	0	1	0	30	30
s_3	1	0	1	0	1	0	0	0	0	50	50
x_B	0	1	0	1	0	1	0	0	0	20	
W	15−M	0	13−M	1	0	−11+M	0	0	1	−220−40M	
t_1	[1]	0	0	−1	0	−1	1	0	0	10	10
y_A	0	0	1	1	0	0	0	1	0	30	
s_3	1	0	0	−1	1	0	0	−1	0	20	20
x_B	0	1	0	1	0	1	0	0	0	20	
W	15−M	0	0	−12+M	0	−11+M	0	−13+M	1	−610−10M	
x_A	1	0	0	−1	0	−1	1	0	0	10	
y_A	0	0	1	1	0	0	0	1	0	30	
s_3	0	0	0	0	1	1	−1	−1	0	10	
x_B	0	1	0	1	0	1	0	0	0	20	
W	0	0	0	3	0	4	−15+M	−13+M	1	−760	

<u>Ans.</u> to Exton, 10 from A and 20 from B; to Whyton, 30

from A; $760

EXERCISE 9.8

1. Minimize $W = 6y_1 + 4y_2$ subject to

$$y_1 - y_2 \geqq 2,$$
$$y_1 + y_2 \geqq 3,$$
$$y_1, y_2 \geqq 0.$$

5. Min. $W = 13y_1 - 3y_2 - 11y_3$ subject to

$$-y_1 + y_2 - y_3 \geqq 1,$$
$$2y_1 - y_2 - y_3 \geqq -1,$$
$$y_1, y_2, y_3 \geqq 0.$$

9. Dual is: Maximize $W = y_1 + 2y_2$ subject to

$$y_1 - y_2 \leqq 4,$$
$$-y_1 + y_2 \leqq 4,$$
$$y_1 + y_2 \leqq 6,$$
$$y_1, y_2 \geqq 0.$$

	y_1	y_2	s_1	s_2	s_3	W		
s_1	1	-1	1	0	0	0	4	
s_2	-1	[1]	0	1	0	0	4	4
s_3	1	1	0	0	1	0	6	6
W	-1	-2	0	0	0	1	0	

	y_1	y_2	s_1	s_2	s_3	W		
s_1	0	0	1	1	0	0	8	
y_2	-1	1	0	1	0	0	4	
s_3	[2]	0	0	-1	1	0	2	1
W	-3	0	0	2	0	1	8	

$$
\begin{array}{c}
\begin{array}{cccccc}
y_1 & y_2 & s_1 & s_2 & s_3 & W
\end{array} \\
\begin{array}{c}
s_1 \\ y_2 \\ y_1 \\ \hline W
\end{array}
\left[
\begin{array}{cccccc|c}
0 & 0 & 1 & 1 & 0 & 0 & 8 \\
0 & 1 & 0 & 1/2 & 1/2 & 0 & 5 \\
1 & 0 & 0 & -1/2 & 1/2 & 0 & 1 \\
\hline
0 & 0 & 0 & 1/2 & 3/2 & 1 & 11
\end{array}
\right]
\end{array}
$$

<u>Ans.</u> $Z = 11$ when $x_1 = 0$, $x_2 = 1/2$, $x_3 = 3/2$

13. Dual is: Maximize $W = -y_1 + 3y_2$ subject to

$$y_1 + y_2 \leqq 6,$$

$$-y_1 + y_2 \leqq 4,$$

$$y_1, \ y_2 \geqq 0.$$

$$
\begin{array}{c}
\begin{array}{ccccc}
y_1 & y_2 & s_1 & s_2 & W
\end{array} \\
\begin{array}{c}
s_1 \\ s_2 \\ \hline W
\end{array}
\left[
\begin{array}{ccccc|cc}
1 & 1 & 1 & 0 & 0 & 6 & 6 \\
-1 & \boxed{1} & 0 & 1 & 0 & 4 & 4 \\
\hline
1 & -3 & 0 & 0 & 1 & 0 &
\end{array}
\right]
\end{array}
$$

$$
\begin{array}{c}
\begin{array}{c}
s_1 \\ y_2 \\ \hline W
\end{array}
\left[
\begin{array}{ccccc|cc}
\boxed{2} & 0 & 1 & -1 & 0 & 2 & 1 \\
-1 & 1 & 0 & 1 & 0 & 4 & \\
\hline
-2 & 0 & 0 & 3 & 1 & 12 &
\end{array}
\right]
\end{array}
$$

$$
\begin{array}{c}
\begin{array}{c}
y_1 \\ y_2 \\ \hline W
\end{array}
\left[
\begin{array}{ccccc|c}
1 & 0 & 1/2 & -1/2 & 0 & 1 \\
0 & 1 & 1/2 & 1/2 & 0 & 5 \\
\hline
0 & 0 & 1 & 2 & 1 & 14
\end{array}
\right]
\end{array}
$$

<u>Ans.</u> $Z = 14$ when $x_1 = 1$, $x_2 = 2$

17. Let y_1 = number of shipping clerk apprentices,

y_2 = number of shipping clerks,

y_3 = number of semiskilled workers,

y_4 = number of skilled workers.

We want to minimize $W = 2y_1 + 5y_2 + 4y_3 + 7y_4$ subject to

$$y_1 + y_2 \qquad\qquad \geqq 60,$$

$$-2y_1 + y_2 \qquad\qquad \geqq 0,$$

$$y_3 + y_4 \geqq 90,$$

$$y_3 - 2y_4 \geqq 0,$$

$$y_1, y_2, y_3, y_4 \geqq 0.$$

The dual is: Maximize $Z = 60x_1 + 0x_2 + 90x_3 + 0x_4$

subject to

$$x_1 - 2x_2 \qquad\qquad \leqq 2,$$

$$x_1 + x_2 \qquad\qquad \leqq 5,$$

$$x_3 + x_4 \leqq 4,$$

$$x_3 - 2x_4 \leqq 7,$$

$$x_1, x_2, x_3, x_4 \geqq 0.$$

	x_1	x_2	x_3	x_4	s_1	s_2	s_3	s_4	Z		
s_1	1	-2	0	0	1	0	0	0	0	2	
s_2	1	1	0	0	0	1	0	0	0	5	
s_3	0	0	[1]	1	0	0	1	0	0	4	4
s_4	0	0	1	-2	0	0	0	1	0	7	7
Z	-60	0	-90	0	0	0	0	0	1	0	

	x_1	x_2	x_3	x_4	s_1	s_2	s_3	s_4	Z		
s_1	[1]	-2	0	0	1	0	0	0	0	2	2
s_2	1	1	0	0	0	1	0	0	0	5	5
x_3	0	0	1	1	0	0	1	0	0	4	
s_4	0	0	0	-3	0	0	-1	1	0	3	
Z	-60	0	0	90	0	0	90	0	1	360	

	x_1	x_2	x_3	x_4	s_1	s_2	s_3	s_4	Z		
x_1	1	-2	0	0	1	0	0	0	0	2	
s_2	0	[3]	0	0	-1	1	0	0	0	3	1
x_3	0	0	1	1	0	0	1	0	0	4	
s_4	0	0	0	-3	0	0	-1	1	0	3	
Z	0	-120	0	90	60	0	90	0	1	480	

	x_1	x_2	x_3	x_4	s_1	s_2	s_3	s_4	Z	
x_1	1	0	0	0	1/3	2/3	0	0	0	4
x_2	0	1	0	0	-1/3	1/3	0	0	0	1
x_3	0	0	1	1	0	0	1	0	0	4
s_4	0	0	0	-3	0	0	-1	1	0	3
Z	0	0	0	90	20	40	90	0	1	600

<u>Ans.</u> 20 shipping clerk apprentices, 40 shipping clerks,
90 semiskilled workers, 0 skilled workers; $600

CHAPTER 9 - REVIEW PROBLEMS

1.   5.   9.

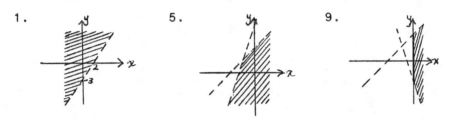

13. Feasible region (see next page) is unbounded. Z is
minimized at the corner point (0,2) where its value is -2.
<u>Ans.</u> Z = -2 when x = 0, y = 2

17. Feasible region appears on next page. The corner points
are (0,0), (0,4), (2,3), and (4,0). Z is maximized at
(2,3) and (4,0) where its value is 36. Thus Z is
maximized at all points on the line segment joining (2,3)
and (4,0).
<u>Ans.</u> Z = 36 when x = (1-t)(2) + 4t = 2 + 2t,
y = (1-t)(3) + 0t = 3 - 3t, and $0 \leqq t \leqq 1$

13.

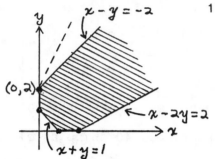

17.

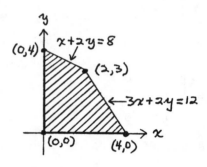

21.

	x_1	x_2	x_3	s	t	W	
	1	2	3	-1	1	0	6
	2	3	1	0	M	1	0

	x_1	x_2	x_3	s	t	W		
t	1	2	$\boxed{3}$	-1	1	0	6	2
W	2-M	3-2M	1-3M	M	0	1	-6M	

	x_1	x_2	x_3	s	t	W	
x_3	1/3	2/3	1	-1/3	1/3	0	2
W	5/3	7/3	0	1/3	$-\frac{1}{3}+M$	1	-2

<u>Ans.</u> $Z = 2$ when $x_1 = 0$, $x_2 = 0$, $x_3 = 2$

25. We write the first constraint as $-x_1 + x_2 + x_3 \geqq 1$.

	x_1	x_2	x_3	s_1	t_1	t_2	W	
	-1	1	1	-1	1	0	0	1
	6	3	2	0	0	1	0	12
	1	2	1	0	M	M	1	0

	x_1	x_2	x_3	s_1	t_1	t_2	W		
t_1	-1	1	1	-1	1	0	0	1	
t_2	$\boxed{6}$	3	2	0	0	1	0	12	2
W	1-5M	2-4M	1-3M	M	0	0	1	-13M	

	x_1	x_2	x_3	s_1	t_1	t_2	W		
t_1	0	$\boxed{3/2}$	4/3	-1	1	1/6	0	3	2
x_1	1	1/2	1/3	0	0	1/6	0	2	4
W	0	$\frac{3}{2}-\frac{3}{2}M$	$\frac{2}{3}-\frac{4}{3}M$	M	0	$-\frac{1}{6}+\frac{5}{6}M$	1	-2-3M	

$$
\begin{array}{c}
\quad\ \ x_1 \quad x_2 \quad x_3 \quad s_1 \quad\ t_1 \quad\ t_2 \quad\ W \\
\begin{array}{c} x_2 \\ x_1 \\ W \end{array}
\left[\begin{array}{cccccccc}
0 & 1 & \boxed{8/9} & -2/3 & 2/3 & 1/9 & 0 & | & 2 \\
1 & 0 & -1/9 & 1/3 & -1/3 & 1/9 & 0 & | & 1 \\
\hline
0 & 0 & -2/3 & 1 & -1+M & -\tfrac{1}{3}+M & 1 & | & -5
\end{array}\right]9/4
\end{array}
$$

$$
\begin{array}{c}
\quad\ \ x_1 \quad x_2 \quad x_3 \quad s_1 \quad\ -Z \\
\begin{array}{c} x_3 \\ x_1 \\ -Z \end{array}
\left[\begin{array}{cccccc}
0 & 9/8 & 1 & -3/4 & 0 & | & 9/4 \\
1 & 1/8 & 0 & 1/4 & 0 & | & 5/4 \\
\hline
0 & 3/4 & 0 & 1/2 & 1 & | & -7/2
\end{array}\right]
\end{array}
$$

Ans. $Z = 7/2$ when $x_1 = 5/4$, $x_2 = 0$, $x_3 = 9/4$

29. Dual is: Maximize $W = 35y_1 + 25y_2$ subject to

$$y_1 + y_2 \leqq 2,$$

$$2y_1 + y_2 \leqq 7,$$

$$3y_1 + y_2 \leqq 8,$$

$$y_1, y_2 \geqq 0.$$

$$
\begin{array}{c}
\quad\ \ y_1 \quad\ y_2 \quad s_1 \quad s_2 \quad s_3 \quad\ W \\
\begin{array}{c} s_1 \\ s_2 \\ s_3 \\ W \end{array}
\left[\begin{array}{cccccccc}
\boxed{1} & 1 & 1 & 0 & 0 & 0 & | & 2 \\
2 & 1 & 0 & 1 & 0 & 0 & | & 7 \\
3 & 1 & 0 & 0 & 1 & 0 & | & 8 \\
\hline
-35 & -25 & 0 & 0 & 0 & 1 & | & 0
\end{array}\right]
\begin{array}{c} 2 \\ 7/2 \\ 8/3 \\ \\ \end{array}
\end{array}
$$

$$
\begin{array}{c}
\begin{array}{c} y_1 \\ s_2 \\ s_3 \\ W \end{array}
\left[\begin{array}{cccccccc}
1 & 1 & 1 & 0 & 0 & 0 & | & 2 \\
0 & -1 & -2 & 1 & 0 & 0 & | & 3 \\
0 & -2 & -3 & 0 & 1 & 0 & | & 2 \\
\hline
0 & 10 & 35 & 0 & 0 & 1 & | & 70
\end{array}\right]
\end{array}
$$

Ans. $Z = 70$ when $x_1 = 35$, $x_2 = 0$, $x_3 = 0$

33. Let x_{AC}, x_{AD}, x_{BC}, and x_{BD} denote the amounts (in hundreds of thousands of gallons) transported from A to C, A to D, B to C, and B to D, respectively. If c is the total transportation cost in thousands of dollars, we want to minimize $c = x_{AC} + 2x_{AD} + 2x_{BC} + 4x_{BD}$ subject to

$$x_{AC} + x_{AD} \leq 6,$$

$$x_{BC} + x_{BD} \leq 6,$$

$$x_{AC} + x_{BC} = 5,$$

$$x_{AD} + x_{BD} = 5,$$

$$x_{AC}, x_{AD}, x_{BC}, x_{BD} \geq 0.$$

	x_{AC}	x_{AD}	x_{BC}	x_{BD}	s_1	s_2	t_3	t_4	W		
	1	1	0	0	1	0	0	0	0	6	
	0	0	1	1	0	1	0	0	0	6	
	1	0	1	0	0	0	1	0	0	5	
	0	1	0	1	0	0	0	1	0	5	
	1	2	2	4	0	0	M	M	1	0	
s_1	1	1	0	0	1	0	0	0	0	6	6
s_2	0	0	1	1	0	1	0	0	0	6	
t_3	[1]	0	1	0	0	0	1	0	0	5	5
t_4	0	1	0	1	0	0	0	1	0	5	
W	1−M	2−M	2−M	4−M	0	0	0	0	1	−10M	
s_1	0	[1]	−1	0	1	0	−1	0	0	1	1
s_2	0	0	1	1	0	1	0	0	0	6	
x_{AC}	1	0	1	0	0	1	1	0	0	5	
t_4	0	1	0	1	0	0	0	1	0	5	5
W	0	2−M	1	4−M	0	0	−1+M	0	1	−5−5M	
x_{AD}	0	1	−1	0	1	0	−1	0	0	1	
s_2	0	0	1	1	0	1	0	0	0	6	6
x_{AC}	1	0	1	0	0	0	1	0	0	5	5
t_4	0	0	[1]	1	−1	0	1	1	0	4	4
W	0	0	3−M	4−M	−2+M	0	1	0	1	−7−4M	

$$
\begin{array}{c|ccccccccc|c}
 & x_{AC} & x_{AD} & x_{BC} & x_{BD} & s_1 & s_2 & t_3 & t_4 & W & \\
\hline
x_{AD} & 0 & 1 & 0 & 1 & 0 & 0 & 0 & 1 & 0 & 5 \\
s_2 & 0 & 0 & 0 & 0 & 1 & 1 & -1 & -1 & 0 & 2 \\
x_{AC} & 1 & 0 & 0 & -1 & 1 & 0 & 0 & -1 & 0 & 1 \\
x_{BC} & 0 & 0 & 1 & 1 & -1 & 0 & 1 & 1 & 0 & 4 \\
\hline
W & 0 & 0 & 0 & 1 & 1 & 1 & -2+M & -3+M & 1 & -19 \\
\end{array}
$$

The minimum value of c is 19, when $x_{AC} = 1$, $x_{AD} = 5$,

$x_{BC} = 4$, and $x_{BD} = 0$.

<u>Ans.</u>   100,000 gal from A to C, 500,000 gal from A to D,

400,000 gal from B to C; $19,000

CHAPTER 9 — MATHEMATICAL SNAPSHOT

1.

	CURATIVE UNITS	TOXIC UNITS	RELATIVE DISCOMFORT
Drug (per ounce)	500	400	1
Radiation (per min.)	1000	600	1
Requirement	≥ 2000	≤ 1400	

Let x_1 = number of ounces of drug and let x_2 = number of
minutes of radiation. We want to minimize the discomfort
D, where $D = x_1 + x_2$, subject to

$$500x_1 + 1000x_2 \geq 2000,$$

$$400x_1 + 600x_2 \leq 1400,$$

$$x_1, x_2 \geq 0.$$

The feasible region is indicated on the following page.

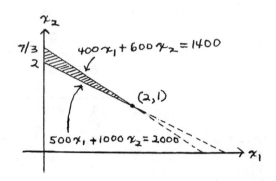

The corner points are $(0,2)$, $\left(0, \frac{7}{3}\right)$, and $(2,1)$. At $(0,2)$,

$D = 0 + 2 = 2$; at $\left(0, \frac{7}{3}\right)$, $D = 0 + \frac{7}{3} = \frac{7}{3}$; at $(2,1)$, $D =$

$2 + 1 = 3$. Thus D is minimum at $(0,2)$.

<u>Ans.</u> 0 ounce of drug, 2 minutes of radiation

10

Limits and Continuity

1. $\lim\limits_{x \to 2} 16 = 16$

5. $\lim\limits_{x \to -1} (x^3-3x^2-2x+1) = (-1)^3-3(-1)^2-2(-1)+1 = -1-3+2+1 = -1$

9. $\lim\limits_{h \to 0} \dfrac{h}{h^2-7h+1} = \dfrac{\lim\limits_{h \to 0} h}{\lim\limits_{h \to 0} (h^2-7h+1)} = \dfrac{0}{0^2-7(0)+1} = 0$

13. $\lim\limits_{x \to -2} \dfrac{x^2+2x}{x+2} = \lim\limits_{x \to -2} \dfrac{x(x+2)}{x+2} = \lim\limits_{x \to -2} x = -2$

17. $\lim\limits_{x \to -1} \dfrac{x^2+2x+1}{x+1} = \lim\limits_{x \to -1} \dfrac{(x+1)^2}{x+1} = \lim\limits_{x \to -1} (x+1) = 0$

21. $\lim\limits_{x\to 4} \dfrac{x^2-9x+20}{x^2-3x-4} = \lim\limits_{x\to 4} \dfrac{(x-4)(x-5)}{(x-4)(x+1)} = \lim\limits_{x\to 4} \dfrac{x-5}{x+1} = -\dfrac{1}{5}$

25. $\lim\limits_{h\to 0} \dfrac{(2+h)^2-2^2}{h} = \lim\limits_{h\to 0} \dfrac{[4+4h+h^2]-4}{h} = \lim\limits_{h\to 0} \dfrac{4h+h^2}{h} =$

$\lim\limits_{h\to 0} \dfrac{h(4+h)}{h} = \lim\limits_{h\to 0} (4+h) = 4$

29. $\lim\limits_{h\to 0} \dfrac{f(x+h)-f(x)}{h} = \lim\limits_{h\to 0} \dfrac{[4-(x+h)]-(4-x)}{h} = \lim\limits_{h\to 0} \dfrac{-h}{h} =$

$\lim\limits_{h\to 0} -1 = -1$

33. a. $\lim\limits_{T_c\to 0} \dfrac{T_h-T_c}{T_h} = \dfrac{T_h-0}{T_h} = \dfrac{T_h}{T_h} = 1$

b. $\lim\limits_{T_c\to T_h} \dfrac{T_h-T_c}{T_h} = \dfrac{T_h-T_h}{T_h} = \dfrac{0}{T_h} = 0$

EXERCISE 10.2

1. a. 2   b. 3   c. does not exist   d. $-\infty$ e. ∞ f. ∞

   g. ∞ h. 0   i. 1   j. 1   k. 1

5. $\lim\limits_{x\to -\infty} 5x$. As x becomes very negative, so does 5x. Thus

   $\lim\limits_{x\to -\infty} 5x = -\infty$.   <u>Ans.</u> $-\infty$

9. $\lim\limits_{x\to -\infty} x^2 = \infty$ since x^2 is positive for $x\to -\infty$. <u>Ans.</u> ∞

13. $\lim\limits_{x \to 5^-} \dfrac{3}{x-5} = -\infty$; $\lim\limits_{x \to 5^+} \dfrac{3}{x-5} = \infty$. So $\lim\limits_{x \to 5} \dfrac{3}{x-5}$ does not exist.

Ans. does not exist

17. $\lim\limits_{x \to \infty} \sqrt{x+10}$. As x becomes very large, so does x+10.

Because square roots of very large numbers are very large,

$\lim\limits_{x \to \infty} \sqrt{x+10} = \infty$.   Ans. ∞

21. $\lim\limits_{x \to \infty} \dfrac{x+2}{x+3} = \lim\limits_{x \to \infty} \dfrac{x}{x} = \lim\limits_{x \to \infty} 1 = 1$

25. $\lim\limits_{t \to \infty} \dfrac{5t^2+2t+1}{4t+7} = \lim\limits_{t \to \infty} \dfrac{5t^2}{4t} = \lim\limits_{t \to \infty} \dfrac{5t}{4} = \lim\limits_{t \to \infty} \left(\dfrac{5}{4}t\right) = \infty$

29. $\lim\limits_{x \to \infty} \dfrac{3-4x-2x^3}{5x^3-8x+1} = \lim\limits_{x \to \infty} \dfrac{-2x^3}{5x^3} = \lim\limits_{x \to \infty} \dfrac{-2}{5} = -\dfrac{2}{5}$

33. $\lim\limits_{w \to \infty} \dfrac{2w^2-3w+4}{5w^2+7w-1} = \lim\limits_{w \to \infty} \dfrac{2w^2}{5w^2} = \lim\limits_{w \to \infty} \dfrac{2}{5} = \dfrac{2}{5}$

37. $\lim\limits_{x \to 1} \dfrac{x^2-3x+1}{x^2+1} = \dfrac{\lim\limits_{x \to 1} (x^2-3x+1)}{\lim\limits_{x \to 1} (x^2+1)} = \dfrac{-1}{2} = -\dfrac{1}{2}$

41. As $x \to 0^+$, $x+x^2$ approaches 0 through positive values. Thus

$\dfrac{2}{x+x^2} \to \infty$.   Ans. ∞

45. As $x \to 0^+$, $\dfrac{3}{x} \to \infty$. Thus $-\dfrac{3}{x} \to -\infty$.   Ans. $-\infty$

49. $\lim\limits_{x \to -\infty} \frac{x+1}{x} = \lim\limits_{x \to -\infty} \frac{x}{x} = \lim\limits_{x \to -\infty} 1 = 1$

53. $g(x)$ a. 0   b. 0   c. 0   d. $-\infty$ e. $-\infty$

57. $\lim\limits_{t \to \infty} \left[20,000 + \frac{10,000}{(t+2)^2} \right] = 20,000 + 0 = 20,000.$ <u>Ans.</u>   20,000

61. 1, 0.5, 0.525, 0.631, 0.912, 0.986, 0.998; conclude
    limit is 1

<u>EXERCISE 10.3</u>

1. $S = 4000e^{0.055(6)} = 4000e^{0.33} \approx \$5564;$
   $5564 - 4000 = \$1564$

5. $e^{0.04} - 1 \approx 0.0408.$ <u>Ans.</u>   4.08%

9. $S = 100e^{0.055(2)} = 100e^{0.11} \approx \$111.63$

13. Effective rate $= e^r - 1.$ Thus $0.05 = e^r - 1,$ $e^r = 1.05,$
    $r = \ln 1.05 \approx 0.04879 \approx 0.0488.$ <u>Ans.</u>   4.88%

17. $3P = Pe^{0.07t},$ $3 = e^{0.07t},$ $0.07t = \ln 3,$ $t = \frac{\ln 3}{0.07} \approx 16.$
    <u>Ans.</u>   16 years

EXERCISE 10.4

1. $f(x) = x^3-5x$; $x = 2$. (i) f is defined at $x = 2$: $f(2) =$
    -2. (ii) $\lim\limits_{x \to 2} f(x) = \lim\limits_{x \to 2} (x^3-5x) = 2^3-5(2) = -2$, which
    exists. (iii) $\lim\limits_{x \to 2} f(x) = -2 = f(2)$. Thus f is continuous
    at $x = 2$.

5. $h(x) = \frac{x-4}{x+4}$; $x = 4$. (i) h is defined at $x = 4$; $h(4) = 0$.
    (ii) $\lim\limits_{x \to 4} h(x) = \lim\limits_{x \to 4} \frac{x-4}{x+4} = \frac{0}{8} = 0$, which exists.
    (iii) $\lim\limits_{x \to 4} h(x) = 0 = h(4)$. Thus h is continuous at $x = 4$.

9. discontinuous at 3 and -3 because at both points the
    denominator of this rational function is zero.

13. f is a polynomial function.

17. none, because f is a polynomial function.

21. none, because g is a polynomial function.

25. $x^3-x = 0$, $x(x^2-1) = 0$, $x(x+1)(x-1) = 0$, $x = 0, \pm 1$.
    Discontinuous at $0, \pm 1$.

29. $f(x) = \begin{cases} 1, & \text{if } x \geq 0, \\ -1, & \text{if } x < 0. \end{cases}$ For $x < 0$, $f(x) = -1$, which is a
    polynomial and hence continuous. For $x > 0$, $f(x) = 1$,
    which is a polynomial and hence continuous. Because
    $\lim\limits_{x \to 0^-} f(x) = \lim\limits_{x \to 0^-} (-1) = -1$ and $\lim\limits_{x \to 0^+} f(x) = \lim\limits_{x \to 0^+} 1 = 1$,

lim f(x) does not exist. Thus f is discontinuous at x = 0.
x→0

Ans. 0

33. $f(x) = \begin{cases} x^2, & \text{if } x > 2, \\ x-1, & \text{if } x < 2. \end{cases}$ For x < 2, f(x) = x-1, which is a

polynomial and hence continuous. For x > 2, f(x) = x^2,
which is a polynomial and hence continuous. Because f is
not defined at x = 2, it is discontinuous there.

Ans. 2

37.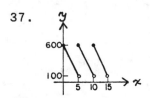

f is continuous at 2.

f is discontinuous at 5.

f is discontinuous at 10.

Ans. yes, no, no

EXERCISE 10.5

1. $x^2-3x-4 > 0$. f(x) = x^2-3x-4 = (x+1)(x-4) = 0 has roots -1
   and 4. By considering the intervals (-∞,-1), (-1,4), and
   (4,∞), we find f(x) > 0 on (-∞,-1) and (4,∞).
   Ans. x < -1, x > 4

5. $2x^2+11x+14 < 0$. f(x)= $2x^2+11x+14$ = (2x+7)(x+2) = 0 has
   roots -7/2 and -2. By considering the intervals
   (-∞,-7/2), (-7/2,-2), and (-2,∞), we find f(x) < 0 on
   (-7/2,-2).   Ans. -7/2 < x < -2

9. $(x+2)(x-3)(x+6) \leq 0$. $f(x) = (x+2)(x-3)(x+6) = 0$ has roots
    -2, 3, and -6. By considering the intervals $(-\infty,-6)$,
    $(-6,-2)$, $(-2,3)$, and $(3,\infty)$, we find $f(x) < 0$ on $(-\infty,-6)$
    and $(-2,3)$. <u>Ans.</u> $x \leq -6$, $-2 \leq x \leq 3$

13. $x^3+4x \geq 0$. $f(x) = x(x^2+4) = 0$ has root 0. By considering
    the intervals $(-\infty,0)$ and $(0,\infty)$, we find $f(x) > 0$ on $(0,\infty)$.
    <u>Ans.</u> $x \geq 0$

17. $\frac{x}{x^2-1} < 0$. $f(x) = \frac{x}{x^2-1}$ is discontinuous when $x = \pm 1$;
    $f(x) = 0$ has root 0. By considering the intervals
    $(-\infty,-1)$, $(-1,0)$, $(0,1)$, and $(1,\infty)$, we find $f(x) < 0$ on
    $(-\infty,-1)$ and $(0,1)$.   <u>Ans.</u> $x < -1$, $0 < x < 1$

21. $\frac{x^2-x-6}{x^2+4x-5} \geq 0$. $f(x) = \frac{x^2-x-6}{x^2+4x-5} = \frac{(x-3)(x+2)}{(x+5)(x-1)}$ is discontinuous
    at $x = -5$ and $x = 1$; $f(x) = 0$ has roots 3 and -2. By
    considering the intervals $(-\infty,-5)$, $(-5,-2)$, $(-2,1)$, $(1,3)$,
    and $(3,\infty)$, we find $f(x) > 0$ on $(-\infty,-5)$, $(-2,1)$, and $(3,\infty)$.
    <u>Ans.</u> $x < -5$, $-2 \leq x < 1$, $x \geq 3$

25. $x^2+2x \geq 2$, or equivalently, $x^2+2x-2 \geq 0$.
    $f(x) = x^2+2x-2 = 0$ has roots $-1\pm\sqrt{3}$. By considering the
    intervals $(-\infty, -1-\sqrt{3})$, $(-1-\sqrt{3}, -1+\sqrt{3})$, and $(-1+\sqrt{3}, \infty)$,
    we find $f(x) > 0$ on $(-\infty, -1-\sqrt{3})$ and $(-1+\sqrt{3}, \infty)$.
    <u>Ans.</u> $x \leq -1-\sqrt{3}$, $x \geq -1+\sqrt{3}$

29.

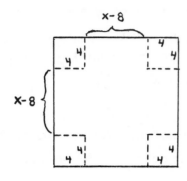

If x is the length of the piece of aluminum, then the box will be 4 by x − 8 by x − 8.

$$4(x - 8)^2 \geq 324$$

$$(x - 8)^2 \geq 81$$

$$x^2 - 16x - 17 \geq 0$$

$$(x - 17)(x + 1) \geq 0.$$

Solving gives x ≤ −1 or x ≥ 17. Since x must be positive, we have x ≥ 17.

<u>Ans.</u> 17 in. by 17 in.

CHAPTER 10 − REVIEW PROBLEMS

1. $\lim\limits_{x \to -1} (2x^2+6x-1) = 2(-1)^2+6(-1)-1 = -5$

5. $\lim\limits_{h \to 0} (x+h) = x+0 = x$

9. As x→∞, x+1→∞. Thus $\lim\limits_{x \to \infty} \frac{2}{x+1} = 0$.   <u>Ans.</u> 0

13. $\lim\limits_{t \to 3^-} \frac{2t-3}{t-3} = -\infty$ and $\lim\limits_{t \to 3^+} \frac{2t-3}{t-3} = \infty$.   Thus $\lim\limits_{t \to 3} \frac{2t-3}{t-3}$ does not exist.   <u>Ans.</u> limit does not exist

17. $\lim\limits_{x \to \infty} \frac{x^2-1}{(3x+2)^2} = \lim\limits_{x \to \infty} \frac{x^2-1}{9x^2+12x+4} = \lim\limits_{x \to \infty} \frac{x^2}{9x^2} = \lim\limits_{x \to \infty} \frac{1}{9} = \frac{1}{9}$

21. $\lim\limits_{x\to\infty} \sqrt{3x}$. As x becomes large, so does 3x. Because the

square roots of large numbers are also large,

$\lim\limits_{x\to\infty} \sqrt{3x} = \infty$.   **Ans.** ∞

25. $\lim\limits_{h\to 0} \dfrac{f(x+h) - f(x)}{h} = \lim\limits_{h\to 0} \dfrac{[8(x+h)-2] - [8x-2]}{h}$

$= \lim\limits_{h\to 0} \dfrac{8h}{h} = \lim\limits_{h\to 0} 8 = 8$

29. (a) $S = 2500e^{0.07(14)} = 2500e^{0.98} \approx \$6661.25$

   (b) $P = 2500e^{-0.07(14)} = 2500e^{-0.98} \approx \$938.28$

33. $f(x) = x+5$; $x = 7$. (i) f is defined at $x = 7$; $f(7) = 12$.

   (ii) $\lim\limits_{x\to 7} f(x) = \lim\limits_{x\to 7} (x+5) = 7+5 = 12$, which exists.

   (iii) $\lim\limits_{x\to 7} f(x) = 12 = f(7)$. Thus f is continuous at $x = 7$.

37. $f(x) = \dfrac{x^2}{x+3}$ is a rational function and the denominator is

zero at $x = -3$. Thus f is discontinuous at $x = -3$.

Ans. $x = -3$

41. $f(x) = \dfrac{4-x^2}{x^2+3x-4} = \dfrac{4-x^2}{(x+4)(x-1)}$ is a rational function and the

denominator is zero only when $x = -4$ or $x = 1$, so f is

discontinuous there.   **Ans.** $x = -4, 1$

45. $x^2+4x-12 > 0$. $f(x) = x^2+4x-12 = (x+6)(x-2) = 0$ has roots
    −6 and 2. By considering the intervals $(-\infty,-6)$, $(-6,2)$,
    and $(2,\infty)$, we find $f(x) > 0$ on $(-\infty,-6)$ and $(2,\infty)$.
    <u>Ans.</u> $x < -6$, $x > 2$

49. $\dfrac{x+5}{x^2-1} < 0$. $f(x) = \dfrac{x+5}{(x+1)(x-1)}$ is discontinuous when $x = \pm 1$,

    and $f(x) = 0$ has root −5. By considering the intervals
    $(-\infty,-5)$, $(-5,-1)$, $(-1,1)$, and $(1,\infty)$, we find $f(x) < 0$ on
    $(-\infty,-5)$ and $(-1,1)$.   <u>Ans.</u> $x < -5$, $-1 < x < 1$

CHAPTER 10 — MATHEMATICAL SNAPSHOT

1. $D = 92.5e^{-rt}$. For 1991, $t = 1$ and $D = 66.8$. Thus

   $66.8 = 92.5e^{-r}$, $e^{-r} = \dfrac{66.8}{92.5}$, $-r = \ln \dfrac{66.8}{92.5}$,

   $r = -\ln \dfrac{66.8}{92.5} \approx 0.326$.   <u>Ans.</u> 32.6%

11

Differentiation

1. $f(x) = x$.

$$f'(x) = \lim_{h \to 0} \frac{f(x + h) - f(x)}{h} = \lim_{h \to 0} \frac{(x + h) - x}{h}$$

$$= \lim_{h \to 0} \frac{h}{h} = \lim_{h \to 0} 1 = 1. \quad \underline{\text{Ans.}} \quad 1$$

5. Let $f(x) = 5 - 4x$.

$$\frac{d}{dx}(5 - 4x) = \lim_{h \to 0} \frac{f(x + h) - f(x)}{h}$$

$$= \lim_{h \to 0} \frac{[5 - 4(x + h)] - [5 - 4x]}{h}$$

$$= \lim_{h \to 0} \frac{-4h}{h} = \lim_{h \to 0} (-4) = -4.$$

9. $f(x) = x^2 + 4x - 8$.

$\frac{d}{dx}(x^2 + 4 - 8)$

$= \lim\limits_{h \to 0} \dfrac{f(x + h) - f(x)}{h}$

$= \lim\limits_{h \to 0} \dfrac{(x + h)^2 + 4(x + h) - 8] - [x^2 + 4x - 8]}{h}$

$= \lim\limits_{h \to 0} \dfrac{x^2 + 2xh + h^2 + 4x + 4h - 8 - x^2 - 4x + 8}{h}$

$= \lim\limits_{h \to 0} \dfrac{2xh + h^2 + 4h}{h}$

$= \lim\limits_{h \to 0} (2x + h + 4) = 2x + 4$.

13. $y = f(x) = \frac{1}{x}$.

$y' = \lim\limits_{h \to 0} \dfrac{f(x + h) - f(x)}{h} = \lim\limits_{h \to 0} \dfrac{\frac{1}{x + h} - \frac{1}{x}}{h}$.

Multiplying the numerator and denominator by $x(x + h)$ gives

$y' = \lim\limits_{h \to 0} \dfrac{x - (x + h)}{h(x)(x + h)} = \lim\limits_{h \to 0} \dfrac{-h}{h(x)(x + h)}$

$= \lim\limits_{h \to 0} \left[- \dfrac{1}{x(x + h)}\right] = - \dfrac{1}{x^2}$.

17. $y = x^2 + 4$.

$y' = \lim\limits_{h \to 0} \dfrac{[(x + h)^2 + 4] - [x^2 + 4]}{h} = \lim\limits_{h \to 0} \dfrac{2xh + h^2}{h}$

$= \lim\limits_{h \to 0} (2x + h) = 2x$.

The slope at $(-2, 8)$ is $y'(-2) = 2(-2) = -4$.

21. $y = x + 4$.

$y' = \lim_{h \to 0} \dfrac{[(x + h) + 4] - [x + 4]}{h} = \lim_{h \to 0} \dfrac{h}{h} = 1$.

If $x = 3$, then $y' = 1$. The tangent line at the point

$(3,7)$ is $y - 7 = 1(x - 3)$, or $y = x + 4$.

25. $y = \dfrac{3}{x + 1}$.

$y' = \lim \dfrac{\dfrac{3}{(x + h) + 1} - \dfrac{3}{x + 1}}{h}$

$= \lim_{h \to 0} \dfrac{\dfrac{3(x + 1) - 3(x + h + 1)}{(x + h + 1)(x + 1)}}{h}$

$= \lim_{h \to 0} \dfrac{-3h}{h(x + h + 1)(x + 1)} = \lim_{h \to 0} \dfrac{-3}{(x + h + 1)(x + 1)}$

$= -\dfrac{3}{(x + 1)^2}$.

If $x = 2$, then $y' = -\dfrac{3}{9} = -\dfrac{1}{3}$. The tangent line at

$(2,1)$ is $y - 1 = -\dfrac{1}{3}(x - 2)$, or $y = -\dfrac{1}{3}x + \dfrac{5}{3}$.

EXERCISE 11.2

1. $f(x) = 5$ is a constant function, so $f'(x) = 0$.

5. $f(x) = 8x^4$, $f'(x) = 8(4x^{4-1}) = 32x^3$

9. $f(x) = 4x^{-14/5}$, $f'(x) = 4 \cdot \left(-\dfrac{14}{5}\right)x^{(-14/5)-1} = -\dfrac{56}{5}x^{-19/5}$

13. $f(p) = \dfrac{13p}{5} + \dfrac{7}{3} = \dfrac{13}{5}p + \dfrac{7}{3}$, $f'(p) = \dfrac{13}{5}(1) + 0 = \dfrac{13}{5}$

17. $\frac{d}{dx}(14x^3 - 6x^2 + 7x - e^3) = 14(3x^2) - 6(2x) + 7(1) - 0$

$$= 42x^2 - 12x + 7$$

21. $f(x) = 2x^{501} - 125x^{100} + 0.2x^{3.4}$

$\quad f'(x) = 2(501x^{500}) - 125(100x^{99}) + 0.2(3.4x^{2.4})$

$\quad\quad = 1002x^{500} - 12{,}500x^{99} + 0.68x^{2.4}$

25. $g(x) = \frac{1}{3}(13 - x^4), \quad g'(x) = \frac{1}{3}(0 - 4x^3) = -\frac{4}{3}x^3$

29. $h'(x) = -2(27 - 14\cdot 5x^4) = -2(27 - 70x^4) = 2(70x^4 - 27)$

33. $f(x) = \frac{1}{x} = x^{-1}, \quad f'(x) = -1x^{-2} = -x^{-2} = -\frac{1}{x^2}$

37. $f(t) = 4\sqrt{t} = 4t^{1/2}, \quad f'(t) = 4\left(\frac{1}{2}t^{-1/2}\right) = 2t^{-1/2} = \frac{2}{\sqrt{t}}$

41. $f(x) = x(3x^2 - 7x + 7) = 3x^3 - 7x^2 + 7x$

$\quad f'(x) = 9x^2 - 14x + 7$

45. $f(x) = x^3(3x)^2 = x^3(9x^2) = 9x^5, \quad f'(x) = 45x^4$

49. $f(q) = \frac{4q^3 + 7q - 4}{q} = 4q^2 + 7 - 4q^{-1}$

$\quad f'(q) = 8q + 4q^{-2} = 8q + \frac{4}{q^2}$

53. $w(x) = \dfrac{x^2 + x^3}{x^2} = 1 + x$, $w'(x) = 0 + 1 = 1$

57. y is a constant, so $y' = 0$ for all x.

61. $y = 3 + x - 5x^2 + x^4$. $y' = 1 - 10x + 4x^3$.
    When $x = 0$, then $y = 3$ and $y' = 1$. Thus an equation of
    the tangent is $y - 3 = 1(x - 0)$, or $y = x + 3$.

65. $z = (1 + b)w_p - bw_c$. $\dfrac{dz}{dw_c} = (1 + b)\dfrac{dw_p}{dw_c} - b$.

    Rewriting the right side and factoring out $1 + b$ give

    $\dfrac{dz}{dw_c} = (1 + b)\dfrac{dw_p}{dw_c} - \dfrac{b(1 + b)}{1 + b}$, $\dfrac{dz}{dw_c} = (1+b)\left[\dfrac{dw_p}{dw_c} - \dfrac{b}{1+b}\right]$.

EXERCISE 11.3

1. (a) $s(4) = 4^2 - 3(4) = 4$ m
   (b) $v = 2t - 3$, $v(4) = 2(4) - 3 = 5$ m/s

5. (a) $s(2) = 2^4 - 2(2^3) + 2 = 2$ m
   (b) $v = 4t^3 - 6t^2 + 1$, $v(2) = 4(2^3) - 6(2^2) + 1 = 9$ m/s

9. $\dfrac{dT}{dT_e} = 0 + 0.27(1 - 0) = 0.27$.

13. $\dfrac{dc}{dq} = 0.3(2q) + 2 = 0.6q + 2$.

    If $q = 3$, then $\dfrac{dc}{dq} = 0.6(3) + 2 = 3.8$.

17. $\bar{c} = 0.01q + 5 + \frac{500}{q}$. $c = \bar{c}q = 0.01q^2 + 5q + 500$.

$\frac{dc}{dq} = 0.02q + 5$, $\frac{dc}{dq}\Big|_{q=50} = 6$, $\frac{dc}{dq}\Big|_{q=100} = 7$.

21. $\frac{dr}{dq} = 0.7$ for all q.

25. $\frac{dc}{dq} = 6.750 - 0.000328(2q) = 6.750 - 0.000656q$.

$\frac{dc}{dq}\Big|_{q=5000} = 6.750 - 0.000656(5000) = 3.47$.

29. $y = 59.3 - 1.5x - 0.5x^2$.

(a) $\frac{dy}{dx} = -1.5 - x$. $\frac{dy}{dx}\Big|_{x=6} = -1.5 - 6 = -7.5$.

(b) Setting $-1.5 - x = -6$ gives $x = 4.5$.

33. $y = 3x^2 + 6$.   (a) $y' = 6x$,   (b) $\frac{y'}{y} = \frac{6x}{3x^2 + 6} = \frac{2x}{x^2 + 2}$,

(c) $6(2) = 12$,   (d) $\frac{4}{4 + 2} = \frac{2}{3} \approx 0.667$,   (e) 66.7%

37. $c = 0.2q^2 + 1.2q + 4$. $\frac{dc}{dq} = 0.4q + 1.2$.

If $q = 5$, then $\frac{dc}{dq} = 0.14(5) + 1.2 = 3.2$.

If $q = 5$, then $c = 15$ and $\frac{dc/dq}{c}(100) = \frac{3.2}{15}(100) \approx 21.3$

41. $\frac{W'}{W} = \frac{0.864t^{-0.568}}{2t^{0.432}} = \frac{0.432}{t}$

EXERCISE 11.5

1. $f'(x) = (4x + 1)(6) + (6x + 3)(4)$

   $\qquad = 24x + 6 + 24x + 12$

   $\qquad = 48x + 18 = 6(8x + 3)$

5. $f'(r) = (3r^2 - 4)(2r - 5) + (r^2 - 5r + 1)(6r)$

   $\qquad = 6r^3 - 15r^2 - 8r + 20 + 6r^3 - 30r^2 + 6r$

   $\qquad = 12r^3 - 45r^2 - 2r + 20$

9. $f'(w) = (8w^2 + 2w - 3)(15w^2) + (5w^3 + 2)(16w + 2)$

   $\qquad = 120w^4 + 30w^3 - 45w^2 + 80w^4 + 10w^3 + 32w + 4$

   $\qquad = 200w^4 + 40w^3 - 45w^2 + 32w + 4$

13. $f'(p) = \frac{3}{2}\left[(p^{1/2} - 4)(4) + (4p - 5)\left(\frac{1}{2}p^{-1/2}\right)\right]$

   $\qquad = \frac{3}{2}(4p^{1/2} - 16 + 2p^{1/2} - \frac{5}{2}p^{-1/2})$

   $\qquad = \frac{3}{2}(6p^{1/2} - 16 - \frac{5}{2}p^{-1/2})$

   $\qquad = \frac{3}{4}(12p^{1/2} - 5p^{-1/2} - 32)$

17. $y = (2x - 1)(3x + 4)(x + 7) = [(2x - 1)(3x + 4)](x + 7)$

   $y' = [(2x-1)(3x+4)][1] + (x+7)[(2x-1)(3) + (3x+4)(2)]$

   $\qquad = 6x^2 + 5x - 4 + (x + 7)[12x + 5]$

   $\qquad = 6x^2 + 5x - 4 + 12x^2 + 89x + 35$

   $\qquad = 18x^2 + 94x + 31.$

21. $y' = \dfrac{(x - 1)(1) - (x + 2)(1)}{(x - 1)^2} = \dfrac{x - 1 - x - 2}{(x - 1)^2} = \dfrac{-3}{(x - 1)^2}$

25. $y' = \dfrac{(x^2 - 5x)(16x - 2) - (8x^2 - 2x + 1)(2x - 5)}{(x^2 - 5x)^2}$

$\quad = \dfrac{16x^3 - 82x^2 + 10x - (16x^3 - 44x^2 + 12x - 5)}{(x^2 - 5x)^2}$

$\quad = \dfrac{-38x^2 - 2x + 5}{(x^2 - 5x)^2}$

29. $g'(x) = \dfrac{(x^{100} + 1)(0) - (1)(100x^{99})}{(x^{100} + 1)^2} = \dfrac{-100x^{99}}{(x^{100} + 1)^2}$

33. $y = \dfrac{3x^2 - x - 1}{\sqrt[3]{x}} = 3x^{5/3} - x^{2/3} - x^{-1/3}$

$\quad y' = 5x^{2/3} - \dfrac{2}{3}x^{-1/3} + \dfrac{1}{3}x^{-4/3} = 5x^{2/3} - \dfrac{2}{1/3} + \dfrac{1}{4/3}$

$\quad = \dfrac{15x^2 - 2x + 1}{3x^{4/3}}$

37. $y' = \dfrac{[(x + 2)(x - 4)](1) - (x - 5)(2x - 2)}{[(x + 2)(x - 4)]^2}$

$\quad = \dfrac{x^2 - 2x - 8 - (2x^2 - 12x + 10)}{[(x + 2)(x - 4)]^2} = \dfrac{-(x^2 - 10x + 18)}{[(x + 2)(x - 4)]^2}$

41. $y = 3x - \dfrac{\dfrac{2}{x} - \dfrac{3}{x - 1}}{x - 2} = 3x - \dfrac{\dfrac{2(x - 1) - 3x}{x(x - 1)}}{x - 2}$

$\quad = 3x + \dfrac{x + 2}{x(x - 1)(x - 2)}$

$\quad y' = 3 + \dfrac{(x^3 - 3x^2 + 2x)[1] - (x + 2)[3x^2 - 6x + 2]}{[x(x - 1)(x - 2)]^2}$

$\quad = 3 - \dfrac{2x^3 + 3x^2 - 12x + 4}{[x(x - 1)(x - 2)]^2}$

45. $y = \frac{6}{x - 1}$, $y' = \frac{(x - 1)[0] - (6)[1]}{(x - 1)^2} = -\frac{6}{(x - 1)^2}$.

$y'(3) = -\frac{6}{2^2} = -\frac{3}{2}$.   The tangent is $y - 3 = -\frac{3}{2}(x - 3)$,

or $y = -\frac{3}{2}x + \frac{15}{2}$.

49. $y = \frac{x}{2x - 6}$. $y' = \frac{(2x - 6)[1] - x[2]}{(2x - 6)^2} = \frac{-6}{(2x - 6)^2}$.

If $x = 1$, then $y = \frac{1}{2 - 6} = -\frac{1}{4}$ and $y' = \frac{-6}{(-4)^2} = \frac{-6}{16} = -\frac{3}{8}$.

Thus $\frac{y'}{y} = \frac{-3/8}{-1/4} = \frac{3}{2} = 1.5$.

53. $p = \frac{108}{q + 2} - 3$. $r = pq = \frac{108q}{q + 2} - 3q$.

$\frac{dr}{dq} = \frac{(q + 2)[108] - (108q)[1]}{(q + 2)^2} - 3 = \frac{216}{(q + 2)^2} - 3$

57. $C = 2 + 2I^{1/2}$. $\frac{dC}{dI} = 0 + 2\left(\frac{1}{2}I^{-1/2}\right) = \frac{1}{\sqrt{I}}$.

When $I = 9$, then $\frac{dC}{dI} = \frac{1}{\sqrt{9}} = \frac{1}{3}$ and $\frac{dS}{dI} = 1 - \frac{1}{3} = \frac{2}{3}$.

61. $\frac{dc}{dq} = 5 \cdot \frac{(q + 3)(2q) - q^2(1)}{(q + 3)^2} = 5 \cdot \frac{q^2 + 6q}{(q + 3)^2} = \frac{5q(q + 6)}{(q + 3)^2}$

65. $y = \frac{0.7355x}{1 + 0.02744x}$.

$\frac{dy}{dx} = \frac{(1 + 0.02744x)(0.7355) - (0.7355x)(0.02744)}{(1 + 0.02744x)^2}$

$= \frac{0.7355}{(1 + 0.02744x)^2}$.

EXERCISE 11.6

1. $\frac{dy}{dx} = \frac{dy}{du} \cdot \frac{du}{dx} = (2u - 2)(2x - 1)$. Expressing the answer in terms of x, we have

$$(2u - 2)(2x - 1) = [2(x^2 - x) - 2](2x - 1)$$
$$= (2x^2 - 2x - 2)(2x - 1)$$
$$= 4x^3 - 2x^2 - 4x^2 + 2x - 4x + 2$$
$$= 4x^3 - 6x^2 - 2x + 2.$$

5. $\frac{dw}{dt} = \frac{dw}{du} \cdot \frac{du}{dt} = (2u)\left[\frac{(t - 1) - (t + 1)}{(t - 1)^2}\right] = 2u\left[\frac{-2}{(t - 1)^2}\right].$

If $t = 3$, then $u = \frac{3 + 1}{3 - 1} = 2$, so $\left.\frac{dw}{dt}\right|_{t=3} = 2(2)\left[\frac{-2}{4}\right] = -2.$

9. $y' = 6(3x + 2)^5 \cdot \frac{d}{dx}(3x + 2) = 6(3x + 2)^5(3) = 18(3x + 2)^5$

13. $y' = -3(x^2 - 2)^{-4} \cdot \frac{d}{dx}(x^2 - 2)$

$$= -3(x^2 - 2)^{-4}(2x)$$

$$= -6x(x^2 - 2)^{-4}$$

17. $y = 2\sqrt[5]{(x^3 + 1)^2} = 2(x^3 + 1)^{2/5}$

$y' = 2\left(\frac{2}{5}\right)(x^3 + 1)^{-3/5}(3x^2) = \frac{12}{5}x^2(x^3 + 1)^{-3/5}$

21. $y = \frac{1}{(x^2 - 3x)^2} = (x^2 - 3x)^{-2}$

$y' = -2(x^2 - 3x)^{-3}(2x - 3) = -2(2x - 3)(x^2 - 3x)^{-3}$

25. $y = \sqrt[3]{7x} + \sqrt[3]{7}x = (7x)^{1/3} + \sqrt[3]{7}x$

$\quad y' = \frac{1}{3}(7x)^{-2/3}(7) + \sqrt[3]{7}(1)$

$\quad\quad = \frac{7}{3}(7x)^{-2/3} + \sqrt[3]{7}$

29. $y = 2x\sqrt{6x - 1} = 2x(6x - 1)^{1/2}$

$\quad y' = 2x\left[\frac{1}{2}(6x - 1)^{-1/2}(6)\right] + \sqrt{6x - 1}(2)$

$\quad\quad = 6x(6x - 1)^{-1/2} + 2\sqrt{6x - 1}$

33. $y = \left(\frac{x - 7}{x + 4}\right)^{10}$

$\quad y' = 10\left(\frac{x - 7}{x + 4}\right)^9\left[\frac{(x + 4)(1) - (x - 7)(1)}{(x + 4)^2}\right]$

$\quad\quad = 10\left(\frac{x - 7}{x + 4}\right)^9\left[\frac{11}{(x + 4)^2}\right] = \frac{110(x - 7)^9}{(x + 4)^{11}}$

37. $y' = \dfrac{(x^2 + 4)^3(2) - (2x - 5)[3(x^2 + 4)^2(2x)]}{(x^2 + 4)^6}$

$\quad = \dfrac{(x^2 + 4)(2) - (2x - 5)[3(2x)]}{(x^2 + 4)^6}$

$\quad = \dfrac{2x^2 + 8 - 12x^2 + 30x}{(x^2 + 4)^6}$

$\quad = \dfrac{-10x^2 + 30x + 8}{(x^2 + 4)^6}$

$\quad = \dfrac{-2(5x^2 - 15x - 4)}{(x^2 + 4)^4}$

41. $y' = 8 + \dfrac{(t + 4)(1) - (t - 1)(1)}{(t + 4)^2} - 2\left(\frac{8t - 7}{4}\right)\left[\frac{1}{4}\cdot 8\right]$

$\quad = 8 + \dfrac{5}{(t + 4)^2} - (8t - 7) = 15 - 8t + \dfrac{5}{(t + 4)^2}$

45.
$$\frac{\left[\begin{array}{l}(x^2-7)^4[(2x+1)(2)(3x-5)(3)+(3x-5)^2(2)]-\\ \qquad\qquad (2x+1)(3x-5)^2[4(x^2-7)^3(2x)]\end{array}\right]}{(x^2-7)^8}$$

49. $y' = 3(x^2 - 7x - 8)^2(2x - 7)$.

If $x = 8$, then slope $= y' = 3(64 - 56 - 8)^2(16 - 7) = 0$.

53. $y' = \dfrac{(x + 1)\left(\frac{1}{2}\right)(7x + 2)^{-1/2}(7) - \sqrt{7x + 2}(1)}{(x + 1)^2}$. If $x = 1$,

then $y' = \dfrac{2\left(\frac{1}{2}\right)\left(\frac{1}{3}\right)7 - 3(1)}{4} = -\dfrac{1}{6}$. The tangent line is

$y - \dfrac{3}{2} = -\dfrac{1}{6}(x - 1)$, or $y = -\dfrac{1}{6}x + \dfrac{5}{3}$.

57. Given $q = 2m$, $p = -0.5q + 20$; $m = 5$. $\dfrac{dr}{dm} = \dfrac{dr}{dq}\cdot\dfrac{dq}{dm}$.

Since $r = pq = -0.5q^2 + 20q$, we have $\dfrac{dr}{dq} = -q + 20$.

For $m = 5$, then $q = 2(5) = 10$, so $\dfrac{dr}{dq} = -10 + 20 = 10$.

Also, $\dfrac{dq}{dm} = 2$. Thus $\dfrac{dr}{dm} = (10)(2) = 20$.

61. $p = 100 - \sqrt{q^2 + 20}$

(a) $\dfrac{dp}{dq} = 0 - \dfrac{1}{2}(q^2 + 20)^{-1/2}(2q) = \dfrac{-q}{\sqrt{q^2 + 20}}$.

(b) $\dfrac{dp/dq}{p} = \dfrac{\dfrac{-q}{\sqrt{q^2 + 20}}}{100 - \sqrt{q^2 + 20}} = -\dfrac{q}{\sqrt{q^2 + 20}\left(100 - \sqrt{q^2 + 20}\right)}$

$= -\dfrac{q}{100\sqrt{q^2 + 20} - q^2 - 20}$

(c) $r = pq = 100q - q\sqrt{q^2 + 20}$.

$$\frac{dr}{dq} = 100 - \left[q \cdot \frac{1}{2}(q^2 + 20)^{-1/2}(2q) + \sqrt{q^2 + 20}(1)\right]$$

$$= 100 - \frac{q^2}{\sqrt{q^2 + 20}} - \sqrt{q^2 + 20}$$

65. $c = \dfrac{5q^2}{\sqrt{q^2 + 3}} + 5000$.

$$\frac{dc}{dq} = \frac{(q^2 + 3)^{1/2}[10q] - (5q^2)\left[\frac{1}{2}(q^2 + 3)^{-1/2}(2q)\right]}{q^2 + 3}.$$

Multiplying numerator and denominator by $(q^2 + 3)^{1/2}$ gives

$$\frac{dc}{dq} = \frac{(q^2 + 3)(10q) - 5q^2(q)}{(q^2 + 3)^{3/2}}$$

$$= \frac{5q^3 + 30q}{(q^2 + 3)^{3/2}} = \frac{5q(q^2 + 6)}{(q^2 + 3)^{3/2}}.$$

69. (a) $l_x = 2000\sqrt{100 - x}$.

$$\frac{d}{dx}(l_x) = 2000\left(\frac{1}{2}\right)(100 - x)^{-1/2}(-1)$$

$$= -\frac{1000}{\sqrt{100 - x}}.$$

If $x = 36$, then $\frac{d}{dx}(l_x) = -\frac{1000}{8} = -125$.

(b) If $x = 36$,

$$\frac{\frac{d}{dx}(l_x)}{l_x} = \frac{-125}{2000(8)} = -\frac{1}{128}.$$

CHAPTER 11 - REVIEW PROBLEMS

1. $f(x) = 2 - x^2$.

    $f'(x)$

    $= \lim\limits_{h \to 0} \dfrac{f(x + h) - f(x)}{h} = \lim\limits_{h \to 0} \dfrac{[2 - (x + h)^2] - (2 - x^2)}{h}$

    $= \lim\limits_{h \to 0} \dfrac{[2 - x^2 - 2hx - h^2] - (2 - x^2)}{h} = \lim\limits_{h \to 0} \dfrac{-2hx - h^2}{h}$

    $= \lim\limits_{h \to 0} \dfrac{-h(2x + h)}{h} = \lim\limits_{h \to 0} -(2x + h) = -2x$

5. $y' = 7(4x^3) - 6(3x^2) + 5(2x) + 0$

    $= 28x^3 - 18x^2 + 10x = 2x(14x^2 - 9x + 5)$

9. $y = \frac{1}{5}(x^2 + 3)$.

    $y' = \frac{1}{5}(2x) = \frac{2x}{5}$

13. $f'(x) = 100(2x^2 + 4x)^{99}(4x + 4)$

    $= 400(x + 1)[(2x)(x + 2)]^{99}$

17. $y' = (8 + 2x)[(4)(x^2 + 1)^3(2x)] + (x^2 + 1)^4[2]$

    $= 2(x^2 + 1)^3[4x(8 + 2x) + (x^2 + 1)]$

    $= 2(x^2 + 1)^3(32x + 8x^2 + x^2 + 1)$

    $= 2(x^2 + 1)^3(9x^2 + 32x + 1)$

21. $y = (4x - 1)^{1/3}$.

    $y' = \frac{1}{3}(4x - 1)^{-2/3}(4) = \frac{4}{3}(4x - 1)^{-2/3}$

25. $h'(x) = (x - 6)^4[3(x + 5)^2] + (x + 5)^3[4(x - 6)^3]$

$\qquad = (x - 6)^3(x + 5)^2[3(x - 6) + 4(x + 5)]$

$\qquad = (x - 6)^3(x + 5)^2(7x + 2)$

29. $y' = 2\left(-\frac{3}{8}\right)x^{-11/8} + \left(-\frac{3}{8}\right)(2x)^{-11/8}(2)$

$\qquad = -\frac{3}{4}x^{-11/8} - \frac{3}{4}(2^{-11/8})x^{-11/8}$

$\qquad = -\frac{3}{4}(1 + 2^{-11/8})x^{-11/8}$

33. $y' = \frac{3}{5}(x^3 + 6x^2 + 9)^{-2/5}(3x^2 + 12x)$

$\qquad = \frac{9}{5}x(x + 4)(x^3 + 6x + 9)^{-2/5}$

37. $y = x^2 - 6x + 4$, $y' = 2x - 6$.
When $x = 1$, then $y = -1$ and $y' = -4$. An equation of the
tangent is $y - (-1) = -4(x - 1)$, or simply $y = -4x + 3$.

41. $f(x) = 4x^2 + 2x + 8$. $f'(x) = 8x + 2$.
$f(1) = 14$ and $f'(1) = 10$. The relative rate of change is
$\frac{f'(1)}{f(1)} = \frac{10}{14} = \frac{5}{7} \approx 0.714$, so the percentage rate of change
is 71.4%.

45. $\frac{dC}{dI} = 0.6 - 0.25\left(\frac{1}{2}\right)I^{-1/2} = 0.6 - \frac{1}{8\sqrt{I}}.$ $\left.\frac{dC}{dI}\right|_{I=16} = 0.569.$
Thus marginal propensity to consume is 0.569 and marginal
propensity to save is $1 - 0.569 = 0.431$.

49. $\frac{dc}{dq} = 0.125 + 0.00878q.$ $\left.\frac{dc}{dq}\right|_{q=70} = 0.7396.$

53. (a) dt/dT when T = 38 is

$$\frac{T}{dT}\left[\frac{4}{3}T - \frac{175}{4}\right]\bigg|_{T=38} = \frac{4}{3}\bigg|_{T=38} = \frac{4}{3}.$$

(b) dt/dT when T = 35 is

$$\frac{d}{dT}\left[\frac{1}{24}T + \frac{11}{4}\right]\bigg|_{T=35} = \frac{1}{24}\bigg|_{T=35} = \frac{1}{24}.$$

12

Additional Differentiation Topics

1. $\frac{dy}{dx} = 4 \cdot \frac{d}{dx}(\ln x) = 4 \cdot \frac{1}{x} = \frac{4}{x}$

5. $y = \ln x^2 = 2 \ln x.$ $\frac{dy}{dx} = 2 \cdot \frac{1}{x} = \frac{2}{x}$

9. $f'(p) = \frac{1}{2p^3 + 3p}(6p^2 + 3) = \frac{6p^2 + 3}{2p^3 + 3p} = \frac{3(2p^2 + 1)}{p(2p^2 + 3)}$

13. $y = \log_3 (2x - 1) = \frac{\ln(2x - 1)}{\ln 3}.$

$$\frac{dy}{dx} = \frac{1}{\ln 3} \cdot \frac{d}{dx}[\ln(2x - 1)]$$

$$= \frac{1}{\ln 3} \cdot \frac{1}{2x - 1}(2)$$

$$= \frac{2}{(2x - 1)(\ln 3)}, \text{ or } \frac{2 \log_3 e}{2x - 1}$$

17. $y = \ln(x^2 + 4x + 5)^3 = 3 \ln(x^2 + 4x + 5)$.

$$\frac{dy}{dx} = 3 \cdot \frac{1}{x^2 + 4x + 5}(2x + 4) = \frac{3(2x + 4)}{x^2 + 4x + 5} = \frac{6(x + 2)}{x^2 + 4x + 5}$$

21. $f(1) = \ln\left(\frac{1 + 1}{1 - 1}\right) = \ln(1 + 1) - \ln(1 - 1)$.

$$f'(1) = \frac{1}{1 + 1} - \frac{1}{1 - 1}(-1) = \frac{(1 - 1) + (1 + 1)}{(1 + 1)(1 - 1)} = \frac{2}{1 - 1^2}$$

25. $y = \ln[(x^2 + 2)^2(x^3 + x - 1)]$

$$= 2 \ln(x^2 + 2) + \ln(x^3 + x - 1).$$

$$\frac{dy}{dx} = 2 \cdot \frac{1}{x^2 + 2}(2x) + \frac{1}{x^3 + x - 1}(3x^2 + 1)$$

$$= \frac{4x}{x^2 + 2} + \frac{3x^2 + 1}{x^3 + x - 1}$$

29. $y = \ln x^3 + \ln^3 x = 3 \ln x + (\ln x)^3$.

$$\frac{dy}{dx} = 3 \cdot \frac{1}{x} + 3(\ln x)^2 \cdot \frac{1}{x} = \frac{3}{x} + \frac{3(\ln x)^2}{x} = \frac{3(1 + \ln^2 x)}{x}$$

33. $y = x \ln\sqrt{x - 1} = \frac{1}{2}x \ln(x - 1)$. By the product rule,

$$\frac{dy}{dx} = \frac{1}{2}\left[x\left(\frac{1}{x - 1}\right) + \ln(x-1) \cdot [1]\right]$$

$$= \frac{x}{2(x - 1)} + \ln\sqrt{x - 1}$$

37. $y = \ln(x^2 - 2x - 2)$, $y' = \frac{2x - 2}{x^2 - 2x - 2}$. The slope of the

tangent line at $x = 3$ is $y'(3) = \frac{6 - 2}{9 - 6 - 2} = 4$. Also, if

$x = 3$, then $y = \ln(9 - 6 - 2) = \ln 1 = 0$. Thus an equation

of the tangent line is $y - 0 = 4(x - 3)$, or $y = 4x - 12$.

41. If $y = \ln f(x)$, then $\frac{dy}{dx} = \frac{1}{f(x)}f'(x) = \frac{f'(x)}{f(x)}$, which is the relative rate of change of $y = f(x)$ with respect to x.

EXERCISE 12.2

1. $y' = 7 \cdot \frac{d}{dx}(e^x) = 7e^x$

5. $y' = e^{3-5x} \cdot \frac{d}{dx}(e^{3-5x}) = e^{3-5x}(-5) = -5e^{3-5x}$

9. By the product rule, $y' = x(e^x) + e^x(1) = e^x(x + 1)$

13. $y = \frac{1}{2}(e^x + e^{-x})$. $y' = \frac{1}{2}[e^x + e^{-x}(-1)] = \frac{e^x - e^{-x}}{2}$

17. $f'(w) = \frac{w^2[e^{2w}(2)] - e^{2w}[2w]}{w^4} = \frac{2e^{2w}(w - 1)}{w^3}$

21. $y = x^3 - 3^x = x^3 - e^{(\ln 3)x}$.
    $y' = 3x^2 - e^{(\ln 3)x}(\ln 3) = 3x^2 - 3^x \ln 3$

25. $y = e^{\ln x} = x$ (by the property that $e^{\ln a} = a$). Thus $y' = 1$.

29. $y = e^x$, $y' = e^x$. When $x = 2$, then $y = e^2$ and $y' = e^2$. Thus an equation of the tangent is $y - e^2 = e^2(x - 2)$, or $y = e^2x - e^2$.

33. $\bar{c} = \dfrac{7000e^{q/700}}{q}$), so $c = \bar{c}q = 7000e^{q/700}$. The marginal

cost function is $\dfrac{dc}{dq} = 7000e^{q/700}\left(\dfrac{1}{700}\right) = 10e^{q/700}$. Thus

$\dfrac{dc}{dq}\Big|_{q=350} = 10e^{0.5}$ and $\dfrac{dc}{dq}\Big|_{q=700} = 10e$.

37. $P = 20{,}000e^{0.03t}$.

$$\dfrac{dP}{dt} = 20{,}000e^{0.03t}(0.03)$$

$$= P(0.03) = 0.03P = kP,$$

where $k = 0.03$.

41. $N = 10^A 10^{-bM} = 10^{A-bM} = e^{(\ln 10)(A-bM)}$.

$$\dfrac{dN}{dM} = e^{(\ln 10)(A-bM)}(\ln 10)(-b)$$

$$= 10^{A-bM}(\ln 10)(-b)$$

$$= -b(10^{A-bM})\ln 10$$

45. $f(t) = 1 - e^{-0.008t}$. $f'(t) = 0.008e^{-0.008t}$.

$f'(100) = 0.008e^{-0.8} \approx (0.008)(0.44933) \approx 0.0036$.

EXERCISE 12.3

1. $2x + 8yy' = 0$

$x + 4yy' = 0,$

$4yy' = -x,$

$y' = -\dfrac{x}{4y}$

5. $\frac{1}{2}x^{-1/2} + \frac{1}{2}y^{-1/2}y' = 0$,

    $x^{-1/2} + y^{-1/2}y' = 0$,

        $y^{-1/2}y' = -x^{-1/2}$,

            $y' = -\dfrac{x^{-1/2}}{y^{-1/2}} = -\dfrac{y^{1/2}}{x^{1/2}} = -\dfrac{\sqrt{y}}{\sqrt{x}} = -\sqrt{\dfrac{y}{x}}$.

9. By the product rule, $xy' + y(1) = 0$, $xy' = -y$, $y' = -\dfrac{y}{x}$

13. $3x^2 + 3y^2y' - 12(xy' + y) = 0$, $3y^2y' - 12xy' = 12y - 3x^2$,

    $y'(3y^2 - 12x) = 12y - 3x^2$, $y'(y^2 - 4x) = 4y - x^2$,

    $y' = \dfrac{4y - x^2}{y^2 - 4x}$

17. $3x^2(3y^2y') + y^3(6x) - 1 + y' = 0$,

                $9x^2y^2y' + y' = 1 - 6xy^3$,

            $y'(9x^2y^2 + 1) = 1 - 6xy^3$,

                    $y' = \dfrac{1 - 6xy^3}{1 + 9x^2y^2}$

21. $[x(e^y y') + e^y(1)] + y' = 0$, $xe^y y' + e^y + y' = 0$,

    $(xe^y + 1)y' = -e^y$, $y' = -\dfrac{e^y}{xe^y + 1}$

25. $3x^2 + 2yy' = 0$, $y' = -\dfrac{3x^2}{2y}$.   At $(-1,2)$, $y' = -\dfrac{3}{4}$.   The

    tangent is given by $y - 2 = -\dfrac{3}{4}(x + 1)$, or $y = -\dfrac{3}{4}x + \dfrac{5}{4}$.

29. $p = \dfrac{20}{(q + 5)^2}$.

$$\frac{d}{dp}(p) = \frac{d}{dp}\left[\frac{20}{(q + 5)^2}\right]$$

$$\frac{d}{dp}(p) = \frac{d}{dp}[20(q + 5)^{-2}]$$

$$1 = -\frac{40}{(q + 5)^3} \cdot \frac{dq}{dp}$$

$$\frac{dq}{dp} = -\frac{(q + 5)^3}{40}$$

33. $\ln \dfrac{f(t)}{1 - f(t)} + \sigma \dfrac{1}{1 - f(t)} = C_1 + C_2 t.$ Thus

$$\ln f(t) - \ln[1 - f(t)] + \sigma[1 - f(t)]^{-1} = C_1 + C_2 t$$

$$\frac{f'(t)}{f(t)} + \frac{f'(t)}{1 - f(t)} + \frac{\sigma f'(t)}{[1 - f(t)]^2} = C_2$$

$$f'(t)\left[\frac{1}{f(t)} + \frac{1}{1 - f(t)} + \frac{\sigma}{[1 - f(t)]^2}\right] = C_2$$

$$f'(t)\left[\frac{[1 - f(t)]^2 + f(t)[1 - f(t)] + \sigma f(t)}{f(t)[1 - f(t)]^2}\right] = C_2$$

$$f'(t)\left[\frac{[1 - f(t)][1 - f(t) + f(t)] + \sigma f(t)}{f(t)[1 - f(t)]^2}\right] = C_2$$

$$f'(t)\left[\frac{[1 - f(t)] + \sigma f(t)}{f(t)[1 - f(t)]^2}\right] = C_2.$$

Thus

$$f'(t) = \frac{C_2 f(t)[1 - f(t)]^2}{\sigma f(t) + [1 - f(t)]}.$$

EXERCISE 12.4

1. $y = (x + 1)^2(x - 1)(x^2 + 3)$. Taking natural logarithms of both sides gives

$$\ln y = \ln\left[(x + 1)^2(x - 1)(x^2 + 3)\right].$$

Using properties of logarithms on the right side gives

$$\ln y = 2 \ln(x + 1) + \ln(x - 1) + \ln(x^2 + 3).$$

Differentiating both sides with respect to x,

$$\frac{y'}{y} = \frac{2}{x + 1} + \frac{1}{x - 1} + \frac{2x}{x^2 + 3}$$

$$y' = y\left[\frac{2}{x + 1} + \frac{1}{x - 1} + \frac{2x}{x^2 + 3}\right].$$

Expressing y in terms of x,

$$y' = (x + 1)^2(x - 1)(x^2 + 3)\left[\frac{2}{x + 1} + \frac{1}{x - 1} + \frac{2x}{x^2 + 3}\right]$$

5. $y = \sqrt{x + 1}\sqrt{x^2 - 2}\sqrt{x + 4}$

$$\ln y = \ln\left(\sqrt{x + 1}\sqrt{x^2 - 2}\sqrt{x + 4}\right)$$

$$\ln y = \frac{1}{2} \ln(x + 1) + \frac{1}{2} \ln(x^2 - 2) + \frac{1}{2} \ln(x + 4)$$

$$\frac{y'}{y} = \frac{1}{2}\left[\frac{1}{x + 1} + \frac{2x}{x^2 - 2} + \frac{1}{x + 4}\right]$$

$$y' = \frac{y}{2}\left[\frac{1}{x + 1} + \frac{2x}{x^2 - 2} + \frac{1}{x + 4}\right]$$

$$= \frac{\sqrt{x + 1}\sqrt{x^2 - 2}\sqrt{x + 4}}{2}\left[\frac{1}{x + 1} + \frac{2x}{x^2 - 2} + \frac{1}{x + 4}\right]$$

9. $y = \dfrac{(2x^2 + 2)^2}{(x + 1)^2(3x + 2)}$

$\ln y = \ln\left[\dfrac{(2x^2 + 2)^2}{(x + 1)^2(3x + 2)}\right]$

$\quad = 2 \ln(2x^2 + 2) - 2 \ln(x + 1) - \ln(3x + 2).$

$\dfrac{y'}{y} = 2 \cdot \dfrac{4x}{2x^2 + 2} - 2 \cdot \dfrac{1}{x + 1} - \dfrac{3}{3x + 2}$

$y' = y\left[\dfrac{8x}{2x^2 + 2} - \dfrac{2}{x + 1} - \dfrac{3}{3x + 2}\right]$

$\quad = \dfrac{(2x^2 + 2)^2}{(x + 1)^2(3x + 2)}\left[\dfrac{4x}{x^2 + 1} - \dfrac{2}{x + 1} - \dfrac{3}{3x + 2}\right]$

13. $y = x^{2x+1}$. Thus $\ln y = \ln x^{2x+1} = (2x + 1) \ln x.$

$\dfrac{y'}{y} = (2x + 1)\dfrac{1}{x} + (\ln x)(2), \quad y' = y\left[\dfrac{2x + 1}{x} + 2 \ln x\right],$

$y' = x^{2x+1}\left[\dfrac{2x + 1}{x} + 2 \ln x\right]$

17. $y = (3x + 1)^{2x}$. Thus $\ln y = \ln[(3x + 1)^{2x}] = 2x \ln(3x+1).$

$\dfrac{y'}{y} = 2\left\{x\left(\dfrac{3}{3x + 1}\right) + [\ln(3x + 1)](1)\right\}$

$y' = 2y\left[\dfrac{3x}{3x + 1} + \ln(3x + 1)\right]$

$\quad = 2(3x + 1)^{2x}\left[\dfrac{3x}{3x + 1} + \ln(3x + 1)\right]$

21. $y = (x + 1)(x + 2)^2(x + 3)^2.$

$\ln y = \ln(x + 1) + 2 \ln(x + 2) + 2 \ln(x + 3)$

$\dfrac{y'}{y} = \dfrac{1}{x + 1} + \dfrac{2}{x + 2} + \dfrac{2}{x + 3} \quad y' = y\left[\dfrac{1}{x + 1} + \dfrac{2}{x + 2} + \dfrac{2}{x + 3}\right].$

When $x = 0$, then $y = 36$ and $y' = 96$. Thus an equation of the tangent line is $y - 36 = 96(x - 0)$, or $y = 96x + 36$.

EXERCISE 12.5

1. $y' = 12x^2 - 24x + 6, \quad y'' = 24x - 24, \quad y''' = 24$

5. $y' = 3x^2 + e^x, \; y'' = 6x + e^x, \; y''' = 6 + e^x, \; y^{(4)} = e^x$

9. $f(p) = \dfrac{1}{6p^3} = \dfrac{1}{6}p^{-3}, \; f'(p) = -\dfrac{1}{2}p^{-4}, \; f''(p) = 2p^{-5},$

$f'''(p) = -10p^{-6} = -\dfrac{10}{p^6}$

13. $y = \dfrac{1}{5x - 6} = (5x - 6)^{-1}$

$\dfrac{dy}{dx} = -5(5x - 6)^{-2}$

$\dfrac{d^2y}{dx^2} = 50(5x - 6)^{-3} = \dfrac{50}{(5x - 6)^3}$

17. $y = \ln[x(x + 1)] = \ln(x) + \ln(x + 1)$

$y' = \dfrac{1}{x} + \dfrac{1}{x + 1} = x^{-1} + (x + 1)^{-1}$

$y'' = -x^{-2} + (-1)(x + 1)^{-2} = -\left[\dfrac{1}{x^2} + \dfrac{1}{(x + 1)^2}\right]$

21. $x^2 + 4y^2 - 16 = 0.$

$2x + 8yy' = 0, \; 8yy' = -2x, \; y' = -\dfrac{x}{4y}.$

$y'' = -\dfrac{4y(1) - x(4y')}{16y^2} = -\dfrac{4y - 4x\left(-\dfrac{x}{4y}\right)}{16y^2} = -\dfrac{4y^2 + x^2}{16y^3}$

$= -\dfrac{16}{16y^3} = -\dfrac{1}{y^3}.$

25. $\sqrt{x} + 4\sqrt{y} = 4$,

$x^{1/2} + 4y^{1/2} = 4$, $\quad \frac{1}{2}x^{-1/2} + 2y^{-1/2}y' = 0$,

$2y^{-1/2}y' = -\frac{1}{2}x^{-1/2}$,

$y' = -\frac{1}{2} \cdot \frac{x^{-1/2}}{2y^{-1/2}} = -\frac{1}{4} \cdot \frac{y^{1/2}}{x^{1/2}}$.

$y'' = -\frac{1}{4}\left[\dfrac{x^{1/2}\left(\frac{1}{2}y^{-1/2}y'\right) - y^{1/2}\left(\frac{1}{2}x^{-1/2}\right)}{x}\right]$

$= -\frac{1}{8}\left[\dfrac{\frac{x^{1/2}}{y^{1/2}}\left(-\frac{y^{1/2}}{4x^{1/2}}\right) - \frac{y^{1/2}}{x^{1/2}}}{x}\right] = -\frac{1}{8}\left[\dfrac{-\frac{1}{4} - \frac{y^{1/2}}{x^{1/2}}}{x}\right]$

$= \frac{1}{8}\left[\dfrac{\frac{1}{4} + \frac{y^{1/2}}{x^{1/2}}}{x}\right] = \frac{1}{8}\left[\dfrac{x^{1/2} + 4y^{1/2}}{4x^{3/2}}\right] = \frac{1}{8}\left[\dfrac{4}{4x^{3/2}}\right] = \dfrac{1}{8x^{3/2}}$

29. $y^2 = e^{x+y}$, $\quad 2yy' = e^{x+y}(1 + y')$, $\quad 2yy' = e^{x+y} + e^{x+y}y'$,

$2yy' - e^{x+y}y' = e^{x+y}$, $\quad y'(2y - e^{x+y}) = e^{x+y}$,

$y' = \dfrac{e^{x+y}}{2y - e^{x+y}} = \dfrac{y^2}{2y - y^2} = \dfrac{y}{2 - y}$.

$y'' = \dfrac{(2 - y)y' - y(-y')}{(2 - y)^2} = \dfrac{2y'}{(2 - y)^2} = \dfrac{2\left(\frac{y}{2 - y}\right)}{(2 - y)^2} = \dfrac{2y}{(2 - y)^3}$

33. $\dfrac{dc}{dq} = 0.6q + 2$, $\quad \dfrac{d^2c}{dq^2} = 0.6$, $\quad \dfrac{d^2c}{dq^2}\bigg|_{q=100} = 0.6$

CHAPTER 12 - REVIEW PROBLEMS

1. $y = 2e^x + e^2 + e^{x^2}$, $\quad y' = 2e^x + 0 + e^{x^2}(2x) = 2(e^x + xe^{x^2})$

5. $y = e^{x^2+4x+5}$, $y' = e^{x^2+4x+5}(2x + 4) = 2(x + 2)e^{x^2+4x+5}$

9. $y = \sqrt{(x - 6)(x + 5)(9 - x)}$

$\ln y = \ln\sqrt{(x - 6)(x + 5)(9 - x)}$

$= \frac{1}{2}\left[\ln(x - 6) + \ln(x + 5) + \ln(9 - x)\right]$.

$\dfrac{y'}{y} = \dfrac{1}{2}\left[\dfrac{1}{x - 6} + \dfrac{1}{x + 5} + \dfrac{-1}{9 - x}\right]$,

$y' = \dfrac{y}{2}\left[\dfrac{1}{x - 6} + \dfrac{1}{x + 5} - \dfrac{1}{9 - x}\right]$

$= \dfrac{\sqrt{(x - 6)(x + 5)(9 - x)}}{2}\left[\dfrac{1}{x - 6} + \dfrac{1}{x + 5} + \dfrac{1}{x - 9}\right]$

13. $f(q) = \ln\left[(q + 1)^2(q + 2)^3\right] = 2 \ln(q + 1) + 3 \ln(q + 2)$.

$f'(q) = \dfrac{2}{q + 1} + \dfrac{3}{q + 2}$

17. $y = \dfrac{4e^{3x}}{xe^{x-1}} = \dfrac{4e^{2x+1}}{x}$.

$y' = 4 \cdot \dfrac{x[e^{2x+1}(2)] - e^{2x+1}[1]}{x^2} = \dfrac{4e^{2x+1}(2x - 1)}{x^2}$.

21. $f(1) = \ln(1 + 1 + 1^2 + 1^3)$.

$f'(1) = \dfrac{1}{1 + 1 + 1^2 + 1^3}[1 + 21 + 31^2] = \dfrac{1 + 41 + 31^2}{1 + 1 + 1^2 + 1^3}$

25. $f(t) = \ln(t^2\sqrt{1 - t}) = 2 \ln t + (1/2) \ln(1 - t)$.

$f'(t) = 2\left(\dfrac{1}{t}\right) + \dfrac{1}{2}\left(\dfrac{1}{1 - t}\right)(-1) = \dfrac{2}{t} + \dfrac{1}{2(t - 1)} = \dfrac{5t - 4}{2t(t - 1)}$

29. $y = e^{x^2-4}$. $y' = e^{x^2-4}[2x] = 2xe^{x^2-4}$.

$y'' = 2(xe^{x^2-4}[2x] + e^{x^2-4} \cdot 1) = 2e^{x^2-4}(2x^2 + 1)$.

At $(2,1)$, $y'' = 2e^0(9) = 18$.

33. $y = e^x$, $y' = e^x$.

If $x = \ln 2$, then $y = e^{\ln 2} = 2$ and $y' = e^{\ln 2} = 2$.

An equation of the tangent line is $y - 2 = 2(x - \ln 2)$,

$y = 2x + 2 - 2 \ln 2$, $y = 2x + 2(1 - \ln 2)$. Alternatively,

since $2 \ln 2 = \ln 2^2 = \ln 4$, the tangent can be written as

$y = 2x + 2 - \ln 4$.

37. $x + xy + y = 5$, $1 + xy' + y(1) + y' = 0$, $(x + 1)y' = -1-y$

$y' = -\dfrac{1 + y}{x + 1}$. $\qquad y'' = -\dfrac{(x + 1)y' - (1 + y)}{(x + 1)^2}$.

At $(2,1)$, $y' = -\dfrac{1 + 1}{2 + 1} = -\dfrac{2}{3}$ and $y'' = -\dfrac{3(-2/3) - 2}{9} = \dfrac{4}{9}$

13

Curve Sketching

We denote the term *critical value* by CV.

1. $y = x^2 + 2$. $y' = 2x = 0$ if $x = 0$. CV: $x = 0$.

$$\begin{array}{c} \diagdown \quad \diagup \\ \hline \Big| \\ 0 \end{array}$$

   Decreasing on $(-\infty, 0)$; increasing on $(0, \infty)$; relative
   minimum when $x = 0$.

5. $y = -(x^3/3) - 2x^2 + 5x - 2$.

   $y' = -x^2 - 4x + 5 = -(x^2 + 4x - 5) = -(x + 5)(x - 1)$.

   CV: $x = -5, 1$.

$$\begin{array}{c} \diagdown \quad \diagup \quad \diagdown \\ \hline \Big|\Big| \\ -5 \qquad 1 \end{array}$$

   Decreasing on $(-\infty, -5)$ and $(1, \infty)$; increasing on $(-5, 1)$;
   relative minimum at $x = -5$; relative maximum at $x = 1$.

9. $y = x^3 - 6x^2 + 9x$.

$y' = 3x^2 - 12x + 9 = 3(x^2 - 4x + 3) = 3(x - 1)(x - 3)$.

CV: $x = 1, 3$.

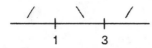

Increasing on $(-\infty, 1)$ and $(3, \infty)$; decreasing on $(1, 3)$; relative maximum when $x = 1$; relative minimum when $x = 3$.

13. $y = -x^5 - 5x^4 + 200$.

$y' = -5x^4 - 20x^3 = -5x^3(x + 4)$.   CV: $x = 0, -4$.

Decreasing on $(-\infty, -4)$ and $(0, \infty)$; increasing on $(-4, 0)$; relative minimum at $x = -4$; relative maximum at $x = 0$.

17. $y = \dfrac{10}{\sqrt{x}} = 10x^{-1/2}$.   [Note: $x > 0$.]

$y' = -5x^{-3/2} = -\dfrac{5}{\sqrt{x^3}} < 0$ for $x > 0$. Decreasing on $(0, \infty)$;

no relative maximum or relative minimum.

21. $y = (x + 2)^3(x - 5)^2$.

$y' = (x + 2)^3[(2)(x - 5)] + (x - 5)^2[(3)(x + 2)^2]$

$= (x + 2)^2(x - 5)[2(x + 2) + 3(x - 5)]$

$= (x + 2)^2(x - 5)(5x - 11)$.

CV: $x = -2, 5, 11/5$.

Increasing on $(-\infty, -2)$, $(-2, 11/5)$ and $(5, \infty)$;   decreasing on $(11/5, 5)$;   relative maximum when $x = 11/5$;   relative minimum when $x = 5$.

25. $y = x^2 - 2 \ln x$.   [Note: $x > 0$.]

$y' = 2x - \dfrac{2}{x} = \dfrac{2x^2 - 2}{x} = \dfrac{2(x^2 - 1)}{x} = \dfrac{2(x + 1)(x - 1)}{x}$.

CV: $x = 1$.

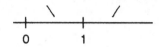

Decreasing on $(0,1)$; increasing on $(1,\infty)$; relative minimum when $x = 1$.

29. $y = x^2 - 6x - 7 = (x - 7)(x + 1)$.
Intercepts $(7,0)$, $(-1,0)$, $(0,-7)$.
$y' = 2x - 6 = 2(x - 3)$.   CV: $x = 3$.
Decreasing on $(-\infty,3)$; increasing on $(3,\infty)$; relative minimum at $x = 3$.

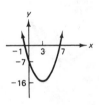

33. $y = 2x^3 - 9x^2 + 12x = x(2x^2 - 9x + 12)$.

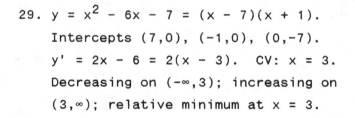

Note that $2x^2 - 9x + 12 = 0$ has no real roots. The only intercept is $(0,0)$.
$y' = 6x^2 - 18x + 12 = 6(x^2 - 3x + 2)$
$= 6(x - 2)(x - 1)$.   CV: $x = 1$ and $x = 2$.
Increasing on $(-\infty,1)$ and $(2,\infty)$; decreasing on $(1,2)$; rel. max. when $x = 1$; rel. min. when $x = 2$.

37. $y = (x - 1)^2(x + 2)^2$.

    Intercepts $(1,0)$, $(-2,0)$, $(0,4)$.

    $y' = (x - 1)^2 \cdot 2(x + 2) + (x + 2)^2 \cdot 2(x - 1)$

    $= 2(x - 1)(x + 2)[(x - 1) + (x + 2)]$

    $= 2(x - 1)(x + 2)(2x + 1)$.

    CV: $x = 1, -2, -\frac{1}{2}$. Decreasing on $(-\infty,-2)$

    and $\left(-\frac{1}{2},1\right)$; increasing on $\left(-2,-\frac{1}{2}\right)$ and

    $(1,\infty)$; rel. min. when $x = -2$ or $x = 1$;

    rel. max. when $x = -\frac{1}{2}$.

41.

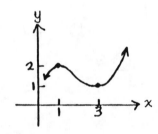

45. $p = 400 - 2q$. Revenue is given by $r = pq = (400 - 2q)q = 400q - 2q^2$. Marginal revenue is $r' = 400 - 4q$. Marginal revenue is increasing when its derivative is positive. But $(r')' = -4 < 0$. Thus marginal revenue is never increasing.

49. $E = 0.71\left(1 - \frac{T_c}{T_h}\right)$. $\frac{dE}{dT_h} = 0.71\left(\frac{T_c}{T_h^2}\right) > 0$, so as T_h increases,

    E increases.

EXERCISE 13.2

1. $f(x) = x^2 - 2x + 3$ and f is continuous over $[-1,2]$.
   $f'(x) = 2x - 2 = 2(x - 1)$. The only critical value is
   $x = 1$. We evaluate f at this point and at the endpoints:
   $f(-1) = 6$, $f(1) = 2$, and $f(2) = 3$. Thus there is an
   absolute maximum when $x = -1$ and an absolute minimum when
   $x = 1$.

5. $f(x) = 4x^3 + 3x^2 - 18x + 3$ and f is continuous over $\left[\frac{1}{2},3\right]$.
   $f'(x) = 12x^2 + 6x - 18 = 6(2x^2 + x - 3) = 6(2x + 3)(x - 1)$.
   The only critical value on $[1/2,3]$ is $x = 1$. We evaluate f
   at this point and the endpoints: $f(1/2) = -19/4$, $f(1) = -8$,
   $f(3) = 84$. There is an absolute maximum when $x = 3$ and an
   absolute minimum when $x = 1$.

EXERCISE 13.3

1. $y = -2x^2 + 4x$. $y' = -4x + 4$. $y'' = -4 < 0$ for all x, so
   the graph is concave down for all x, that is, on $(-\infty,\infty)$.

5. $y = x^4 - 6x^2 + 5x - 6$. $y' = 4x^3 - 12x + 5$.
   $y'' = 12x^2 - 12 = 12(x^2 - 1) = 12(x + 1)(x - 1)$. Possible
   inflection points when $x = \pm 1$. Concave up on $(-\infty,-1)$ and
   on $(1,\infty)$; concave down on $(-1,1)$; inflection points when
   $x = \pm 1$.

9. $y = \dfrac{x^2}{x^2 + 1}$.

$y' = \dfrac{(x^2 + 1)(2x) - x^2(2x)}{(x^2 + 1)^2} = = \dfrac{2x}{(x^2 + 1)^2}$.

$y'' = \dfrac{(x^2 + 1)^2(2) - 2x(2)(x^2 + 1)(2x)}{(x^2 + 1)^4} = \dfrac{(x^2 + 1)(2) - 8x^2}{(x^2 + 1)^3}$

$= \dfrac{2(1 - 3x^2)}{(x^2 + 1)^3} = \dfrac{2(1 + \sqrt{3}x)(1 - \sqrt{3}x)}{(x^2 + 1)^3}$.

Possible inflection points when $x = \pm 1/\sqrt{3}$. Concave down on $(-\infty, -1/\sqrt{3})$ and $(1/\sqrt{3}, \infty)$; concave up on $(-1/\sqrt{3}, 1/\sqrt{3})$; inflection points when $x = \pm 1/\sqrt{3}$.

13. $y = xe^x$. $y' = xe^x + e^x = e^x(x + 1)$.

$y'' = e^x(1) + (x + 1)e^x = e^x(x + 2)$.

$y'' = 0$ if $x = -2$. Concave down on $(-\infty, -2)$; concave up on $(-2, \infty)$; inflection point when $x = -2$.

17. $y = 4x - x^2 = x(4 - x)$. Intercepts $(0,0)$ and $(4,0)$. $y' = 4 - 2x = 2(2 - x)$. CV: $x = 2$. Increasing on $(-\infty, 2)$; decreasing on $(2, \infty)$; rel. max. at $(2,4)$. $y'' = -2$. No possible inflection point. Concave down for all x.

21. $y = \dfrac{x^3}{3} - 4x = \dfrac{x^3 - 12x}{3} = \frac{1}{3}x(x + 2\sqrt{3})(x - 2\sqrt{3})$.

Intercepts $(0,0)$ and $(\pm 2\sqrt{3}, 0)$.

$y' = x^2 - 4 = (x + 2)(x - 2)$. CV: $x = \pm 2$.

Increasing on $(-\infty, -2)$ and $(2, \infty)$;

decreasing on $(-2, 2)$; rel. max. at

(-2, 16/3); rel. min. at (2, -16/3). $y'' = 2x$. Possible inflection point when $x = 0$. Concave down on $(-\infty, 0)$; concave up on $(0, \infty)$; inflection point at $(0,0)$. Symmetric about the origin.

25. $y = 4x^3 - 3x^4 = x^3(4 - 3x)$.
    Intercepts $(0,0)$, $(4/3,0)$.
    $y' = 12x^2 - 12x^3 = 12x^2(1 - x)$.
    CV: $x = 0$ and $x = 1$.
    Increasing on $(-\infty,0)$ and $(0,1)$;
    decreasing on $(1,\infty)$; rel. max. at $(1,1)$.

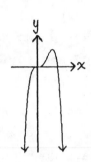

$y'' = 24x - 36x^2 = 12x(2 - 3x)$. Possible inflection points at $x = 0$ and $x = 2/3$. Concave down on $(-\infty, 0)$ and $(2/3,\infty)$; concave up on $(0,2/3)$; inflection point at $(0, 0)$ and $(2/3, 16/27)$.

29. $y = x^3 - 6x^2 + 12x - 6$. Intercept $(0,-6)$.
    $y' = 3x^2 - 12x + 12 = 3(x - 2)^2$.
    CV: $x = 2$. Increasing on $(-\infty,2)$ and $(2,\infty)$.
    $y'' = 6(x - 2)$. Possible inflection point when $x = 2$. Concave down on $(-\infty,2)$; concave up on $(2,\infty)$; inflection point at $(2, 2)$.

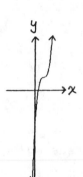

33. $y = 3x^4 - 4x^3 + 1$. Intercepts $(0,1)$
and $(1,0)$ [the latter is found by
inspection of the equation].
No symmetry.

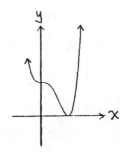

$y' = 12x^3 - 12x^2 = 12x^2(x - 1)$.
CV: $x = 0$ and $x = 1$. Decreasing on
$(-\infty,0)$ and $(0,1)$; increasing on
$(1,\infty)$; relative minimum at $(1, 0)$.

$y'' = 36x^2 - 24x = 12x(3x - 2)$. Possible inflection points
at $x = 0$ and $x = 2/3$. Concave up on $(-\infty,0)$ and $(2/3,\infty)$;
concave down on $(0,2/3)$; inflection points at $(0,1)$ and
$(2/3,11/27)$.

37. $y = x^{1/3}(x - 8)$.
Intercepts $(0,0)$ and $(8,0)$.
Since $y = x^{4/3} - 8x^{1/3}$,
$y' = \frac{4}{3}x^{1/3} - \frac{8}{3}x^{-2/3}$

$\quad = \frac{4}{3}\left[x^{1/3} - \frac{2}{x^{2/3}}\right] = \frac{4(x - 2)}{3x^{2/3}}$.

CV: $x = 0, 2$.
Decreasing on $(-\infty,0)$ and $(0,2)$;
increasing on $(2,\infty)$; relative

minimum at $(2,-6\sqrt[3]{2}) \approx (2,-7.56)$.

$y'' = \frac{4}{9}x^{-2/3} + \frac{16}{9}x^{-5/3}$

$\quad = \frac{4}{9}\left[\frac{1}{x^{2/3}} + \frac{4}{x^{5/3}}\right] = \frac{4(x + 4)}{9x^{5/3}}$.

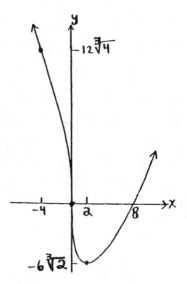

Possible inflection points when
$x = -4, 0$. Concave up on $(-\infty, -4)$ and $(0,\infty)$; concave down
on $(-4,0)$; inflection point at $(-4,12\sqrt[3]{4})$.

41. $y = 2x + 3x^{2/3} = 2x^{2/3}\left(x^{1/3} + \frac{3}{2}\right)$.

Intercepts $(0,0)$ and $(-27/8, 0)$.

$y' = 2 + 2x^{-1/3} = 2\left(1 + \frac{1}{\sqrt[3]{x}}\right)$

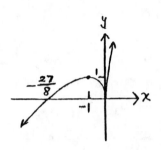

$= 2\left(\frac{\sqrt[3]{x} + 1}{\sqrt[3]{x}}\right)$. CV: $x = 0, -1$.

Increasing on $(-\infty,-1)$ and $(0,\infty)$;
decreasing on $(-1,0)$; rel. max. at $(-1,1)$; rel. min. at
$(0,0)$.

$y'' = -\frac{2}{3}x^{-4/3} = -\frac{2}{3x^{4/3}}$. Possible inflection point at

$x = 0$. Concave down on $(-\infty,0)$ and $(0,\infty)$. Observe that at
the origin the tangent line exists but it is vertical.

45.

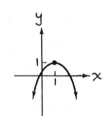

49. $S = f(A) = 12\sqrt[4]{A}$, $0 \leq A \leq 625$. For the given values of
A we have $S' = 3A^{-3/4} > 0$ and $S'' = -(9/4)A^{-7/4} < 0$. Thus
y is increasing and concave down.

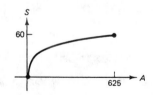

53. $n = f(r) = 0.1 \ln(r) + \frac{7}{r} - 0.8$, $1 \le r \le 10$.

(a) $\frac{dn}{dr} = \frac{0.1}{r} - \frac{7}{r^2} = \frac{0.1r - 7}{r^2} = \frac{0.1(r - 70)}{r^2} < 0$ for

$1 \le r \le 10$. Thus the graph of f is always falling. Also,

$\frac{d^2n}{dr^2} = -\frac{0.1}{r^2} + \frac{14}{r^3} = \frac{14 - 0.1r}{r^3} = \frac{0.1(140 - r)}{r^3} > 0$

for $1 \le r \le 10$ Thus the graph is concave up.

(b) f(r)

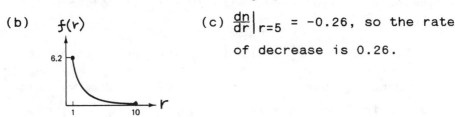

(c) $\left.\frac{dn}{dr}\right|_{r=5} = -0.26$, so the rate of decrease is 0.26.

<u>EXERCISE 13.4</u>

1. $y = x^2 - 5x + 6$. $y' = 2x - 5 = 0$. CV: $x = 5/2$. $y'' = 2$.
$y''(5/2) = 2 > 0$. Thus there is a relative minimum when
$x = 5/2$. Because there is only one relative extremum
and f is continuous, the relative minimum is an absolute
minimum.

5. $y = x^3 - 27x + 1$.

$y' = 3x^2 - 27 = 3(x^2 - 9) = 3(x + 3)(x - 3) = 0$.

CV: $x = \pm 3$. $y'' = 6x$.

$y''(-3) = -18 < 0 \Rightarrow$ relative maximum when $x = -3$

$y''(3) = 18 > 0 \Rightarrow$ relative minimum when $x = 3$

9. $y = 2x^4 + 2.$ $y' = 8x^3 = 0.$ CV: $x = 0.$ $y'' = 24x^2.$
   Since $y''(0) = 0$, the second-derivative test fails. Using
   the first-derivative test, we see that f decreases for
   $x < 0$ and f increases for $x > 0$, so there is a relative
   minimum when $x = 0$.

EXERCISE 13.5

1. $y = f(x) = \frac{x}{x + 1}.$ When $x = -1$ the denominator is zero but
   the numerator is not zero. Thus the line $x = -1$ is a
   vertical asymptote. Testing for horizontal asymptotes,

   $\lim\limits_{x \to \infty} \frac{x}{x + 1} = \lim\limits_{x \to \infty} \frac{x}{x} = \lim\limits_{x \to \infty} 1 = 1$, and $\lim\limits_{x \to -\infty} f(x) = 1.$

   Thus the line $y = 1$ is the only horizontal asymptote.

5. $y = f(x) = \frac{4}{x}.$ When $x = 0$ the denominator is zero but the
   numerator is not zero, so $x = 0$ is a vertical asymptote.
   Taking limits at infinity, $\lim\limits_{x \to \infty} (4/x) = 0 = \lim\limits_{x \to -\infty} (4/x)$, so
   the line $y = 0$ is a horizontal asymptote.

9. $y = f(x) = x^2 - 5x + 8$ is a polynomial function, so there
   are no horizontal or vertical asymptotes.

13. $y = f(x) = \frac{4}{x - 6} + 4 = \frac{4x - 20}{x - 6}.$ From the denominator we
    find that the line $x = 6$ is a vertical asymptote. Taking
    limits at infinity, $\lim\limits_{x \to \infty} f(x) = \lim\limits_{x \to \infty} 4x/x = \lim\limits_{x \to \infty} 4 = 4$, and
    $\lim\limits_{x \to -\infty} f(x) = 4.$ Thus $y = 4$ is a horizontal asymptote.

17. $y = f(x) = \dfrac{x^2 - 3x - 4}{1 + 4x + 4x^2} = \dfrac{x^2 - 3x - 4}{(1 + 2x)^2}$.

From the denominator, $x = -1/2$ is a vertical asymptote.

Also, $\lim\limits_{x\to\infty} f(x) = \lim\limits_{x\to\infty} \dfrac{x^2}{4x^2} = \lim\limits_{x\to\infty} \frac{1}{4} = \frac{1}{4}$, and $\lim\limits_{x\to-\infty} f(x) = \frac{1}{4}$,

so $y = 1/4$ is a horizontal asymptote.

21. $y = \dfrac{3}{x}$. Symmetric about the origin.

Vertical asymptote is $x = 0$.

$\lim\limits_{x\to\infty} 3/x = 0 = \lim\limits_{x\to-\infty} 3/x$, so $y = 0$

is a horizontal asymptote.

$$y' = -\frac{3}{x^2}.$$

CV: none, however $x = 0$ must be
included in the inc.-dec. analysis. Decreasing on $(-\infty,0)$
and $(0,\infty)$.

$y'' = \dfrac{6}{x^3}$. No possible inflection point, but we include

$x = 0$ in the concavity analysis. Concave down on $(-\infty,0)$;
concave up on $(0,\infty)$.

25. $y = f(x) = x^2 + \dfrac{1}{x^2} = \dfrac{x^4 + 1}{x^2}$.

$x \neq 0$, so there is no y-intercept.
Setting $y = 0 \Rightarrow$ no x-intercept.
Replacing x by $-x$ yields symmetry
about the y-axis.

Setting $x^2 = 0$ gives $x = 0$ as the
only vertical asymptote. Because
the degree of the numerator is greater
than the degree of the denominator, no

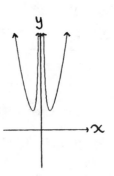

horizontal asymptote exists.

$$y = x^2 + x^{-2}, \quad y' = 2x - 2x^{-3} = 2x - \frac{2}{x^3} = \frac{2x^4 - 2}{x^3} =$$

$$\frac{2(x^4 - 1)}{x^3}. \quad \text{So } y' = \frac{2(x^2 + 1)(x + 1)(x - 1)}{x^3}. \quad \text{CV: } x = \pm 1,$$

but x = 0 must be included in the inc.-dec. analysis.
Decreasing on $(-\infty,-1)$ and $(0,1)$; increasing on $(-1,0)$ and
$(1,\infty)$; rel. min. at $(-1,2)$ and $(1,2)$,

$$y'' = 2 + \frac{6}{x^4} > 0 \text{ for all } x \neq 0. \quad \text{Concave up on } (-\infty,0) \text{ and}$$

$(0,\infty)$.

29. $y = f(x) = \frac{1 + x}{1 - x}$.

Intercepts: Setting x = 0 $\Rightarrow$ y = 1;
setting y = 0 $\Rightarrow$ x = -1. Thus the
only intercepts are $(0,1)$ and $(-1,0)$.
Setting 1 - x = 0 $\Rightarrow$ x = 1 is the
only vertical asymptote.

Since $\lim\limits_{x\to\infty} \frac{1 + x}{1 - x} = \lim\limits_{x\to\infty} \frac{x}{-x} =$

$\lim\limits_{x\to\infty} -1 = -1 = \lim\limits_{x\to-\infty} \frac{1 + x}{1 - x} = -1,$

the only horizontal asymptote
is y = -1.

$$y' = \frac{(1 - x)(1) - (1 + x)(1)}{(1 - x)^2} = \frac{2}{(1 - x)^2}.$$

No critical values, but x = 1 must be considered in the
inc.-dec. analysis. Increasing on $(-\infty,1)$ and $(1,\infty)$.

$$y'' = \frac{4}{(1 - x)^3}. \quad \text{No possible inflection point, but } x = 1$$

must be included in the concavity analysis. Concave up on
$(-\infty,1)$; concave down on $(1,\infty)$.

33. $y = f(x) = x + \frac{1}{x + 1} = \frac{x^2 + x + 1}{x + 1}$.

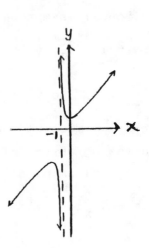

Intercepts: Setting x = 0 $\Rightarrow$ y = 1;
setting y = 0 yields no real roots.
Thus the only intercept is (0,1).
Setting x + 1 = 0 $\Rightarrow$ x = -1 is the
only vertical asymptote. Because
the degree of the numerator is
greater than the degree of the
denominator, there is no horizontal
asymptote.

$y' = \frac{(x + 1)(2x + 1) - (x^2 + x + 1)}{(x + 1)^2}$

$= \frac{x^2 + 2x}{(x + 1)^2} = \frac{x(x + 2)}{(x + 1)^2}$.

CV: 0 and -2, but x = -1 must be included
in the inc.-dec. analysis. Increasing on
$(-\infty, -2)$ and $(0, \infty)$; decreasing on $(-2, -1)$ and $(-1, 0)$;
relative maximum when x = -2; relative minimum when x = 0.

$y'' = \frac{(x + 1)^2(2x + 2) - (x^2 + 2x)[2(x + 1)]}{(x + 1)^4}$

$= \frac{(x + 1)(2x + 2) - (x^2 + 2x)[2]}{(x + 1)^3} = \frac{2}{(x + 1)^3}$.

No possible inflection point, but x = -1 must be included
in the concavity analysis. Concave down on $(-\infty, -1)$;
concave up on $(-1, \infty)$.

37.

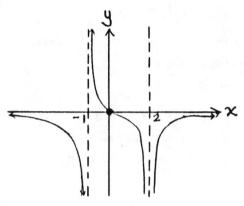

41. $\lim_{t\to\infty} (150 - 76e^{-t}) = \lim_{t\to\infty} \left(150 - \frac{76}{e^t}\right) = 150 - 0 = 150.$ Thus

y = 150 is a horizontal asymptote.

CHAPTER 13 - REVIEW PROBLEMS

1. $y = \frac{3x^2}{x^2 - 16} = \frac{3x^2}{(x + 4)(x - 4)}$.   When x = ±4 the denominator

is zero and the numerator is not zero. Thus x = 4 and

x = -4 are vertical asymptotes.

$\lim_{x\to\infty} \frac{3x^2}{x^2 - 16} = \lim_{x\to\infty} \frac{3x^2}{x^2} = \lim_{x\to\infty} 3 = 3.$ Similarly, $\lim_{x\to-\infty} y = 3.$

Thus y = 3 is the only horizontal asymptote.

5. $f(x) = -x^3 + 6x^2 - 9x.$ $f'(x) = -3x^2 + 12x - 9 =$

$-3(x^2 - 4x + 3) = -3(x-1)(x-3).$ CV: x = 1 and x = 3.

Increasing on (1,3); decreasing on (-∞,1) and (3,∞).

9. $f(x) = \frac{x^6}{6} + \frac{x^3}{3}$. $f'(x) = x^5 + x^2 = x^2(x^3 + 1)$.

CV: $x = 0$ and $x = -1$. Decreasing on $(-\infty,-1)$; increasing on $(-1,0)$ and $(0,\infty)$; relative minimum when $x = -1$.

13. $y = 3x^4 - 4x^3$, $[0,2]$. $y' = 12x^3 - 12x^2 = 12x^2(x - 1)$.

CV: $x = 0$ and $x = 1$. $y(0) = 0$, $y(1) = -1$, $y(2) = 16$.

Absolute maximum when $x = 2$; absolute minimum when $x = 1$.

17. $y = x^3 - 12x + 20$.

Setting $x = 0 \Rightarrow$ y-intercept $(0,20)$.

No symmetry. No asymptotes.

$y' = 3x^2 - 12 = 3(x^2 - 4) = 3(x + 2)(x - 2)$.

CV: $x = \pm2$. Increasing on $(-\infty,-2)$ and

$(2,\infty)$; decreasing on $(-2,2)$;

relative maximum at $(-2,36)$;

relative minimum at $(2,4)$.

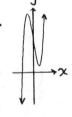

$y'' = 6x$. Possible inflection point when $x = 0$. Concave

up on $(0,\infty)$; concave down on $(-\infty,0)$; inflection point at

$(0,20)$.

21. $y = f(x) = \frac{100(x + 5)}{x^2}$.

Intercept: $(-5,0)$.

No symmetry.

$x = 0$ is the only vertical asymptote.

$\lim_{x\to\infty} y = 100 \lim_{x\to\infty} \frac{x}{x^2} = 100 \lim_{x\to\infty} \frac{1}{x} = 0$,

and $\lim_{x\to-\infty} y = 0$, so $y = 0$ is the only horizontal asymptote.

$y = 100[x^{-1} + 5x^{-2}]$,

$$y' = 100[-x^{-2} - 10x^{-3}] = -100\left[\frac{1}{x^2} + \frac{10}{x^3}\right] = \frac{-100(x + 10)}{x^3}.$$

CV: x = -10, but x = 0 must be included in the analysis
for inc.-dec. Increasing on (-10,0); decreasing on
(-∞,-10) and (0,∞); relative minimum at (-10,-5).

$$y'' = 100[2x^{-3} + 30x^{-4}] = 200\left[\frac{1}{x^3} + \frac{15}{x^4}\right] = \frac{200(x + 15)}{x^4}.$$

Possible inflection point when x = -15, but x = 0 must
also be considered in the concavity analysis. Concave up
on (-15,0) and (0,∞); concave down on (-∞,-15); inflection
point at (-15,-40/9).

25. $f(x) = \frac{1}{\sqrt{2\pi}}e^{-x^2/2}.$

The graph is symmetric about the y-axis. Testing for
horizontal asymptotes: $\lim_{x\to\infty} f(x) = \lim_{x\to-\infty} f(x) = 0.$ Thus
y = 0 is the only horizontal asymptote.

$f'(x) = \frac{-xe^{-x^2/2}}{\sqrt{2\pi}}.$ CV: x = 0. If x < 0, then f'(x) > 0;
if x > 0, then f'(x) < 0. Thus there is a relative (and
absolute) maximum when x = 0.

$f''(x) = -\frac{1}{\sqrt{2\pi}}[xe^{-x^2/2}(-x) + e^{-x^2/2}]$

$\qquad = \frac{e^{-x^2/2}(x + 1)(x - 1)}{\sqrt{2\pi}}.$

Testing f''(x) gives inflection points when x = ±1.

14

Applications of Differentiation

1. $c = 0.05q^2 + 5q + 500$.

   Avg. Cost per unit $= \bar{c} = \dfrac{c}{q} = 0.05q + 5 + \dfrac{500}{q}$.

Thus

$$\bar{c}' = 0.05 - \frac{500}{q^2}.$$

Setting $\bar{c}' = 0$ yields

$$0.05 = \frac{500}{q^2}, \quad q^2 = 10,000, \quad q = \pm 100.$$

We exclude $q = -100$ because q represents number of units.

Since $\bar{c}'' = \dfrac{1000}{q^3} > 0$ for $q > 0$, $\bar{c}$ is an absolute minimum

when $q = 100$.

5. $f(p) = 160 - p - \dfrac{900}{p + 10}$, where $0 \leq p \leq 100$.

   Setting $f'(p) = 0$ gives $-1 + \dfrac{900}{(p + 10)^2} = 0$, $\dfrac{900}{(p + 10)^2} = 1$,

   $(p + 10)^2 = 900$, $p + 10 = \pm 30$, from which $p = 20$.

   (a) Since $f''(p) = \dfrac{-1800}{(p + 10)^3} < 0$ for $p = 20$, we have an

   absolute maximum of $f(20) = 110$ grams.

   (b) $f(0) = 70$ and $f(100) = 51\frac{9}{11}$, so we have an absolute

   minimum of $f(100) = 51\frac{9}{11}$ grams.

9. $p = 42 - 4q$, $\bar{c} = 2 + \dfrac{80}{q}$. Total Cost $= c = \bar{c}q = 2q + 80$.

   Profit $=$ Total Revenue $-$ Total Cost

   $P = pq - c = (42 - 4q)q - (2q + 80)$

   $= -(4q^2 - 40q + 80)$.

   $P' = -(8q - 40)$.

   Setting $P' = 0$ yields $q = 5$. Since $P'' = -8 < 0$, P is
   maximum when $q = 5$. The corresponding value of price p is
   $42 - 4(5) = \$22$.

13. If $x =$ number of $\$0.10$ decreases, then the monthly fee is
    $5 - 0.10x$, and total number of subscribers is $1000 + 100x$.
    Monthly revenue $r =$ (rate)(total no. of subscribers).

    $r = (5 - 0.10x)(1000 + 100x)$

    $r' = (5 - 0.10x)(100) + (1000 + 100x)(-0.10)$

    $= 400 - 20x$.

    Setting $r' = 0$ yields $x = 20$. Since $r'' = -20 < 0$, r is a
    maximum when $x = 20$. This corresponds to a monthly fee of
    $5 - 0.10(20) = \$3$ and a monthly revenue r of $\$9,000$.

17. We are given that 5x + 3(2y) = 3000,
    or y = (3000 - 5x)/6. We want to
    maximize area A where

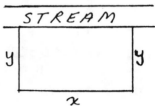

$$A = xy = x\left(\frac{3000 - 5x}{6}\right)$$

$$= \tfrac{1}{6}(3000x - 5x^2).$$

$$A' = \tfrac{1}{6}(3000 - 10x).$$

Setting A' = 0 $\Rightarrow$ x = 300. Since A"(300) = $\tfrac{1}{6}(-10)$ < 0, we

have a maximum at x = 300. Thus y = [3000 - 5(300)]/6 =

250. The dimensions are 300 ft × 250 ft.

21. $V = (12 - 2x)^2 x$

$$= 144x - 48x^2 + 4x^3$$

$$= 4(36x - 12x + x^3).$$

Note: 0 < x < 6.

$$V' = 4(36 - 24x + 3x^2) = 12(x^2 - 8x + 12)$$

$$= 12(x - 6)(x - 2).$$

For 0 < x < 6, setting V' = 0 gives x = 2. Since V' > 0

on (0,2) and V' < 0 on (2,6), V is maximum when x = 2.

Thus the length of the side of the square must be 2 in.,

which results in a volume of $(12 - 4)^2(2) = 128$ in^3.

25. $p = 600 - 2q$, $c = 0.2q^2 + 28q + 200$.

$$\text{Profit} = \text{Total Revenue} - \text{Total Cost}$$

$$P = pq - c$$

$$P = (600 - 2q)q - (0.2q^2 + 28q + 200)$$

$$= -(2.2q^2 - 572q + 200).$$

$$P' = -(4.4q - 572).$$

Setting $P' = 0$ yields $q = 130$. Since $P'' = -4.4 < 0$, P is maximum when $q = 130$. The corresponding price is $p = 340$, and the profit is $P = 36,980$.

If a tax of \$22/unit is imposed on the manufacturer, then the cost equation is

$$c_1 = (0.2q^2 + 28q + 200) + 22q$$

$$= 0.2q^2 + 50q + 200.$$

The demand equation remains the same. Thus

$$P_1 = pq - c_1$$

$$= (600 - 2q)q - (0.2q^2 + 50q + 200)$$

$$= -(2.2q^2 - 550q + 200).$$

$$P_1' = -(4.4q - 550).$$

Setting $P_1' = 0$ yields $q = 125$. Since $P_1'' = -4.4 < 0$, P_1 is maximum when $q = 125$. The corresponding price is $p = 350$ and the profit is $P_1 = 34,175$.

29. Let x = number of people over the 30. Note: $0 \le x \le 10$.

    Revenue = r = (number attending)(charge/person).

$$= (30 + x)(50 - 1.25x)$$

$$= 1500 + 12.5x - 1.25x^2.$$

$$r' = 12.5 - 2.5x.$$

Setting $r' = 0$ yields $x = 5$. Since $r'' = -2.5 < 0$, r is maximum when $x = 5$, that is, when 35 attend.

33. x = tons of chemical A (x ≤ 4), y = (24 - 6x)/(5 - x) = tons of chemical B, profit on A = \$2000/ton, and profit on B = \$1000/ton.

Total Profit = P_T = 2000x + 1000$\left(\dfrac{24 - 6x}{5 - x}\right)$

$$= 2000\left[x + \dfrac{12 - 3x}{5 - x}\right].$$

$$P_T' = 2000\left[1 + \dfrac{(5 - x)(-3) - (12 - 3x)(-1)}{(5 - x)^2}\right]$$

$$= 2000\left[1 - \dfrac{3}{(5 - x)^2}\right]$$

$$= 2000\left[\dfrac{x^2 - 10x + 22}{(5 - x)^2}\right].$$

Setting P_T' = 0 yields (by the quadratic formula)

$$x = \dfrac{10 \pm 2\sqrt{3}}{2} = 5 \pm \sqrt{3}.$$

Because x ≤ 4, choose x = 5 - $\sqrt{3}$. Since P_T is increasing on [0, 5 - $\sqrt{3}$) and decreasing on (5 - $\sqrt{3}$, 4], P_T is a maximum for x = 5 - $\sqrt{3}$ tons. If profit on A is P/ton and profit on B is (P/2)/ton, then

$$P_T = Px + \dfrac{P}{2}\left(\dfrac{24 - 6x}{5 - x}\right) = P\left[x + \dfrac{12 - 6x}{5 - x}\right].$$

$$P_T' = P\left[\dfrac{x^2 - 10x + 22}{(5 - x)^2}\right].$$

Setting P_T' = 0 and using an argument similar to that above, we find that P_T is a maximum when x = 5 - $\sqrt{3}$ tons.

EXERCISE 14.2

1. Let $f(x) = x^3 - 4x + 1$. $f(0) = 1$ and $f(1) = -2$, so $f(0)$
   is closer to 0 than is $f(1)$. We choose $x_1 = 0$.

   $f'(x) = 3x^2 - 4$. $x_{n+1} = x_n - [f(x_n)/f'(x_n)]$.

n	x_n	x_{n+1}
1	2.00000	0.25000
2	0.25000	0.25410
3	0.25410	0.25410

   Because $|x_4 - x_3| < 0.0001$, the root is approximately

   $x_4 = 0.25410$.

5. Let $f(x) = x^3 + x + 16$. $f(-3) = -14$ and $f(-2) = 6$, so
   $f(-2)$ is closer to 0 than is $f(-3)$. We choose $x_1 = -2$.

   $f'(x) = 3x^2 + 1$. $x_{n+1} = x_n - [f(x_n)/f'(x_n)]$.

n	x_n	x_{n+1}
1	-2.00000	-2.46154
2	-2.46154	-2.38977
3	-2.38977	-2.38769
4	-2.38769	-2.38769

   Because $|x_5 - x_4| < 0.0001$, the root is approximately

   $x_5 = -2.38769$.

9. Let $f(x) = x^4 - 2x^3 + x^2 - 3$. $f(1) = -3$ and $f(2) = 1$, so $f(2)$ is closer to 0 than is $f(1)$. We choose $x_1 = 2$.

$f'(x) = 4x^3 - 6x^2 + 2x$. $x_{n+1} = x_n - [f(x_n)/f'(x_n)]$.

n	x_n	x_{n+1}
1	2.00000	1.91667
2	1.91667	1.90794
3	1.90794	1.90785

Because $|x_4 - x_3| < 0.0001$, the root is approximately $x_4 = 1.90785$.

EXERCISE 14.3

1. $y = 3x - 4$. $dy = \frac{d}{dx}(3x - 4) \, dx = 3 \, dx$

5. $u = x^{-2}$. $du = \frac{d}{dx}(x^{-2}) \, dx = -2x^{-3} \, dx = -\frac{2}{x^3} \, dx$

9. $dy = y' \, dx = [(4x + 3)e^{2x^2+3}(4x) + e^{2x^2+3}(4)] \, dx$

$= 4e^{2x^2+3}(4x^2 + 3x + 1) \, dx$

13. $\Delta y = \sqrt{25 - (2.9)^2} - \sqrt{25 - 3^2}$

$= \sqrt{16.59} - \sqrt{16} \approx 4.073 - 4 = 0.073$.

$dy = \frac{-x}{\sqrt{25 - x^2}} \, dx = \frac{-3}{\sqrt{16}}(-0.1) = 0.075$.

17. $\sqrt[3]{63}$. Let $y = f(x) = \sqrt[3]{x}$.

$$f(x + dx) \approx f(x) + dy = \sqrt[3]{x} + \frac{1}{3x^{2/3}} \, dx.$$

If $x = 64$ and $dx = -1$, then

$$\sqrt[3]{63} = f[64 + (-1)] \approx \sqrt[3]{64} + \frac{1}{3(\sqrt[3]{64})^2}(-1) = 4 + \frac{-1}{3 \cdot 4^2} = 3\frac{47}{48}.$$

21. $e^{0.01}$. Let $y = f(x) = e^x$.

$$f(x + dx) \approx f(x) + dy = e^x + e^x \, dx.$$

If $x = 0$ and $dx = 0.01$, then

$$e^{0.01} = f(0 + 0.01) \approx e^0 + e^0(0.01) = 1.01.$$

25. $\frac{dq}{dp} = 6p(p^2 + 5)^2$. $\quad \frac{dp}{dq} = \frac{1}{dq/dp} = \frac{1}{6p(p^2 + 5)^2}$

29. $p = \frac{500}{q + 2}$, $\quad \frac{dp}{dq} = \frac{-500}{(q + 2)^2}$, $\quad \frac{dq}{dp} = \frac{1}{dp/dq} = -\frac{(q + 2)^2}{500}$.

$$\left.\frac{dq}{dp}\right|_{q=18} = -\left.\frac{(q + 2)^2}{500}\right|_{q=18} = -\frac{4}{5}.$$

33. $p = 10/\sqrt{q}$. Approximate p when $q = 24$.

$$p(q + dq) \approx p + dp = \frac{10}{\sqrt{q}} - \frac{5}{\sqrt{q^3}} \, dq.$$

If $q = 25$ and $dq = -1$, then

$$\frac{10}{\sqrt{24}} = p[25 + (-1)] \approx \frac{10}{\sqrt{25}} - \frac{5}{\sqrt{(25)^3}}(-1)$$

$$= 2 + \frac{1}{25} = \frac{51}{25} = 2.04.$$

37. $V = \frac{4}{3}\pi r^3$, $dV = 4\pi r^2\, dr$. Now, the change in r is

$$dr = (6.6 \times 10^{-4}) - (6.5 \times 10^{-4})$$
$$= 0.1 \times 10^{-4} = 10^{-5}.$$

Thus $dV = 4\pi(6.5 \times 10^{-4})^2(10^{-5}) \approx (1.69 \times 10^{-11})\pi \text{ cm}^3$.

EXERCISE 14.4

1. $\eta = \frac{p/q}{dp/dq} = \frac{p/q}{-2} = \frac{30/5}{-2} = -3$, elastic

5. $\eta = \frac{p/q}{-500/(q+2)^2} = \frac{[500/(q+2)]/q}{-500/(q+2)^2} = -\frac{q+2}{q} = -\frac{102}{100} = -1.02$, elastic

9. $q = 600 - 100p$. When $p = 3$, then $q = 300$. $\eta = \frac{p/q}{dp/dq}$.

$\frac{dq}{dp} = -100 \Rightarrow \frac{dp}{dq} = -\frac{1}{100}$. $\eta = \frac{3/300}{-1/100} = -1$, unit elasticity

13. $q = \frac{(p-100)^2}{2}$. $\eta = \frac{p/q}{dp/dq}$. $\frac{dq}{dp} = p - 100 \Rightarrow \frac{dp}{dq} = \frac{1}{p-100}$.

$\eta = \frac{p/q}{1/(p-100)} = \frac{p/[(p-100)^2/2]}{1/(p-100)} = \frac{2p}{p-100}$. If $p = 20$, then $\eta = -1/2$, inelastic

17. $q = 500 - 40p + p^2$. $\eta = \frac{p/q}{dp/dq}$. $\frac{dq}{dp} = -40 + 2p$, so $\frac{dp}{dq} = \frac{1}{-40+2p}$. Thus $\eta = \frac{p/q}{1/(-40+2p)}$. When $p = 15$, then $q = 125$, so $\eta = -\frac{6}{5} = -1.2$. If the price of 15 increases $\frac{1}{2}$%, then demand decreases approximately $\left(\frac{1}{2}\right)(1.2) = 0.6$%.

21. $p = 1000/q^2$. $r = pq = \frac{1000}{q}$. $\frac{dr}{dq} = - \frac{1000}{q^2}$. $\eta = \frac{p/q}{dp/dq} =$

$\frac{1000/q^3}{-2000/q^3} = - \frac{1}{2}$. $p\left(1 + \frac{1}{\eta}\right) = \frac{1000}{q^2}(1 - 2) = - \frac{1000}{q^2} = \frac{dr}{dq}$.

CHAPTER 14 - REVIEW PROBLEMS

1. $q = 80m^2 - 0.1m^4$. $dq/dm = 160m - 0.4m^3 = 0.4m(400 - m^2)$.
   Setting $dq/dm = 0$ yields (for $m \geqq 0$) $m = 0$ or $m = 20$.
   Since q is increasing on $(0,20)$ and decreasing on $(20,\infty)$,
   q is maximum when $m = 20$.

5. $p = 400 - 2q$. $\bar{c} = q + 160 + (2000/q)$. Total Cost = c =
   $\bar{c}q = q^2 + 160q + 2000$. Profit = Total Revenue - Total Cost

$$P = pq - c = (400 - 2q)q - (q^2 + 160q + 2000)$$

$$= -(3q^2 - 240q + 2000).$$

$$P' = -(6q - 240) = -6(q - 40).$$

Setting $P' = 0$ yields $q = 40$. Since $P'' = -6 < 0$, P is
maximum when $q = 40$, and corresponding profit is $P = \$2800$.

9. $N = \frac{14,400 + 120t + 100t^2}{144 + t^2}$, where $t \geqq 0$.

$N' = \frac{(144 + t^2)(120 + 200t) - (14,400 + 120t + 100t^2)(2t)}{(144 + t^2)^2}$

$= \frac{120(144 - t^2)}{(144 + t^2)^2}$. Setting $N' = 0$ gives $t = 12$, from

which $N = 105$. Since $N' > 0$ for $0 \leqq t < 12$ and $N' < 0$ for
$t > 12$, there is an absolute maximum when $t = 12$.

13. $F = \frac{9}{5}C + 32.$ $dF = \frac{9}{5} dC = \frac{9}{5}\left(\frac{1}{2}\right) = \left(\frac{9}{10}\right)^{\circ}.$

17. $x = 4y^2 + 7y - 3.$ $\frac{dy}{dx} = \frac{1}{dx/dy} = \frac{1}{8y + 7}.$

15

Integration

1. $\int 5 \; dx = 5x + C$

5. $\int 5x^{-7} \; dx = 5\int x^{-7} \; dx = 5 \cdot \frac{x^{-7+1}}{-7+1} + C = 5 \cdot \frac{x^{-6}}{-6} + C = -\frac{5}{6x^6} + C$

9. $\int \frac{1}{y^{11/5}} \; dy = \int y^{-11/5} \; dy = \frac{y^{(-11/5)+1}}{(-11/5)+1} + C = \frac{y^{-6/5}}{-6/5} + C =$

$-\frac{5}{6y^{6/5}} + C$

13. $\int (y^5 - 5y) \; dy = \int y^5 \; dy - \int y \; dy = \frac{y^{5+1}}{5+1} - 5 \cdot \frac{y^{1+1}}{1+1} + C =$

$\frac{y^6}{6} - 5 \cdot \frac{y^2}{2} + C = \frac{y^6}{6} - \frac{5y^2}{2} + C$

17. Since 7+e is a constant, $\int(7+e)\ dx = (7+e)x + C$.

21. $\int 3e^x\ dx = 3\int e^x\ dx = 3e^x + C$

25. $\int \frac{-2\sqrt{x}}{3}\ dx = -\frac{2}{3}\int x^{1/2}\ dx = -\frac{2}{3}\cdot\frac{x^{(1/2)+1}}{(1/2)+1} + C =$

$-\frac{2}{3}\cdot\frac{x^{3/2}}{3/2} + C = -\frac{4x^{3/2}}{9} + C$

29. $\int\left(\frac{x^3}{3} - \frac{3}{x^3}\right)\ dx = \frac{1}{3}\int x^3\ dx - 3\int x^{-3}\ dx =$

$\frac{1}{3}\cdot\frac{x^{3+1}}{3+1} - 3\cdot\frac{x^{-3+1}}{-3+1} + C = \frac{1}{3}\cdot\frac{x^4}{4} - 3\cdot\frac{x^{-2}}{-2} + C = \frac{x^4}{12} + \frac{3}{2x^2} + C$

33. $\int\frac{2z-5}{7}\ dz = \frac{1}{7}\int(2z-5)\ dz = \frac{1}{7}\left(2\int z\ dz - \int 5\ dz\right) =$

$\frac{1}{7}\left(2\cdot\frac{z^{1+1}}{1+1} - 5z\right) + C = \frac{1}{7}\left(2\cdot\frac{z^2}{2} - 5z\right) + C = \frac{1}{7}(z^2 - 5z) + C$

37. $\int(2\sqrt{x} - 3\sqrt[4]{x})\ dx = \int(2x^{1/2}-3x^{1/4})\ dx =$

$2\int x^{1/2}\ dx - 3\int x^{1/4}\ dx = 2\cdot\frac{x^{(1/2)+1}}{(1/2)+1} - 3\cdot\frac{x^{(1/4)+1}}{(1/4)+1} + C =$

$2\cdot\frac{x^{3/2}}{3/2} - 3\cdot\frac{x^{5/4}}{5/4} + C = \frac{4x^{3/2}}{3} - \frac{12x^{5/4}}{5} + C$

41. $\int(x^2+5)(x-3)\ dx = \int(x^3-3x^2+5x-15)\ dx =$

$\frac{x^4}{4} - 3\cdot\frac{x^3}{3} + 5\cdot\frac{x^2}{2} - 15x + C = \frac{x^4}{4} - x^3 + \frac{5x^2}{2} - 15x + C$

45. $\int (2u+1)^2 \, du = \int (4u^2+4u+1) \, du = 4\int u^2 \, du + 4\int u \, du + \int 1 \, du =$

$4 \cdot \frac{u^3}{3} + 4 \cdot \frac{u^2}{2} + u + C = \frac{4u^3}{3} + 2u^2 + u + C$

49. $\int \frac{e^6 + e^x}{2} \, dx = \frac{1}{2}\int (e^6+e^x) \, dx = \frac{1}{2}\left(\int e^6 \, dx + \int e^x \, dx\right) =$

$\frac{1}{2}(e^6 x + e^x) + C$

EXERCISE 15.2

1. $dy/dx = 3x-4$. $y = \int (3x-4) \, dx = \frac{3x}{2} - 4x + C$. Because

$y(-1) = \frac{13}{2}$, then $\frac{13}{2} = \frac{3(-1)^2}{2} - 4(-1) + C$. Thus $C = 1$.

Ans. $y = (3x^2/2)-4x+1$

5. $y'' = -x^2-2x$. $y' = \int (-x^2-2x) \, dx = -(x^3/3)-x^2+C_1$.

$y'(1) = 0$ implies $0 = (-1/3)-1+C_1$, or $C_1 = 4/3$. Thus

$y' = (x^3/3)-x^2+(4/3)$. $y = \int \left(\frac{x^3}{3} - x^2 + \frac{4}{3}\right) \, dx =$

$(-x^4/12)-(x^3/3)+(4x/3)+C_2$. $y(1) = 1$ implies

$1 = (-1/12)-(1/3)+(4/3)+C_2$, or $C_2 = 1/12$.

Ans. $y = (-x^4/12)-(x^3/3)+(4x/3)+(1/12)$

9. $dr/dq = 0.7$. $r = \int 0.7 \, dq = 0.7q + C$. When $q = 0$, then

$r = 0$, so $0 = 0 + C$, or $C = 0$. Thus $r = 0.7q$. Since

$r = pq$, then $p = r/q = (0.7q)/q = 0.7$. Ans. $p = 0.7$

13. $dc/dq = 1.35$. $c = \int 1.35 \, dq = 1.35q + C$. When $q = 0$, then $c = 200$, so $200 = 0 + C$, or $C = 200$. <u>Ans.</u> $c = 1.35q+200$

17. $G = \int [-(P/25)+2] \, dP = -(P^2/50)+2P+C$. When $P = 10$, then $G = 38$, so $38 = -2+20+C$. Thus $C = 20$.

<u>Ans.</u> $G = -(1/50)P^2+2P+20$

21. $dc/dq = 0.003q^2-0.4q+40$. $c = \int(0.003q^2 - 0.4q + 40) \, dq =$

$0.003 \cdot \frac{q^3}{3} - 0.04 \cdot \frac{q^2}{2} + 40q + C = 0.001q^3 - 0.2q^2 + 40q + C$.

When $q = 0$, then $c = 5000$, so $5000 = 0 - 0 + 0 + C$, or

$C = 5000$. Thus $c = 0.001q^3 - 0.2q^2 + 40q + 5000$. When

$q = 100$, then $c = 8000$. Since

$$\text{Avg. Cost} = \bar{c} = \frac{\text{Total Cost}}{\text{Quantity}} = \frac{c}{q},$$

when $q = 100$, $\bar{c} = 8000/100 = 80$. (Note that $dc/dq = 27.50$ when $q = 50$ is not relevant to problem.) <u>Ans.</u> $80

<u>EXERCISE 15.3</u>

1. $\int (x+5)^7 \, dx = \int (x+5)^7 \, [dx] = \frac{(x+5)^8}{8} + C$

5. $\int (3y^2+6y)(y^3+3y^2+1)^{2/3} \, dx = \int (y^3+3y^2+1)^{2/3}[(3y^2+6y) \, dy] =$

$\frac{(y^3+3y^2+1)^{5/3}}{5/3} + C = \frac{3}{5}(y^3+3y^2+1)^{5/3} + C$

9. $\displaystyle\int\sqrt{x+10}\ dx = \int(x+10)^{1/2}[dx] = \frac{(x+10)^{3/2}}{3/2} + C =$

$\displaystyle\frac{2(x+10)^{3/2}}{3} + C$

13. $\displaystyle\int x(x^2+3)^{12}\ dx = \frac{1}{2}\int(x^2+3)^{12}[2x\ dx] = \frac{1}{2}\cdot\frac{(x^2+3)^{13}}{13} + C =$

$\displaystyle\frac{(x^2+3)^{13}}{26} + C$

17. $\displaystyle\int 3e^{3x}\ dx = \int e^{3x}[3\ dx] = e^{3x} + C$

21. $\displaystyle\int xe^{5x^2}\ dx = \frac{1}{10}\int e^{5x^2}[10x\ dx] = \frac{1}{10}e^{5x^2} + C$

25. $\displaystyle\int\frac{1}{x+5}\ dx = \int\frac{1}{(x+5)}[dx] = \ln|x+5| + C$

29. $\displaystyle\int\frac{6z}{(z^2-6)^5}\ dz = 6\cdot\frac{1}{2}\int(z^2-6)^{-5}[2z\ dz] = 3\cdot\frac{(z^2-6)^{-4}}{-4} + C =$

$\displaystyle -\frac{3}{4}(z^2-6)^{-4} + C$

33. $\displaystyle\int\frac{s^2}{s^3+5}\ ds = \frac{1}{3}\int\frac{1}{s^3+5}[3s^2\ ds] = \frac{1}{3}\ln|s^3+5| + C$

37. $\displaystyle\int\sqrt{5x}\ dx = \frac{1}{5}\int(5x)^{1/2}[5\ dx] = \frac{1}{5}\cdot\frac{(5x)^{3/2}}{3/2} + C =$

$\displaystyle\frac{2}{15}(5x)^{3/2} + C = \frac{2}{15}(5x)(5x)^{1/2} = \frac{2}{3}x\sqrt{5x} + C$

41. $\int 2y^3 e^{y^4+1} \, dy = 2\int y^3 e^{y^4+1} \, dy = 2\cdot\frac{1}{4}\int e^{y^4+1}[4y^3 \, dy] =$

$2\cdot\frac{1}{4}\cdot e^{y^4+1} + C = \frac{1}{2}e^{y^4+1} + C$

45. $\int (e^{-5x}+2e^x) \, dx = \int e^{-5x} \, dx + 2\int e^x \, dx =$

$- \frac{1}{5}\int e^{-5x}[-5 \, dx] + 2\int e^x \, dx = - \frac{1}{5}e^{-5x} + 2e^x + C$

49. $\int \frac{x^2+2}{x^3+6x} \, dx = \frac{1}{3}\int \frac{1}{x^3+6x}[(3x^2+6) \, dx] = \frac{1}{3} \ln|x^3+6x| + C$

53. $\int x(2x^2+1)^{-1} \, dx = \int \frac{x}{2x^2+1} \, dx = \frac{1}{4}\int \frac{1}{2x^2+1}[4x \, dx] =$

$\frac{1}{4} \ln(2x^2+1) + C$

57. $\int (2x^3+x)(x^4+x^2) \, dx = \frac{1}{2}\int (x^4+x^2)^1[2(2x^3+x) \, dx] =$

$\frac{1}{2}\cdot\frac{(x^4+x^2)^2}{2} + C = \frac{1}{4}(x^4+x^2)^2 + C$

61. $\int x(2x+1)e^{4x^3+3x^2-4} \, dx = \frac{1}{6}\int e^{4x^3+3x^2-4}[6x(2x+1) \, dx] =$

$\frac{1}{6}e^{4x^3+3x^2-4} + C$

65. $\int (dx/\sqrt{2x}) = \frac{1}{2}\int (2x)^{-1/2}[2 \, dx] = \frac{1}{2}\cdot\frac{(2x)^{1/2}}{1/2} + C = \sqrt{2x} + C$

69. $\int \left[\frac{x}{x^2+1} + \frac{x^5}{(x^6+1)^2} \right] dx = \int \frac{x}{x^2+1} dx + \int \frac{x^5}{(x^6+1)^2} dx =$

$\frac{1}{2}\int \frac{1}{x^2+1}[2x\ dx] + \frac{1}{6}\int (x^6+1)^{-2}[6x^5\ dx] =$

$\frac{1}{2}\ln(x^2+1) + \frac{1}{6}\cdot\frac{(x^6+1)^{-1}}{-1} + C = \frac{1}{2}\ln(x^2+1) - \frac{1}{6(x^6+1)} + C$

73. $\int \left[\sqrt{2x+3} - \frac{x}{x^2+3} \right] dx = \int (2x+3)^{1/2}\ dx - \int \frac{x}{x^2+3}\ dx =$

$\frac{1}{2}\int (2x+3)^{1/2}[2\ dx] - \frac{1}{2}\int \frac{1}{x^2+3}[2x\ dx] =$

$\frac{1}{2}\cdot\frac{(2x+3)^{3/2}}{3/2} - \frac{1}{2}\ln(x^2+3) + C = \frac{1}{3}(2x+3)^{3/2} - \ln\sqrt{x^2+3} + C$

77. $y' = (3-2x)^2$. $y = \int (3-2x)^2\ dx = -\frac{1}{2}\int (3-2x)^2[-2\ dx] =$

$-\frac{1}{2}\cdot\frac{(3-2x)^3}{3} + C = -\frac{1}{6}(3-2x)^3 + C$. $y(0) = 1$ implies

$1 = -\frac{1}{6}(27) + C$, so $C = \frac{11}{2}$. <u>Ans.</u> $y = -\frac{1}{6}(3-2x)^3 + \frac{11}{2}$

81. Note that $r > 0$. Thus $C = \int \left(\frac{Rr}{2K} + \frac{B_1}{r} \right) dr =$

$\int \frac{Rr}{2K}\ dr + \int \frac{B_1}{r}\ dr = \frac{R}{2K}\int r\ dr + B_1\int \frac{1}{r}\ dr =$

$\frac{R}{2K}\cdot\frac{r^2}{2} + B_1\ \ln(r) + B_2 = \frac{Rr^2}{4K} + B_1\ \ln(r) + B_2$.

<u>Ans.</u> $\frac{Rr^2}{4K} + B_1\ \ln(r) + B_2$

EXERCISE 15.4

1. $\int \frac{2x^4+3x^3-x^2}{x^3} \, dx = \int \left(\frac{2x^4}{x^3} + \frac{3x^3}{x^3} - \frac{x^2}{x^3}\right) dx = \int \left(2x + 3 - \frac{1}{x}\right) dx =$

$2 \cdot \frac{x^2}{2} + 3x - \ln|x| + C = x^2 + 3x - \ln|x| + C$

5. $\int \frac{3}{\sqrt{4-5x}} \, dx = 3 \int (4-5x)^{-1/2} \, dx = 3 \cdot \left(-\frac{1}{5}\right) \int (4-5x)^{-1/2} [-5 \, dx] =$

$- \frac{3}{5} \cdot \frac{(4-5x)^{1/2}}{1/2} + C = - \frac{6}{5}\sqrt{4-5x} + C$

9. $\int 2x(7-e^{x^2/4}) \, dx = \int (14x-2xe^{x^2/4}) \, dx =$

$14 \int x \, dx - 2 \int xe^{x^2/4} \, dx = 14 \int x \, dx - 2 \cdot 2 \int e^{x^2/4} \left[\frac{1}{2}x \, dx\right] =$

$14 \cdot \frac{x^2}{2} - 4 \cdot e^{x^2/4} + C = 7x^2 - 4e^{x^2/4} + C$

13. $\int \frac{e^{7/x}}{x^2} \, dx = \int e^{7/x} \cdot \frac{1}{x^2} \, dx = - \frac{1}{7} \int e^{7/x} \left[- \frac{7}{x^2} \, dx\right] = - \frac{1}{7}e^{7/x} + C$

17. $\int \frac{\ln x}{x} \, dx = \int (\ln x) \left[\frac{1}{x} \, dx\right] = \frac{(\ln x)^2}{2} + C = \frac{1}{2}(\ln^2 x) + C$

21. $\int x\sqrt{e^{x^2+3}} \, dx = \int x(e^{x^2+3})^{1/2} \, dx = \int e^{(x^2+3)/2}[x \, dx] =$

$e^{(x^2+3)/2} + C$

25. $\int\left[\dfrac{x^3}{\sqrt{x^4-1}} - \ln 4\right]\,dx = \dfrac{1}{4}\int(x^4-1)^{-1/2}[4x^3\,dx] - \int(\ln 4)\,dx =$

$\dfrac{1}{4}\cdot\dfrac{(x^4-1)^{1/2}}{1/2} - (\ln 4)x + C = \dfrac{1}{2}\sqrt{x^4-1} - (\ln 4)x + C$

29. By long division, $\dfrac{6x^2-11x+5}{3x-1} = 2x - 3 + \dfrac{2}{3x-1}$.   Thus

$\int\dfrac{6x^2-11x+5}{3x-1}\,dx = \int\left(2x - 3 + \dfrac{2}{3x-1}\right)\,dx =$

$2\int x\,dx - \int 3\,dx + 2\cdot\dfrac{1}{3}\int\dfrac{1}{3x-1}[3\,dx] = x^2 - 3x + \dfrac{2}{3}\ln|3x-1| + C$

33. $\int\dfrac{xe^{x^2}}{\sqrt{e^{x^2}+2}}\,dx = \dfrac{1}{2}\int(e^{x^2}+2)^{-1/2}[2xe^{x^2}\,dx] = \dfrac{1}{2}\cdot\dfrac{(e^{x^2}+2)^{1/2}}{1/2} + C =$

$\sqrt{e^{x^2}+2} + C$

37. $\int\sqrt{x}\sqrt{(8x)^{3/2}+3}\,dx = \int(8^{3/2}x^{3/2} + 3)^{1/2}\cdot x^{1/2}\,dx =$

$\dfrac{2}{3\cdot 8^{3/2}}\int(8^{3/2}x^{3/2} + 3)^{1/2}\left[8^{3/2}\cdot\dfrac{3}{2}\cdot x^{1/2}\,dx\right] =$

$\dfrac{2}{3\cdot 16\sqrt{2}}\cdot\dfrac{(8^{3/2}x^{3/2} + 3)^{3/2}}{3/2} + C = \dfrac{1}{36\sqrt{2}}[(8x)^{3/2}+3]^{3/2} + C$

41. $e^{\ln(x+2)}$ is simply x+2.   Thus

$\int e^{\ln(x+2)}\,dx = \int(x+2)\,dx = \dfrac{x^2}{2} + 2x + C$

45. $\frac{dc}{dq} = \frac{20}{q+5}$. $c = \int \frac{20}{q+5} \, dq = 20 \int \frac{1}{q+5} \, dq = 20 \ln|q+5| + C$.

When q = 0, then c = 2000, so 2000 = 20 ln(5) + C, or

C = 2000 - 20 ln 5.   Hence c = 20 ln|q+5| + 2000 - 20 ln 5 =

20(ln|q+5| - ln 5) + 2000 = 20 ln|(q+5)/5| + 2000.

<u>Ans.</u>   c = 20 ln|(q+5)/5| + 2000

49. $\frac{dC}{dI} = \frac{3}{4} - \frac{1}{6\sqrt{I}}$. $C = \int \left[\frac{3}{4} - \frac{I^{-1/2}}{6} \right] dI =$

$\int \frac{3}{4} \, dI - \frac{1}{6} \int I^{-1/2} \, dI = \frac{3}{4} I - \frac{1}{6} \cdot \frac{I^{1/2}}{1/2} + C_1 = \frac{3}{4} I - \frac{\sqrt{I}}{3} + C_1$.

Thus $C = \frac{3}{4} I - \frac{\sqrt{I}}{3} + C_1$.   C(25) = 23 implies that

$23 = \frac{3}{4} \cdot 25 - \frac{5}{3} + C_1$, so $C_1 = \frac{71}{12}$.

<u>Ans.</u> $C = \frac{3}{4} I - \frac{1}{3} \sqrt{I} + \frac{71}{12}$

<u>EXERCISE 15.5</u>

1. 5 + 6 + 7 + 8 + 9 = 35

5. 5 + 20 = 25

9. $0 + \frac{3}{2} + \left(-\frac{8}{3} \right) = -\frac{7}{6}$

13. $\sum\limits_{k=1}^{4} (2k-1)$

17. $\displaystyle\sum_{k=1}^{450} k = \frac{450(451)}{2} = 101,475$

21. $\displaystyle\sum_{i=1}^{6} 3i^2 = 3\sum_{i=1}^{6} i^2 = 3\cdot\frac{6(7)(13)}{6} = 273$

EXERCISE 15.6

1. $f(x) = x$, $y = 0$, $x = 1$. S_3, $\Delta x = 1/3$.

$$S_3 = \tfrac{1}{3}f\left(\tfrac{1}{3}\right) + \tfrac{1}{3}f\left(\tfrac{2}{3}\right) + \tfrac{1}{3}f\left(\tfrac{3}{3}\right) = \tfrac{1}{3}\left[f\left(\tfrac{1}{3}\right) + f\left(\tfrac{2}{3}\right) + f\left(\tfrac{3}{3}\right)\right]$$

$$= \tfrac{1}{3}\left[\tfrac{1}{3} + \tfrac{2}{3} + \tfrac{3}{3}\right] = \tfrac{1}{3}\cdot\tfrac{6}{3} = \tfrac{2}{3}. \qquad \underline{\text{Ans.}} \quad 2/3 \text{ sq unit}$$

5. $f(x) = x$, $y = 0$, $x = 1$. $\Delta x = 1/n$.

$$S_n = \tfrac{1}{n}f\left(\tfrac{1}{n}\right) + \cdots + \tfrac{1}{n}f\left(n\cdot\tfrac{1}{n}\right) = \tfrac{1}{n}\left[f\left(\tfrac{1}{n}\right) + \cdots + f\left(n\cdot\tfrac{1}{n}\right)\right]$$

$$= \tfrac{1}{n}\left[\tfrac{1}{n} + \cdots + \tfrac{n}{n}\right] = \tfrac{1}{n^2}[1 + \cdots + n] = \tfrac{1}{n^2}\cdot\tfrac{n(n+1)}{2}$$

$$= \tfrac{1}{2}\cdot\tfrac{n+1}{n} = \tfrac{1}{2}\left[1 + \tfrac{1}{n}\right]. \qquad \lim_{n\to\infty} S_n = \tfrac{1}{2}. \qquad \underline{\text{Ans.}} \quad 1/2 \text{ sq unit}$$

9. $f(x) = 2x^2$, $y = 0$, $x = 2$. $\Delta x = 2/n$.

$$S_n = \tfrac{2}{n}f\left(\tfrac{2}{n}\right) + \cdots + \tfrac{2}{n}f\left(n\cdot\tfrac{2}{n}\right) = \tfrac{2}{n}\left[f\left(\tfrac{2}{n}\right) + \cdots + f\left(n\cdot\tfrac{2}{n}\right)\right]$$

$$= \tfrac{2}{n}\left[2\left(\tfrac{2}{n}\right)^2 + \cdots + 2\left(n\cdot\tfrac{2}{n}\right)^2\right] = \tfrac{16}{n^3}[1^2 + \cdots + n^2]$$

$$= \tfrac{16}{n^3}\cdot\tfrac{n(n+1)(2n+1)}{6} = \tfrac{8}{3}\cdot\tfrac{2n^2+3n+1}{n^2} = \tfrac{8}{3}\left[2 + \tfrac{3}{n} + \tfrac{1}{n^2}\right].$$

$$\lim_{n\to\infty} S_n = \tfrac{16}{3}. \qquad \underline{\text{Ans.}} \quad 16/3 \text{ sq units}$$

13. $\int_0^3 -4x \, dx.$ Let $f(x) = -4x.$ $\Delta x = 3/n.$

$S_n = \frac{3}{n}f\left(\frac{3}{n}\right) + \dots + \frac{3}{n}f\left(n \cdot \frac{3}{n}\right) = \frac{3}{n}\left[f\left(\frac{3}{n}\right) + \dots + f\left(n \cdot \frac{3}{n}\right)\right]$

$= \frac{3}{n}\left[-4\left(\frac{3}{n}\right) - \dots - 4\left(n \cdot \frac{3}{n}\right)\right] = -\frac{36}{n^2}[1 + \dots + n]$

$= -\frac{36}{n^2} \cdot \frac{n(n+1)}{2} = -18 \cdot \frac{n+1}{n} = -18\left[1 + \frac{1}{n}\right].$

$\int_0^3 -4x \, dx = \lim_{n \to \infty} S_n = -18.$ <u>Ans.</u> -18

EXERCISE 15.7

1. $\int_0^2 5 \, dx = 5x \Big|_0^2 = 10 - 0 = 10$

5. $\int_{-3}^1 (2x-3) \, dx = (x^2-3x) \Big|_{-3}^1 = -2 - (18) = -20$

9. $\int_{-2}^{-1} (3w^2-w-1) \, dw = \left(w^3 - \frac{w^2}{2} - w\right) \Big|_{-2}^{-1} = -\frac{1}{2} - (-8) = \frac{15}{2}$

13. $\int_{-1}^1 \sqrt[3]{x^5} \, dx = \int_{-1}^1 x^{5/3} \, dx = \frac{3x^{8/3}}{8} \Big|_{-1}^1 = \frac{3}{8} - \frac{3}{8} = 0$

17. $\int_{-1}^1 (z+1)^5 \, dz = \frac{(z+1)^6}{6} \Big|_{-1}^1 = \frac{32}{3} - 0 = \frac{32}{3}$

21. $\int_1^8 \frac{4}{y} \, dy = 4 \ln|y| \Big|_1^8 = 4(\ln 8 - \ln 1) = 4(\ln 8 - 0) = 4 \ln 8$

25. $\int_4^5 \frac{2}{(x-3)^3} \, dx = 2\int_4^5 (x-3)^{-3} \, dx = 2 \cdot \frac{(x-3)^{-2}}{-2} \Big|_4^5 = -\frac{1}{(x-3)^2} \Big|_4^5 =$

$-\frac{1}{4} - (-1) = \frac{3}{4}$

29. $\int_0^1 x^2 \sqrt[3]{7x^3+1} \, dx = \frac{1}{21}\int_0^1 (7x^3+1)^{1/3}[21x^2 \, dx] =$

$\frac{1}{21} \cdot \frac{(7x^3+1)^{4/3}}{4/3} \Big|_0^1 = \frac{(7x^3+1)^{4/3}}{28} \Big|_0^1 = \frac{16}{28} - \frac{1}{28} = \frac{15}{28}$

33. $\int_0^1 (e^x - e^{-2x}) \, dx = \int_0^1 e^x \, dx - \left(-\frac{1}{2}\right)\int_0^1 e^{-2x}[-2 \, dx] =$

$\left(e^x + \frac{e^{-2x}}{2}\right) \Big|_0^1 = \left(e + \frac{e^{-2}}{2}\right) - \left(1 + \frac{1}{2}\right) = e + \frac{1}{2e^2} - \frac{3}{2}$

37. $\int_1^3 (x+1)e^{x^2+2x} \, dx = \frac{1}{2}\int_1^3 e^{x^2+2x}[2(x+1) \, dx] = \frac{1}{2}e^{x^2+2x} \Big|_1^3 =$

$\frac{1}{2}\left(e^{15} - e^3\right) = \frac{e^3}{2}(e^{12} - 1)$

41. The total number receiving between a and b dollars equals the number N(a) receiving a or more dollars minus the number N(b) receiving b or more dollars. Thus

$N(a) - N(b) = \int_b^a -Ax^{-B} \, dx.$ <u>Ans.</u> $\int_b^a -Ax^{-B} \, dx$

45. $\int_{36}^{64} 10,000\sqrt{100-t}\ dt = (-1)(10,000)\int_{36}^{64}(100-t)^{1/2}[(-1)\ dt] =$

$-\frac{2}{3}(10,000)(100-t)^{3/2}\Big|_{36}^{64} = -\frac{2}{3}(10,000)[216 - 512] \approx$

1,973,333.   **Ans.** 1,973,333

49. $\int_{400}^{900}\frac{1000}{\sqrt{100q}}\ dq = \int_{400}^{900}\frac{1000}{10\sqrt{q}}\ dq = 100\int_{400}^{900}q^{-1/2}\ dq =$

$100\cdot\frac{q^{1/2}}{1/2}\Big|_{400}^{900} = 200\sqrt{q}\Big|_{400}^{900} = 200(30 - 20) = 200(10) =$

2000.   **Ans.** $2000

53. $G = \int_{-R}^{R} i\ dx = ix\Big|_{-R}^{R} = iR - (-iR) = 2Ri.$ **Ans.** 2Ri

EXERCISE 15.8

In Problems 1-33, answers are assumed to be expressed in square units.

1. y = 4x, x = 2. Region appears below.

area $= \int_0^2 4x\ dx = 2x^2\Big|_0^2 = 8 - 0 = 8$

5. y = x-1, x = 5. Region appears below.

area $= \int_1^5 (x-1)\ dx = \left(\frac{x^2}{2} - x\right)\Big|_1^5 = \frac{15}{2} - \left(-\frac{1}{2}\right) = \frac{16}{2} = 8$

9. $y = x^2+2$, $x = -1$, $x = 2$. Region appears below.

area $= \int_{-1}^{2} (x^2+2)\ dx = \left(\frac{x^3}{3} + 2x\right)\Big|_{-1}^{2} = \frac{20}{3} - \left(-\frac{7}{3}\right) = \frac{27}{3} = 9$

1.

5.

9.

13. $y = 9-x^2$. Region appears below.

area $= \int_{-3}^{3} (9-x^2)\ dx = \left(9x - \frac{x^3}{3}\right)\Big|_{-3}^{3} = 18 - (-18) = 36$

17. $y = 3+2x-x^2$. Region appears below.

area $= \int_{-1}^{3} (3+2x-x^2)\ dx = \left(3x + x^2 - \frac{x^3}{3}\right)\Big|_{-1}^{3}$

$= 9 - \left(-\frac{5}{3}\right) = \frac{32}{3}$

21. $y = \sqrt{x+9}$, $x = -9$, $x = 0$. Region appears below.

area $= \int_{-9}^{0} \sqrt{x+9}\ dx = \int_{-9}^{0} (x+9)^{1/2}\ dx = \frac{(x+9)^{3/2}}{3/2}\Big|_{-9}^{0}$

$= \frac{2(x+9)^{3/2}}{3}\Big|_{-9}^{0} = 18 - 0 = 18$

13.

17.

21.

25. $y = \sqrt[3]{x}$, $x = 2$. Region appears below.

$$\text{area} = \int_0^2 \sqrt[3]{x}\, dx = \int_0^2 x^{1/3}\, dx = \frac{3x^{4/3}}{4}\Big|_0^2 = \frac{3(2)^{4/3}}{4} - 0$$

$$= \frac{3(2\sqrt[3]{2})}{4} = \frac{3}{2}\sqrt[3]{2}$$

29. $y = x + \frac{2}{x}$, $x = 1$, $x = 2$. Region appears below.

$$\text{area} = \int_1^2 \left(x + \frac{2}{x}\right) dx = \left(\frac{x^2}{2} + 2\ln|x|\right)\Big|_1^2$$

$$= (2 + 2\ln 2) - \frac{1}{2} = \frac{3}{2} + 2\ln 2 = \frac{3}{2} + \ln 4$$

33. $y = 2x - x^2$, $x = 1$, $x = 3$. Region appears below.

$$\text{area} = \int_1^2 (2x-x^2)\, dx + \int_2^3 -(2x-x^2)\, dx$$

$$= \left(x^2 - \frac{x^3}{3}\right)\Big|_1^2 - \left(x^2 - \frac{x^3}{3}\right)\Big|_2^3$$

$$= \left[\frac{4}{3} - \frac{2}{3}\right] - \left[0 - \frac{4}{3}\right] = \frac{6}{3} = 2$$

25.

29.

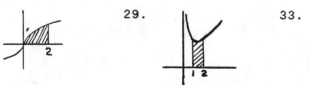

33.

37. (a) $P(0 \leq x \leq 1) = \int_0^1 \frac{1}{8}x\, dx = \frac{x^2}{16}\Big|_0^1 = \frac{1}{16} - 0 = \frac{1}{16}$

(b) $P(2 \leq x \leq 4) = \int_2^4 \frac{1}{8}x\, dx = \frac{x^2}{16}\Big|_2^4 = 1 - \frac{1}{4} = \frac{3}{4}$

(c) $P(x \geq 3) = \int_3^4 \frac{1}{8}x\, dx = \frac{x^2}{16}\Big|_3^4 = 1 - \frac{9}{16} = \frac{7}{16}$

<u>Ans.</u> (a) $\frac{1}{16}$; (b) $\frac{3}{4}$; (c) $\frac{7}{16}$

EXERCISE 15.9

In Problems 1-21, the answers are assumed to be expressed in square units.

1. $y = x^2$, $y = 2x$. Region appears below. $x^2 = 2x$,

   $x^2 - 2x = 0$, $x(x-2) = 0$, so $x = 0, 2$.

   $$\text{area} = \int_0^2 (2x - x^2)\, dx = \left(x^2 - \frac{x^3}{3}\right)\Big|_0^2 = \left(4 - \frac{8}{3}\right) - 0 = \frac{4}{3}$$

5. $y = x^2 + 3$, $y = 9$. Region appears below. $x^2 + 3 = 9$, $x^2 = 6$,

   $x = \pm\sqrt{6}$.

   $$\text{area} = \int_{-\sqrt{6}}^{\sqrt{6}} [9 - (x^2 + 3)]\, dx = \int_{-\sqrt{6}}^{\sqrt{6}} (6 - x^2)\, dx$$

   $$= \left(6x - \frac{x^3}{3}\right)\Big|_{-\sqrt{6}}^{\sqrt{6}} = \left(6\sqrt{6} - \frac{6\sqrt{6}}{3}\right) - \left(-6\sqrt{6} + \frac{6\sqrt{6}}{3}\right)$$

   $$= 8\sqrt{6}$$

9. $y = 4 - x^2$, $y = -3x$. Region appears below. $-3x = 4 - x^2$,

   $x^2 - 3x - 4 = 0$, $(x+1)(x-4) = 0$, so $x = -1, 4$.

   $$\text{area} = \int_{-1}^4 [(4 - x^2) - (-3x)]\, dx = \left(4x - \frac{x^3}{3} + \frac{3x^2}{2}\right)\Big|_{-1}^4$$

   $$= \left(16 - \frac{64}{3} + 24\right) - \left(-4 + \frac{1}{3} + \frac{3}{2}\right) = \frac{125}{6}$$

1.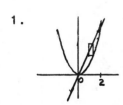

5.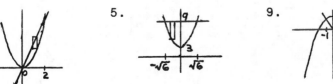

9.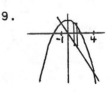

13. $2y = 4x-x^2$, $2y = x-4$. Region appears below.

$x-4 = 4x-x^2$, $x^2-3x-4 = 0$, $(x+1)(x-4) = 0$, so $x = -1$, 4.
Note that the y-values of the curves are given by

$y = \frac{4x-x^2}{2}$ and $y = \frac{x-4}{2}$.

area $= \int_{-1}^{4} \left[\left(\frac{4x-x^2}{2} \right) - \left(\frac{x-4}{2} \right) \right] dx = \int_{-1}^{4} \left(\frac{3}{2}x - \frac{x^2}{2} + 2 \right) dx$

$= \left(\frac{3x^2}{4} - \frac{x^3}{6} + 2x \right) \Big|_{-1}^{4} = \left(12 - \frac{64}{6} + 8 \right) - \left(\frac{3}{4} + \frac{1}{6} - 2 \right)$

$= \frac{125}{12}$

17. $y = 8-x^2$, $y = x^2$, $x = -1$, $x = 1$. Region appears below.
$x^2 = 8-x^2$, $2x^2 = 8$, $x^2 = 4$, $x = \pm 2$.

area $= \int_{-1}^{1} [(8-x^2)-x^2] dx = \int_{-1}^{1} (8-2x^2) dx$

$= \left(8x - \frac{2x^3}{3} \right) \Big|_{-1}^{1} = \left(8 - \frac{2}{3} \right) - \left(-8 + \frac{2}{3} \right) = \frac{44}{3}$

21. $y = x^3$, $y = x$. Region appears below. $x^3 = x$, $x^3-x = 0$,
$x(x^2-1) = 0$, $x(x+1)(x-1) = 0$, so $x = 0$, ± 1.

area $= \int_{-1}^{0} (x^3-x) dx + \int_{0}^{1} (x-x^3) dx$

$= \left(\frac{x^4}{4} - \frac{x^2}{2} \right) \Big|_{-1}^{0} + \left(\frac{x^2}{2} - \frac{x^4}{4} \right) \Big|_{0}^{1}$

$= \left[0 - \left(\frac{1}{4} - \frac{1}{2} \right) \right] + \left[\left(\frac{1}{2} - \frac{1}{4} \right) - 0 \right] = \frac{1}{2}$

13.   17.   21.

25. $\dfrac{\text{Area between curve and diag.}}{\text{Area under diagonal}} = \dfrac{\int_0^1 \left[x - \left(\frac{20}{21}x^2 + \frac{1}{21}x\right)\right] \, dx}{\int_0^1 x \, dx}$.

Numerator $= \int_0^1 \left[\frac{20}{21}x - \frac{20}{21}x^2\right] \, dx = \frac{20}{21}\int_0^1 (x-x^2) \, dx$

$= \frac{20}{21}\left(\frac{x^2}{2} - \frac{x^3}{3}\right)\Big|_0^1 = \frac{20}{21}\left[\left(\frac{1}{2} - \frac{1}{3}\right) - 0\right] = \frac{20}{21} \cdot \frac{1}{6} = \frac{10}{63}$.

Denominator $= \int_0^1 x \, dx = \frac{x^2}{2}\Big|_0^1 = \frac{1}{2}$.

Coefficient of inequality $= \frac{10/63}{1/2} = \frac{20}{63}$.   Ans. $\frac{20}{63}$

EXERCISE 15.10

1. D: $p = 20 - 0.8q$ ⎱   Equil. pt. $= (q_0, p_0) = (8, 13.6)$
   S: $p = 4 + 1.2q$ ⎰

   $CS = \int_0^8 [(20 - 0.8q) - 13.6] \, dq = \int_0^8 (6.4 - 0.8q) \, dq$

   $\quad = (6.4q - 0.4q^2)\Big|_0^8 = (51.2 - 25.6) - 0 = 25.6$.

   $PS = \int_0^8 [13.6 - (4 + 1.2q)] \, dq = \int_0^8 (9.6 - 1.2q) \, dq$

   $\quad = (9.6q - 0.6q^2)\Big|_0^8 = (76.8 - 38.4) - 0 = 38.4$.

   Ans. CS $= 25.6$, PS $= 38.4$

5. D: q = 100(10-p) }   Equil. pt. = (q_0, p_0) = (400, 6).

   S: q = 80(p-1)   }

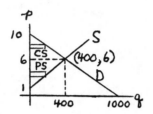

$$CS = \int_6^{10} 100(10-p)\ dp = 100\left(10p - \frac{p^2}{2}\right)\Big|_6^{10}$$

$$= 100[(100-50) - (60-18)] = 800.$$

$$PS = \int_1^6 80(p-1)\ dp = 80\left(\frac{p^2}{2} - p\right)\Big|_1^6$$

$$= 80\left[(18 - 6) - \left(\frac{1}{2} - 1\right)\right] = 1000.$$

<u>Ans.</u> CS = 800, PS = 1000

CHAPTER 15 - REVIEW PROBLEMS

1. $\int (x^3+2x-7)\ dx = \frac{x^4}{4} + 2\cdot\frac{x^2}{2} - 7x + C = \frac{x^4}{4} + x^2 - 7x + C$

5. $\int \frac{2}{(x+5)^3}\ dx = 2\int(x+5)^{-3}\ dx = \frac{2(x+5)^{-2}}{-2} + C = -(x+5)^{-2} + C$

9. $\int_0^1 \sqrt[3]{3t+8}\ dt = \frac{1}{3}\int_0^1 (3t+8)^{1/3}[3\ dt] = \frac{1}{3}\cdot\frac{(3t+8)^{4/3}}{4/3}\Big|_0^1 =$

   $\frac{(3t+8)^{4/3}}{4}\Big|_0^1 = \frac{11\sqrt[3]{11}}{4} - 4$

13. $\int \dfrac{\sqrt[4]{z} - \sqrt[3]{z}}{\sqrt{z}}\ dz = \int\left(\dfrac{z^{1/4}}{z^{1/2}} - \dfrac{z^{1/3}}{z^{1/2}}\right)\ dz = \int\left(z^{-1/4} - z^{-1/6}\right)\ dz =$

$\dfrac{z^{3/4}}{3/4} - \dfrac{z^{5/6}}{5/6} + C = \dfrac{4z^{3/4}}{3} - \dfrac{6z^{5/6}}{5} + C$

17. $\int x^2\sqrt{3x^3+2}\ dx = \tfrac{1}{9}\int(3x^3+2)^{1/2}[9x^2\ dx] = \tfrac{1}{9}\cdot\dfrac{(3x^3+2)^{3/2}}{3/2} + C =$

$\tfrac{1}{9}\cdot\dfrac{2(3x^3+2)^{3/2}}{3} + C = \tfrac{2}{27}(3x^3+2)^{3/2} + C$

21. $\int\left(\dfrac{1}{x} + \dfrac{2}{x^2}\right)\ dx = \int\dfrac{1}{x}\ dx + 2\int x^{-2}\ dx = \ln|x| + 2\cdot\dfrac{x^{-1}}{-1} + C =$

$\ln|x| - \dfrac{2}{x} + C$

25. $\displaystyle\int_{\sqrt{3}}^{2} 7x\sqrt{4-x^2}\ dx = 7\int_{\sqrt{3}}^{2} x(4-x^2)^{1/2}\ dx =$

$7\cdot\left(-\tfrac{1}{2}\right)\displaystyle\int_{\sqrt{3}}^{2}(4-x^2)^{1/2}[-2x\ dx] = -\dfrac{7}{2}\cdot\dfrac{(4-x^2)^{3/2}}{3/2}\bigg|_{\sqrt{3}}^{2} =$

$-\dfrac{7}{3}\cdot(4-x^2)^{3/2}\bigg|_{\sqrt{3}}^{2} = -\dfrac{7}{3}(0 - 1) = \dfrac{7}{3}$

29. $\int\dfrac{\sqrt{t}-3}{t^2}\ dt = \int\left[\dfrac{t^{1/2}}{t^2} - \dfrac{3}{t^2}\right]\ dt = \int(t^{-3/2}-3t^{-2})\ dt =$

$\dfrac{t^{-1/2}}{-1/2} - 3\cdot\dfrac{t^{-1}}{-1} + C = -2t^{-1/2} + 3t^{-1} + C = \dfrac{3}{t} - \dfrac{2}{\sqrt{t}} + C$

33. $y = \int(e^{2x}+3)\ dx = \int e^{2x}\ dx + \int 3\ dx = \tfrac{1}{2}\int e^{2x}[2\ dx] + \int 3\ dx =$

$\tfrac{1}{2}e^{2x} + 3x + C.$ $y(0) = -\tfrac{1}{2}$ implies that $-\tfrac{1}{2} = \tfrac{1}{2} + 0 + C,$

so $C = -1.$ <u>Ans.</u> $y = \tfrac{1}{2}e^{x} + 3x - 1$

In Problems 37-49, answers are assumed to be expressed in square units.

37. $y = \sqrt{x+4}$, x = 0.   Region appears below.

$$\text{area} = \int_{-4}^{0} \sqrt{x+4}\ dx = \int_{-4}^{0} (x+4)^{1/2}[dx] = \frac{x+4}{3/2}^{3/2}\Big|_{-4}^{0}$$

$$= \frac{2(x+4)^{3/2}}{3}\Big|_{-4}^{0} = \frac{16}{3} - 0 = \frac{16}{3}$$

41. $y = \frac{1}{x} + 3$, x = 1, x = 3.   Region appears below.

$$\text{area} = \int_{1}^{3}\left(\frac{1}{x} + 3\right) dx = (\ln|x| + 3x)\Big|_{1}^{3} = [\ln(3) + 9] - 3$$

$$= 6 + \ln 3$$

37.

41.

45. $y = x^2+4x-5$, y = 0.   Region appears below.

$x^2+4x-5 = 0$, (x+5)(x-1) = 0, so x = -5, 1.

$$\text{area} = \int_{-5}^{1} -(x^2+4x-5)\ dx = -\left(\frac{x^3}{3} + 2x^2 - 5x\right)\Big|_{-5}^{1}$$

$$= -\left(\frac{1}{3} + 2 - 5\right) + \left(-\frac{125}{3} + 50 + 25\right) = 36$$

49. $y = \ln x$, x = 0, y = 0, y = 1.   Region appears below.

Because $y = \ln x$, then $x = e^y$.

$$\text{area} = \int_{0}^{1} e^y\ dy = e^y\Big|_{0}^{1} = e - 1$$

45.

49.

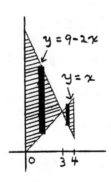

53. $\int_{10}^{20}(275-q-0.3q^2)\,dq = \left(275q - \frac{q^2}{2} - \frac{0.3q^3}{3}\right)\Big|_{10}^{20} =$

$(5500-200-800) - (2750-50-100) = 1900.$ <u>Ans.</u> \$1900

57. $y = 9-2x$, $y = x$; from $x = 0$ to $x = 4$.

$x = 9-2x$, $3x = 9$, so $x = 3$.

area $= \int_{0}^{3}[(9-2x)-x]\,dx + \int_{3}^{4}[x-(9-2x)]\,dx$

$= \int_{0}^{3}(9-3x)\,dx + \int_{3}^{4}(3x-9)\,dx$

$= \left(9x - \frac{3x^2}{2}\right)\Big|_{0}^{3} + \left(\frac{3x^2}{2} - 9x\right)\Big|_{3}^{4}$

$= \left[\left(27 - \frac{27}{2}\right) - 0\right] + \left[(24 - 36) - \left(\frac{27}{2} - 27\right)\right]$

$= 15$ square units

61. $Q = \int_0^R 2\pi r v \ dr = 2\pi \int_0^R r \cdot \frac{(P_1 - P_2)(R^2 - r^2)}{4\eta L} \ dr$

$= \frac{\pi(P_1 - P_2)}{2\eta L} \int_0^R r(R^2 - r^2) \ dr = \frac{\pi(P_1 - P_2)}{2\eta L} \int_0^R (R^2 r - r^3) \ dr$

$= \frac{\pi(P_1 - P_2)}{2\eta L} \left(\frac{R^2 r^2}{2} - \frac{r^4}{4} \right) \Big|_0^R = \frac{\pi(P_1 - P_2)}{2\eta L} \left[\left(\frac{R^4}{2} - \frac{R^4}{4} \right) - 0 \right]$

$= \frac{\pi(P_1 - P_2)}{2\eta L} \left(\frac{R^4}{4} \right) = \frac{\pi R^4 (P_1 - P_2)}{8\eta L}$, as was to be shown.

CHAPTER 15 — MATHEMATICAL SNAPSHOT

1. $\int_0^5 f(t) \ dt = \int_0^5 (50 - 2t) \ dt = (50t - t^2) \Big|_0^5$

$= (250 - 25) - 0 = 225 = 225.$

$\int_{10}^{15} f(t) \ dt = \int_{10}^{15} (50 - 2t) \ dt = (50t - t^2) \Big|_{10}^{15}$

$= (750 - 225) - (500 - 100) = 125.$

Ans. 225; 125

16

Methods and Applications of Integration

1. $\int xe^{-x}\,dx$. Letting $u = x$, $dv = e^{-x}\,dx$, then $du = dx$,

   $v = -e^{-x}$. $\int xe^{-x}\,dx = -xe^{-x} - \int -e^{-x}\,dx =$

   $-xe^{-x} - \int e^{-x}[-\,dx] = -xe^{-x} - e^{-x} + C = -e^{-x}(x+1) + C$.

5. $\int \ln(4x)\,dx$. Letting $u = \ln(4x)$, $dv = dx$, then $du =$

   $(1/x)\,dx$, $v = x$. $\int \ln(4x)\,dx = x\,\ln(4x) - \int x\left(\frac{1}{x}\,dx\right) =$

   $x\,\ln(4x) - \int dx = x\,\ln(4x) - x + C = x[\ln(4x)-1] + C$.

9. $\int \dfrac{x}{(2x+1)^2}\,dx$. Letting $u = x$, $dv = (2x+1)^{-2}\,dx$, then

   $du = dx$, $v = \dfrac{(2x+1)^{-1}}{-2} = -\dfrac{1}{2(2x+1)}$. Thus

$$\int \frac{x}{(2x+1)^2} \, dx = -\frac{x}{2(2x+1)} - \int -\frac{1}{2(2x+1)} \, dx =$$

$$-\frac{x}{2(2x+1)} + \frac{1}{2} \cdot \frac{1}{2} \int \frac{1}{2x+1} [2 \, dx] = -\frac{x}{2(2x+1)} + \frac{1}{4} \ln|2x+1| + C.$$

13. $\displaystyle\int_0^1 xe^{-x^2} \, dx = -\frac{1}{2} \int_0^1 e^{-x^2}(-2x \, dx)$ (Form: $\int e^u \, du$)

$$= -\frac{1}{2} e^{-x^2} \Big|_0^1 = -\frac{1}{2}(e^{-1} - 1) = \frac{1}{2}(1 - e^{-1})$$

17. $\int x^2 e^x \, dx$. Letting $u = x^2$, $dv = e^x \, dx$, then $du = 2x \, dx$

and $v = e^x$.

$$\int x^2 e^x \, dx = x^2 e^x - \int e^x (2x \, dx) = x^2 e^x - 2\int xe^x \, dx.$$

For $\int xe^x \, dx$, let $u = x$, $dv = e^x \, dx$. Then $du = dx$, $v = e^x$

and

$$\int xe^x \, dx = xe^x - \int e^x \, dx = xe^x - e^x + C_1 = e^x(x-1) + C_1.$$

Thus $\int x^2 e^x \, dx = x^2 e^x - 2[e^x(x-1)] + C = e^x(x^2-2x+2) + C.$

21. area $= \displaystyle\int_1^{e^3} (\ln x) \, dx$. Letting $u = \ln x$, $dv = dx$, then

$du = (1/x) \, dx$, $v = x$.

$$\text{area} = \int_1^{e^3} (\ln x) \, dx = (x \ln x)\Big|_1^{e^3} - \int_1^{e^3} x \cdot \frac{1}{x} \, dx =$$

$$(x \ln x)\Big|_1^{e^3} - \int_1^{e^3} dx = [x \ln(x) - x]\Big|_1^{e^3} =$$

$$[e^3 \cdot 3 - e^3] - [1 \cdot 0 - 1] = 2e^3 + 1 \qquad \underline{\text{Ans.}} \quad 2e^3 + 1 \text{ sq units}$$

EXERCISE 16.2

1. $\dfrac{5x-2}{x^2-x} = \dfrac{5x-2}{x(x-1)} = \dfrac{A}{x} + \dfrac{B}{x-1}$. $5x-2 = A(x-1) + Bx$.

   If $x = 1$, then $3 = B$. If $x = 0$, then $-2 = -A$, or $A = 2$.

   $\displaystyle\int\dfrac{5x-2}{x^2-x}\,dx = \int\left(\dfrac{2}{x} + \dfrac{3}{x-1}\right)\,dx$.

   <u>Ans.</u> $2\ \ln|x| + 3\ \ln|x-1| + C = \ln|x^2(x-1)^3| + C$

5. $\dfrac{3x^3-3x+4}{4x^2-4} = \dfrac{1}{4}\cdot\dfrac{3x^3-3x+4}{x^2-1} = \dfrac{1}{4}\left(3x + \dfrac{4}{x^2-1}\right)$.

   $\dfrac{4}{x^2-1} = \dfrac{4}{(x-1)(x+1)} = \dfrac{A}{x-1} + \dfrac{B}{x+1}$. $4 = A(x+1) + B(x-1)$.

   If $x = -1$, then $4 = -2B$, or $B = -2$. If $x = 1$, then

   $4 = 2A$, or $A = 2$.

   $\displaystyle\int\dfrac{3x^3-3x+4}{4x^2-4}\,dx = \dfrac{1}{4}\int\left(3x + \dfrac{2}{x-1} + \dfrac{-2}{x+1}\right)\,dx$.

   <u>Ans.</u> $(1/4)[(3x^2/2) + 2\ \ln|x-1| - 2\ \ln|x+1|] + C =$

   $(1/4)[(3x^2/2) + \ln\{(x-1)/(x+1)\}^2] + C$

9. $\displaystyle\int\dfrac{3x^5+4x^3-x}{x^6+2x^4-x^2-2}\,dx = \dfrac{1}{2}\int\dfrac{1}{x^6+2x^4-x^2-2}[2(3x^5+4x^3-x)\,dx]$.

   (Form: $\int(1/u)\,du$.) (Partial fractions not required.)

   <u>Ans.</u> $(1/2)\ \ln|x^6+2x^4-x^2-2| + C$

13. $\dfrac{x^2+8}{x^3+4x} = \dfrac{x^2+8}{x(x^2+4)} = \dfrac{A}{x} + \dfrac{Bx+C}{x^2+4}$. $x^2+8 = A(x^2+4) + (Bx+C)x$.

   $x^2+8 = (A+B)x^2 + Cx + 4A$. Thus $A+B = 1$, $C = 0$, $4A = 8$.

   This gives $A = 2$, $B = -1$, $C = 0$. Thus

$$\int \frac{x^2+8}{x^3+4x} \, dx = \int \left(\frac{2}{x} + \frac{-x}{x^2+4}\right) dx = 2\int \frac{1}{x} \, dx - \frac{1}{2}\int \frac{1}{x^2+4}[2 \, dx].$$

<u>Ans.</u> $2 \ln|x| - \frac{1}{2} \ln(x^2+4) + C = \frac{1}{2} \ln[x^4/(x^2+4)] + C$

17. $\dfrac{14x^3+24x}{(x^2+1)(x^2+2)} = \dfrac{Ax+B}{x^2+1} + \dfrac{Cx+D}{x^2+2}.$

$14x^3+24x = (x^2+2)(Ax+B) + (x^2+1)(Cx+D)$

$\qquad\qquad = (A+C)x^3 + (B+D)x^2 + (2A+C)x + (2B+D).$

Thus A+C = 14, B+D = 0, 2A+C = 24, 2B+D = 0.

This gives A = 10, B = 0, C = 4, D = 0.

$$\int \frac{14x^3+24x}{(x^2+1)(x^2+2)} \, dx = \int \left(\frac{10x}{x^2+1} + \frac{4x}{x^2+2}\right) dx$$

$$= 5\int \frac{1}{x^2+1}[2 \, dx] + 2\int \frac{1}{x^2+2}[2 \, dx].$$

<u>Ans.</u> $5 \ln(x^2+1) + 2 \ln(x^2+2) + C = \ln[(x^2+1)^5(x^2+2)^2] + C$

21. $\dfrac{2-2x}{x^2+7x+12} = \dfrac{2-2x}{(x+3)(x+4)} = \dfrac{A}{x+3} + \dfrac{B}{x+4}.$ $2-2x = A(x+4)+B(x+3).$

If x = -4, then 10 = -B, or B = -10.   If x = -3, then

8 = A.

$$\int_0^1 \frac{2-2x}{x^2+7x+12} \, dx = \int_0^1 \left(\frac{8}{x+3} + \frac{-10}{x+4}\right) dx =$$

$$\Big[8 \ln|x+3| - 10 \ln|x+4|\Big]\Big|_0^1.$$

<u>Ans.</u> $18 \ln(4) - 10 \ln(5) - 8 \ln(3)$

EXERCISE 16.3

1. Form. 5 with $u = x$, $a = 6$, $b = 7$. Then $du = dx$.

   <u>Ans.</u> $\frac{1}{6} \ln\left|\frac{x}{6+7x}\right| + C$

5. Form. 12 with $u = x$, $a = 2$, $b = 3$, $c = 4$, $k = 5$. Then

   $du = dx$.   <u>Ans.</u> $\frac{1}{2}\left[\frac{4}{5} \ln|4+5x| - \frac{2}{3} \ln|2+3x|\right] + C$

9. Form. 9 with $u = x$, $a = 1$, $b = 1$. Then $du = dx$.

   $\int \frac{2\ dx}{x(1+x)^2} = 2\int \frac{dx}{x(1+x)^2} = 2\left[\frac{1}{1+x} + \ln\left|\frac{x}{1+x}\right|\right] + C$

13. Form. 23 with $u = x$, $a^2 = 3$. Then $du = dx$.

    <u>Ans.</u> $\frac{1}{2}\left(x\sqrt{x^2-3} - 3 \ln\left|x+\sqrt{x^2-3}\right|\right) + C$

17. Form. 39 with $u = x$, $n = 2$, $a = 1$. Then $du = dx$.

    $\int x^2 e^x\ dx = x^2 e^x - 2\int x e^x\ dx$. Applying Form. 38 on $\int x e^x\ dx$

    with $u = x$, $a = 1$ (so $du = dx$) gives $\int x e^x\ dx =$

    $e^x(x-1) + C_1$. Thus $\int x^2 e^x\ dx = x^2 e^x - 2[e^x(x-1)] + C =$

    $e^x[x^2-2(x-1)] + C = e^x(x^2-2x+2) + C$.

    <u>Ans.</u> $e^x(x^2-2x+2) + C$

21. Form. 7 with $u = x$, $a = 1$, $b = 3$. Then $du = dx$.

    <u>Ans.</u> $\frac{1}{9}\left(\ln\left|1+3x\right| + \frac{1}{1+3x}\right) + C$

25. Form. 42 with u = 3x, n = 5. Then du = 3 dx.

$\int x^5 \ln(3x) \, dx = \frac{1}{3^6} \int (3x)^5 \ln(3x) \, [3 \, dx].$

Ans. $\frac{1}{3^6} \left[\frac{(3x)^6 \ln(3x)}{6} - \frac{(3x)^6}{36} \right] + C = \frac{x^6}{36}[6 \ln(3x) - 1] + C$

29. Form. 27 with u = 2x, a^2 = 13. Then du = 2 dx.

$\int \frac{dx}{\sqrt{4x^2-13}} = \frac{1}{2} \int \frac{1}{\sqrt{(2x)^2-13}} [2 \, dx].$

Ans. $\frac{1}{2} \ln|2x + \sqrt{4x^2-13}| + C$

33. Form. 21 with u = 2x, a^2 = 9. Then du = 2 dx.

$\int \frac{dx}{x^2\sqrt{9-4x^2}} = 2 \int \frac{[2 \, dx]}{(2x)^2\sqrt{9-(2x)^2}} = 2 \left[- \frac{\sqrt{9-4x^2}}{9(2x)} \right] + C.$

Ans. $- \frac{\sqrt{9-4x^2}}{9x} + C$

37. Can be put in the form $\int u^n \, du$.

$\int x\sqrt{2x^2+1} \, dx = \frac{1}{4} \int (2x^2+1)^{1/2} [4x \, dx] = \frac{1}{4} \cdot \frac{(2x^2+1)^{3/2}}{\frac{3}{2}} + C$

Ans. $\frac{1}{6}(2x^2+1)^{3/2} + C$

41. Integration by parts or formula 42. For formula 42, let

u = x, n = 3. Then du = dx. Ans. $\frac{x^4}{4} \left[\ln(x) - \frac{1}{4} \right] + C$

45. Integration by parts (applied twice) or formula 43 and
    then formula 41. For formula 43, let u = x, n = 0,

m = 2.   Then du = dx. $\int \ln^2 x \, dx = x \ln^2 x - 2\int \ln x \, dx$.

Now we apply formula 41 to the last integral with u = x

(so du = dx).   Ans. $x(\ln x)^2 - 2x(\ln x) + 2x + C$

49. Can be put in the form $\int u^n \, du$.

$$\int_0^1 \frac{2x \, dx}{\sqrt{8-x^2}} = -\int_0^1 (8-x^2)^{-1/2}[-2x \, dx] = - \left. \frac{(8-x^2)^{1/2}}{1/2} \right|_0^1 =$$

$$= -2(8-x^2)^{1/2} \Big|_0^1 = -2(\sqrt{7} - \sqrt{8}) = -2(\sqrt{7} - 2\sqrt{2}) =$$

$2(2\sqrt{2} - \sqrt{7})$.   Ans. $2(2\sqrt{2} - \sqrt{7})$

53. Partial fractions or formula 5.   For formula 5, let u = q,
a = 1, b = -1.   Then du = dq.

$$\int_{q_0}^{q_n} \frac{dq}{q(1-q)} = \ln\left|\frac{q}{1-q}\right| \Big|_{q_0}^{q_n} = \ln\left|\frac{q_n}{1-q_n}\right| - \ln\left|\frac{q_0}{1-q_0}\right|.$$

Ans. $\ln\left|\frac{q_n(1-q_0)}{q_0(1-q_n)}\right|$

57. (a) $\int_0^{10} 400e^{0.06(10-t)} \, dt = 400\int_0^{10} e^{0.6-0.06t} \, dt$

$$= 400\int_0^{10} e^{0.6} e^{-0.06t} \, dt = 400e^{0.6}\int_0^{10} e^{-0.06t} \, dt$$

$$= 400e^{0.6}\left(\frac{1}{-0.06}\right)\int_0^{10} e^{-0.06t}[-0.06 \, dt] \qquad \left[\text{Form } \int e^u \, du\right]$$

$$= \frac{400e^{0.6}}{-0.06} e^{-0.06t} \Big|_0^{10} = \frac{400e^{0.6}}{-0.06}[e^{-0.6} - 1]$$

$$\approx \frac{400(1.8221)}{-0.06}[0.54881 - 1] \approx 5481. \qquad \text{Ans.}\quad \$5481$$

(b) $\int_0^5 40te^{0.04(5-t)}\, dt = 40\int_0^5 te^{0.2}e^{-0.04t}\, dt$

$= 40e^{0.2}\int_0^5 te^{-0.04t}\, dt$

$= 40e^{0.2}\left[\dfrac{e^{-0.04t}}{0.0016}(-0.04t-1)\right]\Big|_0^5$ (Form. 38: u = t,
                                                   a = -0.04; du = dt)

$= \dfrac{40e^{0.2}}{0.0016}[e^{-0.2}(-0.2 - 1) - 1(-1)]$

$\approx \dfrac{40(1.2214)}{0.0016}[0.017524] \approx 535.$ <u>Ans.</u> $535

<u>Ans.</u>   (a) $5481; (b) $535

EXERCISE 16.4

1. $\bar{f} = \dfrac{1}{4-0}\int_0^4 x^2\, dx = \dfrac{1}{4}\cdot\dfrac{x^3}{3}\Big|_0^4 = \dfrac{16}{3} - 0 = \dfrac{16}{3}$

5. $\bar{f} = \dfrac{1}{2-(-2)}\int_{-2}^2 4t^3\, dt = \dfrac{1}{4}t^4\Big|_{-2}^2 = 4 - 4 = 0$

9. $\bar{P} = \dfrac{1}{100-0}\int_0^{100}(396q-2.1q^2-400)\, dq =$

$\dfrac{1}{100}(198q^2 - 0.7q^3 - 400q)\Big|_0^{100} =$

$\dfrac{1}{100}(1{,}980{,}000 - 700{,}000 - 40{,}000) - 0 = 12{,}400.$

<u>Ans.</u> $12,400

EXERCISE 16.5

1. $f(x) = x^2$, $n = 5$, $a = 0$, $b = 1$. Trapezoidal.

$h = \frac{b-a}{n} = \frac{1}{5} = 0.2$.

$$f(0) = 0.0000$$
$$2f(0.2) = 0.0800$$
$$2f(0.4) = 0.3200$$
$$2f(0.6) = 0.7200$$
$$2f(0.8) = 1.2800$$
$$f(1) = \underline{1.0000}$$
$$3.4000$$

$\int_0^1 x^2 \, dx \approx \frac{0.2}{2}(3.4000) = 0.340$.

Actual value: $\int_0^1 x^2 \, dx = \left.\frac{x^3}{3}\right|_0^1 = \frac{1}{3} \approx 0.333$.

Ans. 0.340; 0.333

5. $f(x) = \frac{x}{x+1}$, $n = 4$, $a = 0$, $b = 2$. Trapezoidal.

$h = \frac{b-a}{n} = \frac{2}{4} = 0.5$.

$$f(0) = 0.0000$$
$$2f(0.5) = 0.6667$$
$$2f(1) = 1.0000$$
$$2f(1.5) = 1.2000$$
$$f(2) = \underline{0.6667}$$
$$3.5334$$

$\int_0^2 \frac{x}{x+1} \, dx \approx \frac{0.5}{2}(3.5334) \approx 0.883$.   Ans. 0.883

9. a = 1, b = 5, h = 1.

$$f(1) = 0.4000 \qquad = 0.4000$$
$$4f(2) = 4(0.6000) \quad = 2.4000$$
$$2f(3) = 2(1.2000) \quad = 2.4000$$
$$4f(4) = 4(0.8000) \quad = 3.2000$$
$$f(5) = 0.5000 \qquad = \underline{0.5000}$$
$$8.9000$$

$$\int_1^5 f(x)\ dx \approx \tfrac{1}{3}(8.9000) \approx 2.967. \qquad \underline{Ans.} \quad 2.967$$

13. $f(x) = \sqrt{1-x^2}$, a = 0, b = 1, n = 4, h = $\frac{1-0}{4}$ = 0.25.

Simpson.

$$f(0) = 1.0000$$
$$4f(0.25) = 3.8730$$
$$2f(0.50) = 1.7321$$
$$4f(0.75) = 2.6458$$
$$f(1) = \underline{0.0000}$$
$$9.2509$$

$$\int_0^1 \sqrt{1-x^2}\ dx \approx \frac{0.25}{3}(9.2509) \approx 0.771. \qquad \underline{Ans.} \quad 0.771$$

EXERCISE 16.6

1. $y' = 2xy^2$. $\frac{dy}{dx} = 2xy^2$. $\frac{dy}{y^2} = 2x\ dx$. $\int \frac{dy}{y^2} = \int 2x\ dx$.

$-\frac{1}{y} = x^2 + C$. $\qquad \underline{Ans.} \quad y = -\frac{1}{x^2 + C}$

5. $\frac{dy}{dx} = y$, $y > 0$. $\frac{dy}{y} = dx$. $\int\frac{dy}{y} = \int dx$. $\ln y = x + C_1$.

$y = e^{x+C_1} = e^{C_1}e^x = Ce^x$, where $C = e^{C_1}$.

<u>Ans.</u> $y = Ce^x$, $C > 0$

9. $y' = \frac{1}{y}$, $y > 0$, $y(2) = 2$. $\frac{dy}{dx} = \frac{1}{y}$. $y\,dy = dx$.

$\int y\,dy = \int dx$. $\frac{y^2}{2} = x + C$. Since $y(2) = 2$, then

$\frac{2^2}{2} = 2 + C$, so $C = 0$. Thus $y^2 = 2x$ or $y = \sqrt{2x}$ (since

$y > 0$). <u>Ans.</u> $y = \sqrt{2x}$

13. $(4x^2+3)^2y' - 4xy^2 = 0$, $y(0) = 3/2$. $(4x^2+3)^2\frac{dy}{dx} - 4xy^2 = 0$,

$(4x^2+3)^2\frac{dy}{dx} = 4xy^2$, $\frac{dy}{y^2} = \frac{4x}{(4x^2+3)^2}\,dx$.

$\int\frac{dy}{y^2} = \int\frac{4x}{(4x^2+3)^2}\,dx$, $\int y^{-2}\,dy = 4\cdot\frac{1}{8}\int(4x^2+3)^{-2}[8x\,dx]$.

$-\frac{1}{y} = -\frac{1}{2(4x^2+3)} + C$. Since $y(0) = \frac{3}{2}$, then

$-\frac{1}{3/2} = -\frac{1}{2(3)} + C$, so $C = -\frac{1}{2}$. Thus

$$-\frac{1}{y} = -\frac{1}{2(4x^2+3)} - \frac{1}{2} = -\frac{1 + (4x^2+3)}{2(4x^2+3)}$$

$$= -\frac{4x^2+4}{2(4x^2+3)} = -\frac{4(x^2+1)}{2(4x^2+3)} = -\frac{2(x^2+1)}{4x^2+3}.$$

<u>Ans.</u> $y = \frac{4x^2+3}{2(x^2+1)}$

17. Let N be the population (in billions) at time t, where t is the number of years past 1930. N follows exponential growth, so $N = N_0 e^{kt}$. When t = 0, then N = 2, so $N_0 = 2$. Thus $N = 2e^{kt}$. Since N = 3 when t = 30, then $3 = 2e^{30k}$, $3/2 = e^{30k}$, 30k = ln(3/2), or k = ln(3/2)/30. Thus $N = 2e^{t \ln(3/2)/30} \approx 2e^{t(0.40547/30)} \approx 2e^{(0.013516)t}$. For year 2000, t = 70, so $N \approx 2e^{(0.013516)70} \approx 2e^{0.946}$.

Ans. $2e^{0.946}$ billion

21. Let N be the amount of ^{14}C present in scroll t years after scroll was made. Then $N = N_0 e^{-\lambda t}$, where N_0 is amount of ^{14}C present when t = 0. We want to find t when $N = 0.7N_0$.

$0.7N_0 = N_0 e^{-\lambda t}$, $0.7 = e^{-\lambda t}$, $-\lambda t = \ln 0.7$,

$-\lambda t = \ln 7 - \ln 10 \approx 1.94591 - 2.30259 = -0.35668$,

$t \approx 0.35668/\lambda$. By Eq. 15, $\lambda \approx 0.69315/5600$, so

$t \approx 0.35668(5600/0.69315) \approx 2900$.   Ans.   2900 years

25. $N = N_0 e^{-\lambda t}$. When t = 2, then N = 10. Thus $10 = N_0 e^{-2\lambda}$,

$N_0 = 10e^{2\lambda}$. By Eq. 15, 6 = (ln 2)/λ, λ = (ln 2)/6. Thus

$N_0 = 10e^{2(\ln 2)/6} \approx 10e^{0.69315/3} \approx 10e^{0.23} \approx 12.6$.

Ans.   12.6 units

EXERCISE 16.7

1. $N = M/(1+ be^{-ct})$. Since $M = 40{,}000$, and $N = 20{,}000$ when $t = 0$, 70 have $20{,}000 = \frac{40{,}000}{1+b}$. Thus $1+b = \frac{40{,}000}{20{,}000} = 2$, or $b = 1$. Hence $N = \frac{40{,}000}{1+e^{-ct}}$. When $t = 5$, then $N = 25{,}000$.

Thus $25{,}000 = \frac{40{,}000}{1+e^{-5c}}$, $1+e^{-5c} = \frac{40{,}000}{25{,}000} = \frac{8}{5}$,

$e^{-5c} = \frac{8}{5} - 1 = \frac{3}{5}$, $e^{-c} = \left(\frac{3}{5}\right)^{1/5}$. Hence $N = \frac{40{,}000}{1+(3/5)^{t/5}}$.

When $t = 10$, then $N = \frac{40{,}000}{1+(3/5)^2} \approx 29{,}412$. Ans. $29{,}400$

5. $N = M/(1+be^{-ct})$. Since $M = 100{,}000$, and $N = 500$ when $t = 0$, we have $500 = \frac{100{,}000}{1+b}$, $1+b = \frac{100{,}000}{500} = 200$, $b = 199$. Hence $N = \frac{100{,}000}{1+199e^{-ct}}$. If $t = 1$, then $N = 1000$.

Thus $1000 = \frac{100{,}000}{1+199e^{-c}}$, $1+199e^{-c} = \frac{100{,}000}{1000} = 100$,

$199e^{-c} = 99$, $e^{-c} = \frac{99}{199}$. Hence $N = \frac{100{,}000}{1+199\left(\frac{99}{199}\right)^t}$.

If $t = 2$, then $N = \frac{100{,}000}{1+199\left(\frac{99}{199}\right)^2} \approx 1990$. Ans. 1990

9. $\frac{dT}{dt} = k(T-a)$ where $a = 10$. $\frac{dT}{T-a} = k\, dt$, $\int \frac{dT}{T-a} = \int k\, dt$.
Thus $\ln(T-10) = kt + C$. At $t = 0$, $T = 32$. Thus $\ln(22-10) = 0 + C$, so $C = \ln 22$ and $\ln(T-10) = kt + \ln 22$, $\ln(T-10) - \ln 22 = kt$. Hence $\ln\left(\frac{T-10}{22}\right) = kt$.

If $t = 1$, then $T = 30$. Thus $\ln\left(\frac{30-10}{22}\right) = k\cdot 1$, so
$k = \ln(20/22) = \ln(10/11) = \ln(1/1.1) = -\ln 1.1 \approx$

-0.09531. Hence $\ln\left(\frac{T-10}{22}\right) \approx -0.09531t$. If $T = 37$, then

$\ln\left(\frac{27}{22}\right) \approx -0.09531t$, $\ln\left(\frac{2.7}{2.2}\right) \approx -0.09531t$,

$t \approx \dfrac{\ln 2.7 - \ln 2.2}{-0.09531} \approx \dfrac{0.99325 - 0.78846}{-0.09531} \approx \dfrac{0.20479}{-0.09531} \approx$

-2.15. Note: 2.15 hr corresponds to 2 hr 9 min.

3:15 AM - 2 hr 9 min = 1:06 AM.   Ans.   1:06 AM

13. $\dfrac{dN}{dt} = k(M-N)$, $\int\dfrac{dN}{M-N} = \int k\, dt$, $-\ln(M-N) = kt + C$. If $t = 0$,

then $N = N_0$, so $-\ln(M-N_0) = C$. Thus $-\ln(M-N) =$

$kt - \ln(M-N_0)$, $\ln(M-N_0) - \ln(M-N) = kt$, $\ln\dfrac{M-N_0}{M-N} = kt$,

$\ln\dfrac{M-N}{M-N_0} = -kt$, $\dfrac{M-N}{M-N_0} = e^{-kt}$, $M-N = (M-N_0)e^{-kt}$,

$N = M-(M-N_0)e^{-kt}$.   Ans. $N = M-(M-N_0)e^{-kt}$

EXERCISE 16.8

1. $\displaystyle\int_3^\infty \frac{1}{x^2}\, dx = \lim_{r\to\infty} \int_3^r x^{-2}\, dx = \lim_{r\to\infty} \left.\frac{x^{-1}}{-1}\right|_3^r = \lim_{r\to\infty} \left.\left(-\frac{1}{x}\right)\right|_3^r =$

$\lim_{r\to\infty} \left(-\frac{1}{r} + \frac{1}{3}\right) = 0 + \frac{1}{3} = \frac{1}{3}$

5. $\displaystyle\int_1^\infty e^{-x}\, dx = \lim_{r\to\infty} -\int_1^r e^{-x}[-dx] = \lim_{r\to\infty} \left. -e^{-x}\right|_1^r =$

$\lim_{r\to\infty} (-e^{-r} + e^{-1}) = \lim_{r\to\infty} \left(-\frac{1}{e^r} + \frac{1}{e}\right) = 0 + \frac{1}{e} = \frac{1}{e}$

9. $\displaystyle\int_{-\infty}^{-2} \frac{1}{(x+1)^3}\, dx = \lim_{r\to-\infty} \int_{r}^{-2} (x+1)^{-3}\, dx = \lim_{r\to-\infty} \frac{(x+1)^{-2}}{-2}\Big|_{r}^{-2} =$

$\displaystyle\lim_{r\to-\infty} -\frac{1}{2(x+1)^2}\Big|_{r}^{-2} = \lim_{r\to-\infty} \left[-\frac{1}{2} + \frac{1}{2(r+1)^2}\right] = -\frac{1}{2} + 0 = -\frac{1}{2}$

13. (a) $\displaystyle\int_{800}^{\infty} \frac{k}{x^2}\, dx = 1, \quad \lim_{r\to\infty} k\int_{800}^{r} x^{-2}\, dx = 1, \quad \lim_{r\to\infty} -\frac{k}{x}\Big|_{800}^{r} = 1,$

$\displaystyle\lim_{r\to\infty} \left(-\frac{k}{r} + \frac{k}{800}\right) = 1, \quad 0 + \frac{k}{800} = 1, \quad k = 800.$

(b) $\displaystyle\int_{1200}^{\infty} \frac{800}{x^2}\, dx = \lim_{r\to\infty} 800\int_{1200}^{r} x^{-2}\, dx = \lim_{r\to\infty} -\frac{800}{x}\Big|_{1200}^{r}$

$\displaystyle= \lim_{r\to\infty} \left(-\frac{800}{r} + \frac{800}{1200}\right) = 0 + \frac{2}{3} = \frac{2}{3}.$

<u>Ans.</u> (a) 800; (b) 2/3

17. area $\displaystyle= \int_{0}^{\infty} e^{-2x}\, dx = \lim_{r\to\infty} -\frac{1}{2}\int_{0}^{r} e^{-2x}[-2\ dx] = \lim_{r\to\infty} -\frac{e^{-2x}}{2}\Big|_{0}^{r} =$

$\displaystyle\lim_{r\to\infty} \left[-\frac{1}{2e^{2r}} + \frac{1}{2}\right] = 0 + \frac{1}{2} = \frac{1}{2}.$ <u>Ans.</u> $\frac{1}{2}$ sq unit

CHAPTER 16 - REVIEW PROBLEMS

1. Integration by parts or formula 42. For integration by parts, let u = ln x, dv = x dx. Then du = $\frac{1}{x}$ dx and

v = $\frac{x^2}{2}$. Thus $\displaystyle\int x \ln x\, dx = \ln x \left(\frac{x^2}{2}\right) - \int \frac{x^2}{2}\cdot\frac{1}{x}\, dx =$

$\frac{x^2}{2} \ln(x) - \int \frac{x}{2} dx = \frac{x^2}{2} \ln(x) - \frac{x^2}{4} + C =$

$\frac{x^2}{4}[2 \ln(x) - 1] + C.$ For formula 42, let u = x (so du =

dx) and n = 1.   Ans. $\frac{x^2}{4}[2 \ln(x) - 1] + C$

5. By partial fractions, $\int \frac{x \, dx}{(2+3x)(3+x)} = \int \left[\frac{-2/7}{2+3x} + \frac{3/7}{3+x}\right] dx =$

$-\frac{2}{21} \ln|2+3x| + \frac{3}{7} \ln|3+x| + C.$ Alternatively, by formula

12, with u = x (so du = dx), a = 2, b = 3, c = 3, and

k = 1, $\int \frac{x \, dx}{(2+3x)(3+x)} = \frac{1}{7}\left[3 \ln|3+x| - \frac{2}{3} \ln|2+3x|\right] + C.$

Ans. $\frac{1}{21}(9 \ln|3+x| - 2 \ln|2+3x|) + C$

9. Formula 21 with u = 4x (so du = 4 dx) and a^2 = 9.

$\int \frac{dx}{x^2\sqrt{9-16x^2}} = 4\int \frac{[4 \, dx]}{(4x)^2\sqrt{9-(4x)^2}} = 4\left[-\frac{\sqrt{9-16x^2}}{9(4x)}\right] + C.$

Ans. $-\frac{\sqrt{9-16x^2}}{9x} + C$

13. Integration by parts or formula 38. For integration by

parts, let u = x and dv = e^{7x} dx. Then du = dx and v =

$\frac{1}{7}e^{7x}$. Thus $\int xe^{7x} dx = x\cdot\frac{1}{7}e^{7x} - \int \frac{1}{7}e^{7x} dx =$

$\frac{x}{7}e^{7x} - \frac{1}{7}\cdot\frac{1}{7}\int e^{7x}[7 \, dx] = \frac{x}{7}e^{7x} - \frac{1}{49}e^{7x} + C.$ For formula 38,

let u = x (so du = dx) and a = 7.   Ans. $\frac{e^{7x}}{49}(7x-1) + C$

17. Division or formula 3. For division,

$$\int \frac{2x}{3+2x}\ dx = \int \left[1 - \frac{3}{3+2x}\right]\ dx = x - 3\cdot\frac{1}{2}\int \frac{1}{3+2x}[2\ dx] =$$

$x - \frac{3}{2}\ \ln|3+2x|\ +$ C. To apply formula 3, write the

integral as $2\int \frac{x}{3+2x}\ dx$ and let u = x (so du = dx), a = 3

and b = 2.   Ans. $x - \frac{3}{2}\ \ln|3+2x|\ +$ C

21. f(x) = 1/(x+1), n = 6, a = 0, b = 3. $h = \frac{b-a}{n} = \frac{3-0}{6} = 0.5$.

   (a) Trapezoidal

            f(0) = 1.0000

        2f(0.5) = 1.3333

          2f(1) = 1.0000

        2f(1.5) = 0.8000

          2f(2) = 0.6667

        2f(2.5) = 0.5714

           f(3) = <u>0.2500</u>

                5.6214

   $\frac{0.5}{2}(5.6214) \approx 1.405$

   (b) Simpson

            f(0) = 1.0000

        4f(0.5) = 2.6667

          2f(1) = 1.0000

        4f(1.5) = 1.6000

          2f(2) = 0.6667

        4f(2.5) = 1.1429

           f(3) = <u>0.2500</u>

                8.3263

   $\frac{0.5}{3}(8.3263) \approx 1.388$

Ans. (a) 1.405; (b) 1.388

25. $\int_{3}^{\infty} \frac{1}{x^3}\ dx = \lim_{r\to\infty} \int_{3}^{r} x^{-3}\ dx = \lim_{r\to\infty} \frac{x^{-2}}{-2}\Big|_{3}^{r} = \lim_{r\to\infty} -\frac{1}{2x^2}\Big|_{3}^{r} =$

$\lim_{r\to\infty} \left[-\frac{1}{2r^2} + \frac{1}{18}\right] = 0 + \frac{1}{18} = \frac{1}{18}$

29. $N = N_0 e^{kt}$. Since $N = 100,000$ when $t = 0$, then $N_0 =$

100,000. Thus $N = 100,000e^{kt}$. Since $N = 120,000$ when

$t = 15$, then $120,000 = 100,000e^{15k}$, $1.2 = e^{15k}$,

$\ln 1.2 = 15k$, or $k = (\ln 1.2)/15$. Thus

$N = 100,000e^{t \ln(1.2)/15} = 100,000(e^{\ln 1.2})^{t/15} =$

$100,000(1.2)^{t/15}$. For 1995, $t = 30$ and

$N = 100,000(1.2)^{30/15} = 100,000(1.2)^2 = 144,000$.

Ans. 144,000

33. $N = \dfrac{450}{1+be^{-ct}}$. If $t = 0$, then $N = 2$. Thus $2 = \dfrac{450}{1+b}$,

$1+b = \dfrac{450}{2} = 225$, $b = 224$. So $N = \dfrac{450}{1+224e^{-ct}}$. If $t = 6$,

then $N = 300$. Thus $300 = \dfrac{450}{1+224e^{-6c}}$, $1+224e^{-6c} = \dfrac{450}{300} = \dfrac{3}{2}$,

$224e^{-6c} = \dfrac{3}{2} - 1 = \dfrac{1}{2}$, $e^{-6c} = \dfrac{1}{448}$, $e^{6c} = 448$,

$6c = \ln 448 \approx 6.10479$, $c \approx 1.02$.

Ans. $N = \dfrac{450}{1+224e^{-1.02t}}$

37. $\displaystyle\int_0^\infty f(x)\,dx = \lim_{r\to\infty}\int_0^r (0.008e^{-0.01x} + 0.00004e^{-0.0002x})\,dx =$

$\displaystyle\lim_{r\to\infty} (-0.8e^{-0.01x} - 0.2e^{-0.0002x})\Big|_0^r =$

$\displaystyle\lim_{r\to\infty} \left(-\frac{0.8}{e^{0.01r}} - \frac{0.2}{e^{0.0002r}} + 0.8 + 0.2\right) =$

$0 - 0 + 0.8 + 0.2 = 1$

CHAPTER 16 — MATHEMATICAL SNAPSHOT

1. $C = 2000$, $w_0 = 200$. $w_{eq} = \dfrac{C}{17.5} = \dfrac{2000}{17.5} \approx 114$.

$$w(t) = \frac{C}{17.5} + \left(w_0 - \frac{C}{17.5}\right)e^{-0.005t}$$

$$= \frac{2000}{17.5} + \left(200 - \frac{2000}{17.5}\right)e^{-0.005t}.$$

Letting $w(t) = 175$ and solving for t gives

$$175 = \frac{2000}{17.5} + \left(200 - \frac{2000}{17.5}\right)e^{-0.005t}$$

$$175 - \frac{2000}{17.5} = \left(200 - \frac{2000}{17.5}\right)e^{-0.005t}$$

$$\frac{175 - \frac{2000}{17.5}}{200 - \frac{2000}{17.5}} = e^{-0.005t}$$

$$-0.005t = \ln\left[\frac{175 - \frac{2000}{17.5}}{200 - \frac{2000}{17.5}}\right]$$

$$t = \frac{\ln\left[\dfrac{175 - \frac{2000}{17.5}}{200 - \frac{2000}{17.5}}\right]}{-0.005} \approx 69$$

Ans.   114; 69

17

Continuous Random Variables

1. a. $P(1<X<2) = \int_1^2 \frac{1}{6}(x+1)\ dx = \left.\frac{(x+1)^2}{12}\right|_1^2 = \frac{9}{12} - \frac{4}{12} = \frac{5}{12}.$

   b. $P(X<2.5) = \int_1^{2.5} \frac{1}{6}(x+1)\ dx = \left.\frac{(x+1)^2}{12}\right|_1^{2.5} = \frac{49}{48} - \frac{4}{12}$

   $= \frac{11}{16} = 0.6875.$

   c. $P(X \geqq \frac{3}{2}) = \int_{3/2}^3 \frac{1}{6}(x+1)\ dx = \left.\frac{(x+1)^2}{12}\right|_{3/2}^3 = \frac{16}{12} - \frac{25}{48}$

   $= \frac{13}{16} = 0.8125.$

   d. $\int_1^c \frac{1}{6}(x+1)\ dx = \frac{1}{2},\ \left.\frac{(x+1)^2}{12}\right|_1^c = \frac{1}{2},\ \frac{(c+1)^2}{12} - \frac{1}{3} = \frac{1}{2},$

   $(c+1)^2 - 4 = 6,\ (c+1)^2 = 10,\ c+1 = \pm\sqrt{10},\ c = -1\pm\sqrt{10}.$

   We choose $c = -1+\sqrt{10}$ since $1 < c < 3$.   <u>Ans.</u> $-1+\sqrt{10}$

5. a. $f(x) = \begin{cases} 1/(b-a), & \text{if } a \leq x \leq b, \\ 0, & \text{otherwise.} \end{cases}$

   b. $\mu = \int_a^b x\left(\frac{1}{b-a}\right) dx = \frac{x^2}{2(b-a)}\Big|_a^b = \frac{b^2-a^2}{2(b-a)} = \frac{a+b}{2}$.

   c. $\sigma^2 = \int_a^b x^2\left(\frac{1}{b-a}\right) dx - \mu^2 = \frac{x^3}{3(b-a)}\Big|_a^b - \left(\frac{a+b}{2}\right)^2$

   $= \frac{b^3-a^3}{3(b-a)} - \frac{(a+b)^2}{4} = \frac{b^2+ab+a^2}{3} - \frac{a^2+2ab+b^2}{4}$

   $= \frac{b^2-2ab+a^2}{12} = \frac{(b-a)^2}{12}$.

   Thus $\sigma = \frac{b-a}{\sqrt{12}}$.   Ans. $\frac{(b-a)^2}{12}$; $\frac{b-a}{\sqrt{12}}$

9. a. $\int_0^4 kx\, dx = 1$, $\frac{kx^2}{2}\Big|_0^4 = 1$, $8k = 1$, $k = \frac{1}{8}$.   Ans. $\frac{1}{8}$

   b. $P(2<X<3) = \int_2^3 \frac{x}{8}\, dx = \frac{x^2}{16}\Big|_2^3 = \frac{9}{16} - \frac{4}{16} = \frac{5}{16}$.

   c. $P(X>2.5) = \int_{2.5}^4 \frac{x}{8}\, dx = \frac{x^2}{16}\Big|_{2.5}^4 = 1 - \frac{25}{64} = \frac{39}{64} = 0.609$.

   d. $P(X>0) = P(0 \leq X \leq 4) = 1$.

   e. $\mu = \int_0^4 x\left(\frac{x}{8}\right) dx = \frac{x^3}{24}\Big|_0^4 = \frac{64}{24} - 0 = \frac{8}{3}$.

   f. $\sigma^2 = \int_0^4 x^2\left(\frac{x}{8}\right) dx - \mu^2 = \frac{x^4}{32}\Big|_0^4 - \left(\frac{8}{3}\right)^2$

   $= 8 - \frac{64}{9} = \frac{8}{9}$.   Thus $\sigma = \frac{\sqrt{8}}{3} = \frac{2\sqrt{2}}{3}$.   Ans. $\frac{2\sqrt{2}}{3}$

   g. $P(X<c) = \frac{1}{2}$, $\int_0^c \frac{x}{8}\, dx = \frac{1}{2}$, $\frac{x^2}{16}\Big|_0^c = \frac{1}{2}$, $\frac{c^2}{16} = \frac{1}{2}$,

   $c^2 = 8$, $c = \pm 2\sqrt{2}$.   We choose $c = 2\sqrt{2}$ since $0 < c < 4$.

   Ans. $2\sqrt{2}$

h. $P(3<X<5) = P(3<X<4) = \int_3^4 \frac{x}{8}\, dx = \frac{x^2}{16}\Big|_3^4 = \frac{16}{16} - \frac{9}{16} = \frac{7}{16}.$

13. $P(X>1) = 1 - P(X\leq1) = 1 - \int_0^1 3e^{-3x}\, dx = 1 - (-e^{-3x})\Big|_0^1$

$$= 1 - (-e^{-3} + 1) = 1 - (-0.04979 + 1) = 0.050.$$

Ans.   0.050

EXERCISE 17.2

1. a. $P(0<Z<1.8) = A(1.8) = 0.4641$

    b. $P(0.45<Z<2.81) = A(2.81) - A(0.45)$

$$= 0.4975 - 0.1736 = 0.3239$$

    c. $P(Z>-1.22) = 0.5 + A(1.22) = 0.5 + 0.3888 = 0.8888$

    d. $P(Z\leq2.93) = 0.5 + A(2.93) = 0.5 + 0.4983 = 0.9983$

    e. $P(-2.61<Z\leq1.4) = A(2.61) + A(1.4)$

$$= 0.4955 + 0.4192 = 0.9147$$

    f. $P(Z>0.07) = 0.5 - A(0.07) = 0.5 - 0.0279 = 0.4721$

5. $P(Z>z_0) = 0.8599,\ 0.5 + A(-z_0) = 0.8599,\ A(-z_0) = 0.3599,$

   $-z_0 = 1.08,\ z_0 = -1.08.$ Ans. -1.08

9. a. $P(X<22) = P\left(Z<\frac{22-16}{4}\right) = P(Z<1.5) = 0.5 + A(1.5)$

$$= 0.5 + 0.4332 = 0.9332$$

    b. $P(X<10) = P\left(Z<\frac{10-16}{4}\right) = P(Z<-1.5) = 0.5 - A(1.5)$

$$= 0.5 - 0.4332 = 0.0668$$

c. $P(10.8 < X < 12.4) = P\left(\frac{10.8-16}{4} < Z < \frac{12.4-16}{4}\right)$

$$= P(-1.3 < Z < -0.9) = A(1.3) - A(0.9)$$

$$= 0.4032 - 0.3159 = 0.0873$$

13. Since $\sigma^2 = 9$, $\sigma = 3$. Thus $P(19 < X \leq 28) = P\left(\frac{19-25}{3} < Z \leq \frac{28-25}{3}\right) =$

    $P(-2 < Z \leq 1) = A(2) + A(1) = 0.4772 + 0.3413 = 0.8185$.

17. Let X be score on test. $P(X > 630) = P\left(Z > \frac{630-500}{100}\right) =$

    $P(Z > 1.3) = 0.5 - A(1.3) = 0.5 - 0.4032 = 0.0968$.

    <u>Ans.</u> 9.68%

21. Let X be I.Q. of a child in population.

    (a) $P(X > 125) = P\left(Z > \frac{125-100.4}{11.6}\right) = P(Z > 2.12) =$

       $0.5 - A(2.12) = 0.5 - 0.4830 = 0.0170$. Thus 1.7% of
       the children have I.Q.'s greater than 125.

    (b) If x_0 is the value, then $P(X > x_0) = 0.90$. Thus

       $P\left(Z > \frac{x_0-100.4}{11.6}\right) = 0.90$ or $0.5 + A\left(-\frac{x_0-100.4}{11.6}\right) = 0.90$.

       Hence $A\left(-\frac{x_0-100.4}{11.6}\right) = 0.4$, so $-\frac{x_0-100.4}{11.6} = 1.28$, or

       $x_0 = 85.552 \approx 85.6$.

    <u>Ans.</u> (a) 1.7%; (b) 85.6

1. $n = 150$, $p = 0.4$, $q = 0.6$, $\mu = np = 150(0.4) = 60$,

   $\sigma = \sqrt{npq} = \sqrt{150(0.4)(0.6)} = \sqrt{36} = 6$.

   $P(X \leq 52) = P(X \leq 52.5)$. $z = \dfrac{52.5-60}{6} = -1.25$.

   $P(X \leq 52) = P(X \leq 52.5) \approx P(Z \leq -1.25) = 0.5 - A(1.25)$

              $= 0.5 - 0.3944 = 0.1056$;

   $P(X \geq 74) = P(X \geq 73.5) \approx P\left(Z \geq \dfrac{73.5-60}{6}\right) = P(Z \geq 2.25)$

              $= 0.5 - A(2.25) = 0.5 - 0.4878 = 0.0122$.

   <u>Ans.</u>   0.1056; 0.0122

5. Let $X = $ no. of times 5 occurs.   Then X is binomial with

   $n = 300$, $p = 1/6$, $q = 5/6$, $\mu = np = 50$, $\sigma = \sqrt{npq} =$

   $\sqrt{41.666} = 6.45$.

   $P(45 \leq X \leq 60) = P(44.5 \leq X \leq 60.5) \approx P\left(\dfrac{44.5-50}{6.45} \leq Z \leq \dfrac{60.5-50}{6.45}\right)$

              $= P(-0.85 \leq Z \leq 1.63) = A(0.85) + A(1.63)$

              $= 0.3023 + 0.4484 = 0.7507$.   <u>Ans.</u>   0.7507

9. Let $X = $ no. of correct answers.   Then X is binomial and

   $p = 0.5$, $q = 0.5$.

   If $n = 20$, then $\mu = np = 20(0.5) = 10$, $\sigma = \sqrt{npq} =$

   $\sqrt{20(0.5)(0.5)} = \sqrt{5} = 2.24$, and

   $P(X \geq 12) = P(X \geq 11.5) \approx P\left(Z \geq \dfrac{11.5-10}{2.24}\right) = P(Z \geq 0.67)$

              $= 0.5 - A(0.67) = 0.5 - 0.2486 = 0.2514$.

   If $n = 100$, then $\mu = np = 100(0.5) = 50$, $\sigma = \sqrt{npq} =$

   $\sqrt{100(0.5)(0.5)} = \sqrt{25} = 5$, and

$$P(X \geq 60) = P(X \geq 59.5) \approx P\left(Z \geq \frac{59.5-50}{5}\right) = P(Z \geq 1.9)$$

$$= 0.5 - A(1.9) = 0.5 - 0.4713 = 0.0287.$$

Ans. 0.2514; 0.0287

CHAPTER 17 - REVIEW PROBLEMS

1. a. $P(0 \leq X \leq 1) = 1$, $\int_0^1 \left(\frac{1}{3} + kx^2\right) dx = 1$, $\left.\left(\frac{x}{3} + \frac{kx^3}{3}\right)\right|_0^1 = 1$,

$\frac{1}{3} + \frac{k}{3} = 1$, $\frac{k}{3} = \frac{2}{3}$, $k = 2$.   Ans. 2

b. $P\left(\frac{1}{2} < X < \frac{3}{4}\right) = \int_{1/2}^{3/4} \left(\frac{1}{3} + 2x^2\right) dx = \left.\left(\frac{x}{3} + \frac{2x^3}{3}\right)\right|_{1/2}^{3/4} =$

$\left.\frac{1}{3}(x + 2x^3)\right|_{1/2}^{3/4} = \frac{1}{3}\left[\left(\frac{3}{4} + \frac{27}{32}\right) - \left(\frac{1}{2} + \frac{1}{4}\right)\right] = \frac{9}{32}.$

c. $P\left(X \geq \frac{1}{2}\right) = \int_{1/2}^1 \left(\frac{1}{3} + 2x^2\right) dx = \left.\left(\frac{x}{3} + \frac{2x^3}{3}\right)\right|_{1/2}^1 =$

$\left.\frac{1}{3}(x + 2x^3)\right|_{1/2}^1 = \frac{1}{3}\left[(1 + 2) - \left(\frac{1}{2} + \frac{1}{4}\right)\right] = \frac{3}{4}.$

d. If $0 \leq x \leq 1$, $F(x) = \int_0^x \left(\frac{1}{3} + 2t^2\right) dt =$

$\left.\left(\frac{t}{3} + \frac{2t^3}{3}\right)\right|_0^x = \frac{x}{3} + \frac{2x^3}{3}.$

Ans. $F(x) = \begin{cases} 0, & \text{if } x < 0 \\ \frac{x}{3} + \frac{2x^3}{3}, & \text{if } 0 \leq x \leq 1 \\ 1, & \text{if } x > 1 \end{cases}$

5. $P(X > 22) = P\left(Z > \frac{22-20}{4}\right) = P(Z > 0.5) = 0.5 - A(0.5)$

$$= 0.5 - 0.1915 = 0.3085$$

9. $P(X<16) = P\left(Z<\frac{16-20}{4}\right) = P(Z<-1) = 0.5 - A(1)$

              $= 0.5 - 0.3413 = 0.1587$

13. Let X = height of an individual. X is normally
    distributed with μ = 68 and σ = 2.

    $P(X>72) = P\left(Z>\frac{72-68}{2}\right) = P(Z>2) = 0.5 - A(2)$

            $= 0.5 - 0.4772 = 0.0228.$ <u>Ans.</u> 0.0228

18

Multivariable Calculus

1. $f(2,1) = 4(2) - (1)^2 + 3 = 8 - 1 + 3 = 10$

5. $h(-3,3,5,4) = \dfrac{-3(3)}{5^2 - 4^2} = \dfrac{-9}{25 - 16} = \dfrac{-9}{9} = -1$

9. $F(2,0,-1) = 3$

13. $f(400, 400, 80) = 400(400)/80 = 2000$

17. A plane parallel to the x,y-plane has the form
    z = constant. Because (2,7,6) lies on the plane, the
    equation is z = 6. <u>Ans.</u> z = 6

21. $3x+6y+2z = 12$ can be put in
    the form $Ax+By+Cz+D = 0$, so
    the graph is a plane. The
    intercepts are $(4,0,0)$,
    $(0,2,0)$, and $(0,0,6)$.

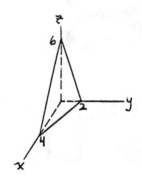

25. $z = 4-x^2$. The x,z-trace
    is $z = 4-x^2$, which is a
    parabola. For any fixed
    value of y, we obtain
    the parabola $z = 4-x^2$.

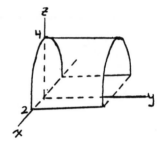

EXERCISE 18.2

1. $f_x(x,y) = 4(2x) + 0 + 0 = 8x$;

   $f_y(x,y) = 0 + 3(2y) + 0 = 6y$

5. $g_x(x,y) = (3x^2)y^2 + 2(2x)y - 3(1)y + 0 = 3x^2y^2 + 4xy - 3y$;

   $g_y(x,y) = x^3(2y) + 2x^2(1) - 3x(1) + 4(1)$

   $\qquad\qquad = 2x^3y + 2x^2 - 3x + 4$

9. $h(s,t) = \frac{s^2+4}{t-3}$. $h_s(s,t) = \frac{1}{t-3}(2s)$. Since $h(s,t) =$

$(s^2+4)(t-3)^{-1}$, then $h_t(s,t) = (s^2+4)[(-1)(t-3)^{-2}(1)]$.

<u>Ans.</u> $h_s(s,t) = 2s/(t-3)$; $h_t(s,t) = -(s^2+4)/(t-3)^2$

13. $h(x,y) = \frac{x^2+3xy+y^2}{\sqrt{x^2+y^2}}$.

$h_x(x,y) = \dfrac{(x^2+y^2)^{1/2}[2x+3y] - (x^2+3xy+y^2)\left[\frac{1}{2}(x^2+y^2)^{-1/2}(2x)\right]}{\left[(x^2+y^2)^{1/2}\right]^2}$

$= \dfrac{(x^2+y^2)^{-1/2}\left[(x^2+y^2)(2x+3y) - (x^2+3xy+y^2)x\right]}{x^2+y^2}$

$= \dfrac{2x^3+3x^2y+2xy^2+3y^3-x^3-3x^2y-xy^2}{(x^2+y^2)^{3/2}} = \dfrac{x^3+xy^2+3y^3}{(x^2+y^2)^{3/2}}$;

$h_y(x,y) = \dfrac{(x^2+y^2)^{1/2}[3x+2y] - (x^2+3xy+y^2)\left[\frac{1}{2}(x^2+y^2)^{-1/2}(2y)\right]}{\left[(x^2+y^2)^{1/2}\right]^2}$

$= \dfrac{(x^2+y^2)^{-1/2}\left[(x^2+y^2)(3x+2y) - (x^2+3xy+y^2)y\right]}{x^2+y^2}$

$= \dfrac{3x^3+2x^2y+3xy^2+2y^3-x^2y-3xy^2-y^3}{(x^2+y^2)^{3/2}} = \dfrac{3x^3+x^2y+y^3}{(x^2+y^2)^{3/2}}$.

17. $x = 5x \ln(x^2+y)$.

$\frac{\partial z}{\partial x} = 5\left\{x\left[\frac{1}{x^2+y}(2x)\right] + \ln(x^2+y)\ [1]\right\} = 5\left[\frac{2x^2}{x^2+y} + \ln(x^2+y)\right]$;

$\frac{\partial z}{\partial y} = 5x\left(\frac{1}{x^2+y}[1]\right) = \frac{5x}{x^2+y}$

21. $f(r,s) = e^{3-r} \ln(7-s)$.

$f_r(r,s) = \ln(7-s)\left[e^{3-r}(-1)\right] = -e^{3-r} \ln(7-s)$;

$f_s(r,s) = e^{3-r}\left[\frac{1}{7-s}(-1)\right] = \frac{e^{3-r}}{s-7}$

25. $g_r(r,s,t) = e^{s+t}[2r+0] = 2re^{s+t}$;

$g_s(r,s,t) = e^{s+t}[0+21s^2] + (r^2+7s^3)[e^{s+t}(1)]$

$= (7s^3+21s^2+r^2)e^{s+t}$;

$g_t(r,s,t) = (r^2+7s^3)[e^{s+t}(1)] = e^{s+t}(r^2+7s^3)$

29. $g(x,y,z) = e^x\sqrt{y+2x}$. $g_z(x,y,z) = e^x\left[\frac{1}{2}(y+2z)^{-1/2}(2)\right] =$

$e^x/\sqrt{y+2z}$. $g_z(0,1,4) = 1/\sqrt{1+8} = 1/3$. __Ans.__ $1/3$

33. $F(b,C,T,i) = \frac{bT}{C} + \frac{iC}{2}$. $\frac{\partial F}{\partial C} = \frac{\partial}{\partial C}\left[\frac{bT}{C}\right] + \frac{\partial}{\partial C}\left[\frac{iC}{2}\right] = -\frac{bT}{C^2} + \frac{i}{2}$.

EXERCISE 18.3

1. $c = 4x+0.3y^2+2y+500$. $\partial c/\partial y = 0.6y+2$. When $x = 20$ and $y = 30$, then $\partial c/\partial y = 0.6(30)+2 = 20$. __Ans.__ 20

5. In order to avoid confusing the number "1" with the letter "1", we shall use "L" to denote the letter "1".

$\partial P/\partial k = 1.582(0.764)L^{0.192}k^{-0.236} = 1.208648L^{0.192}k^{-0.236}$

$\partial P/\partial L = 1.582(0.192)L^{-0.808}k^{0.764} = 0.303744L^{-0.808}k^{0.764}$

9. $q_A = 100p_A^{-1}p_B^{-1/2}$; $q_B = 500p_B^{-1}p_A^{-1/3}$.

$\partial q_A/\partial p_A = 100(-1)p_A^{-2}p_B^{-1/2} = -100/(p_A^2 p_B^{1/2})$,

$\partial q_A/\partial p_B = 100(-1/2)p_A^{-1}p_B^{-3/2} = -50/(p_A p_B^{3/2})$,

$\partial q_B/\partial p_A = 500(-1/3)p_B^{-1}p_A^{-4/3} = -500/(3p_B p_A^{4/3})$,

$\partial q_B/\partial p_B = 500(-1)p_B^{-2}p_A^{-1/3} = -500/(p_B^2 p_A^{1/3})$.

Since $\partial q_A/\partial p_B < 0$ and $\partial q_B/\partial p_A < 0$, the products are complementary.

13. $\partial z/\partial x = 1120$. If a staff manager with an MBA degree had an extra year of work experience before the degree, the manager would receive $1120 per year in extra compensation.

17. (a) $\frac{\partial R}{\partial E_r} = 2.5945 - 0.1608E_r - 0.0277I_r$.

If $E_r = 18.8$ and $I_r = 10$, then $\partial R/\partial E_r = -0.70554$.

Since $\partial R/\partial E_r < 0$, such a candidate should not be so advised.

(b) $\partial R/\partial N = 0.8579 - 0.0122N$. If $\partial R/\partial N < 0$, then $N > 70.3$.

<u>Ans.</u> (a) no; (b) 70%

EXERCISE 18.4

1. $2x + 0 + 2z\frac{\partial z}{\partial x} = 0$. $2z\frac{\partial z}{\partial x} = -2x$, $\frac{\partial z}{\partial x} = -\frac{2x}{2z} = -\frac{x}{z}$.

5. $x^2 - 2y - z^2 + y(x^2z^2) = 20$.

    $2x - 0 - 2z\frac{\partial z}{\partial x} + y\left[x^2\cdot 2z\frac{\partial z}{\partial x} + z^2\cdot 2x\right] = 0$,

    $\left(2x^2yz - 2z\right)\frac{\partial z}{\partial x} = -2x - 2xyz^2$, $\frac{\partial z}{\partial x} = \frac{-2x(1+yz^2)}{2z(x^2y-1)} = \frac{x(yz^2+1)}{z(1-x^2y)}$.

9. $\frac{1}{z}\frac{\partial z}{\partial x} + \frac{\partial z}{\partial x} - y = 0$. $\left(\frac{1}{z} + 1\right)\frac{\partial z}{\partial x} = y$, $\left(\frac{1+z}{z}\right)\frac{\partial z}{\partial x} = y$,

    $\frac{\partial z}{\partial x} = \frac{yz}{1+z}$.

13. $\left[x\cdot 2z\frac{\partial z}{\partial x} + z^2\cdot 1\right] + y\frac{\partial z}{\partial x} - 0 = 0$. $(2xz+y)\frac{\partial z}{\partial x} = -z^2$,

    $\frac{\partial z}{\partial x} = -\frac{z^2}{2xz+y}$.   If $x = 2$, $y = -2$, $z = 3$, then $\frac{\partial z}{\partial x} = -\frac{9}{12-2} =$

    $-\frac{9}{10}$.   <u>Ans.</u> $-\frac{9}{10}$

17. $\dfrac{(rs)\left[2t\frac{\partial t}{\partial r}\right] - (s^2+t^2)[s]}{(rs)^2} = 0$. $2rst\frac{\partial t}{\partial r} - s(s^2+t^2) = 0$,

    $2rst\frac{\partial t}{\partial r} = s(s^2+t^2)$, $\frac{\partial t}{\partial r} = \frac{s(s^2+t^2)}{2rst} = \frac{s^2+t^2}{2rt}$.   If $r = 1$,

    $s = 2$, $t = 4$, then $\frac{\partial t}{\partial r} = \frac{4+16}{2\cdot 1\cdot 4} = \frac{20}{8} = \frac{5}{2}$.   <u>Ans.</u> $\frac{5}{2}$

EXERCISE 18.5

1. $f_x(x,y) = 4(2x)y = 8xy;$ $f_{xy}(x,y) = 8x$

5. $f_y(x,y) = 4[e^{2xy}(2x)] = 8xe^{2xy}$

    $f_{yx}(x,y) = 8[x(e^{2xy} \cdot 2y) + e^{2xy}(1)] = 8e^{2xy}(2xy+1)$

    $f_{yxy}(x,y) = 8[e^{2xy}(2x) + (2xy+1)(e^{2xy} \cdot 2x)]$

                $= 8e^{2xy}(2x)[1+(2xy+1)] = 8e^{2xy}(2x)[2+2xy]$

                $= 32x(1+xy)e^{2xy}$

9. $\frac{\partial z}{\partial x} = \frac{1}{2}(x^2+y^2)^{-1/2}[2x] = x(x^2+y^2)^{-1/2}$

    $\frac{\partial^2 z}{\partial x^2} = x\left[-\frac{1}{2}(x^2+y^2)^{-3/2}[2x]\right] + (x^2+y^2)^{-1/2}[1]$

       $= (x^2+y^2)^{-3/2}\left[-x^2 + (x^2+y^2)\right] = y^2(x^2+y^2)^{-3/2}$

13. $f_k(L,k) = 30L^3k^5-7Lk^6.$ $f_{kk}(L,k) = 150L^3k^4-42Lk^5.$

     $f_{kkL}(L,k) = 450L^2k^4-42k^5.$ Thus $f_{kkL}(2,1) =$

     $450(4)(1)-(42)(1) = 1758.$ <u>Ans.</u>   1758

17. $f_x(x,y) = 24x^2+4xy^2.$ $f_y(x,y) = 4x^2y+20y^3.$

     $f_{xy}(x,y) = 8xy.$ $f_{yx}(x,y) = 8xy.$

     Thus $f_{xy}(x,y) = f_{yx}(x,y).$

21. $2z\frac{\partial z}{\partial y} + 2y = 0.$ $\frac{\partial z}{\partial y} = -\frac{2y}{2z} = -\frac{y}{z}.$ $\frac{\partial^2 z}{\partial y^2} = -\frac{z(1) - y\cdot\frac{\partial z}{\partial y}}{z^2} =$

$-\frac{z - y\left(-\frac{y}{z}\right)}{z^2} = -\frac{z^2+y^2}{z^3}.$ From original equation,

$z^2+y^2 = 3x^2.$ Thus $\frac{\partial^2 z}{\partial y^2} = -\frac{3x^2}{z^3}.$ <u>Ans.</u> $-\frac{z^2+y^2}{z^3} = -\frac{3x^2}{z^3}$

EXERCISE 18.6

1. $z = 5x+3y,$ $x = 2r+3s,$ $y = r-2s.$

$\frac{\partial z}{\partial r} = \frac{\partial z}{\partial x}\frac{\partial x}{\partial r} + \frac{\partial z}{\partial y}\frac{\partial y}{\partial r} = (5)(2) + (3)(1) = 13$

$\frac{\partial z}{\partial s} = \frac{\partial z}{\partial x}\frac{\partial x}{\partial s} + \frac{\partial z}{\partial y}\frac{\partial y}{\partial s} = (5)(3) + (3)(-2) = 9$

5. $w = x^2z^2+xyz+yz^2,$ $x = 5t,$ $y = 2t+3,$ $z = 6-t.$

$\frac{dw}{dt} = \frac{\partial w}{\partial x}\frac{dx}{dt} + \frac{\partial w}{\partial y}\frac{dy}{dt} + \frac{\partial w}{\partial t}\frac{dz}{dt}$

$\quad = (2xz^2+yz)(5) + (xz+z^2)(2) + (2x^2z+xy+2yz)(-1)$

$\quad = 5(2xz^2+yz) + 2(xz+z^2) - (2x^2z+xy+2yz)$

9. $w = x^2+xyz+y^3z^2,$ $x = r-s^2,$ $y = rs,$ $z = 2r-5s.$

$\frac{\partial w}{\partial s} = \frac{\partial w}{\partial x}\frac{\partial x}{\partial s} + \frac{\partial w}{\partial y}\frac{\partial y}{\partial s} + \frac{\partial w}{\partial z}\frac{\partial z}{\partial s}$

$\quad = (2x+yz)(-2s) + (xz+3y^2z^2)(r) + (xy+2y^3z)(-5)$

$\quad = -2s(2x+yz) + r(xz+3y^2z^2) - 5(xy+2y^3z)$

13. $z = (4x+3y)^3$, $x = r^2s$, $y = r-2s$; $r = 0$, $s = 1$.

$\frac{\partial z}{\partial r} = \frac{\partial z}{\partial x}\frac{\partial x}{\partial r} + \frac{\partial z}{\partial y}\frac{\partial y}{\partial r} = 12(4x+3y)^2(2rs) + 9(4x+3y)^2(1) =$

$3(4x+3y)^2(8rs+3)$. When $r = 0$, $s = 1$, then $x = 0$, $y = -2$,

and $\partial z/\partial r = 324$. <u>Ans.</u> 324

17. $p = aP-whL$, where $P = f(l,k)$ and $l = Lg(h)$.

$\frac{\partial p}{\partial L} = a\frac{\partial P}{\partial L} - wh = a\left[\frac{\partial P}{\partial l}\frac{\partial l}{\partial L} + \frac{\partial P}{\partial k}\frac{\partial k}{\partial L}\right] - wh$

$\quad = a\left[\frac{\partial P}{\partial l}g(h) + \frac{\partial P}{\partial k}\cdot 0\right] - wh = a\frac{\partial P}{\partial l}g(h) - wh.$

$\frac{\partial p}{\partial h} = a\frac{\partial P}{\partial h} - wL = a\left[\frac{\partial P}{\partial l}\frac{\partial l}{\partial h} + \frac{\partial P}{\partial k}\frac{\partial k}{\partial h}\right] - wL$

$\quad = a\left[\frac{\partial P}{\partial l}Lg'(h) + \frac{\partial P}{\partial k}\cdot 0\right] - wL = a\frac{\partial P}{\partial l}Lg'(h) - wL.$

<u>Ans.</u> $\frac{\partial p}{\partial L} = a\frac{\partial P}{\partial l}g(h) - wh$; $\frac{\partial p}{\partial h} = a\frac{\partial P}{\partial l}Lg'(h) - wL$

EXERCISE 18.7

1. $f(x,y) = x^2+y^2-5x+4y+xy$.

$\begin{cases} f_x(x,y) = 2x+y-5 = 0 \\ f_y(x,y) = x+2y+4 = 0. \end{cases}$ Crit. pt.: $(14/3, -13/3)$.

<u>Ans.</u> $(14/3,-13/3)$

5. $f(x,y,z) = 2x^2+xy+y^2+100-z(x+y-200)$.

$\begin{cases} f_x(x,y,z) = 4x+y-z = 0 \\ f_y(x,y,z) = x+2y-z = 0 \\ f_z(x,y,z) = -x-y+200 = 0. \end{cases}$

Crit. pt.: $(50, 150, 350)$. <u>Ans.</u> $(50, 150, 350)$

9. $f(x,y) = y-y^2-3x-6x^2$.

$$\begin{cases} f_x(x,y) = -3-12x = 0 \\ f_y(x,y) = 1-2y = 0. \end{cases}$$ Crit. pt.: $(-1/4,1/2)$.

$f_{xx}(x,y) = -12$, $f_{yy}(x,y) = -2$, $f_{xy}(x,y) = 0$.   At

$(-1/4,1/2)$, $D = (-12)(-2)-0^2 = 24 > 0$ and $f_{xx}(x,y) =$

$-12 < 0$; thus rel. max.   Ans. $(-1/4,1/2)$, rel. max.

13. $f(x,y) = (1/3)(x^3+8y^3) - 2(x^2+y^2) + 1$.

$$\begin{cases} f_x(x,y) = x^2-4x = 0 \\ f_y(x,y) = 8y^2-4y = 0. \end{cases}$$

Crit. pt.: $(0,0)$, $(4,1/2)$, $(0,1/2)$, $(4,0)$.

$f_{xx}(x,y) = 2x-4$, $f_{yy}(x,y) = 16y-4$, $f_{xy}(x,y) = 0$.

At $(0,0)$, $D = (-4)(-4)-0^2 = 16 > 0$ and $f_{xx}(x,y) = -4 < 0$;

thus rel. max.   At $(4,1/2)$, $D = (4)(4)-0^2 = 16 > 0$ and

$f_{xx}(x,y) = 4 > 0$; thus rel. min.   At $(0,1/2)$, $D =$

$(-4)(4)-0^2 = -16 < 0$; thus neither.   At $(4,0)$, $D =$

$(4)(-4)-0^2 = -16 < 0$; thus neither.   Ans. $(0,0)$, rel.

max.; $(4,1/2)$, rel. min.; $(0,1/2)$, $(4,0)$, neither

17. $f(p,q) = pq-(1/p)-(1/q)$.

$$\begin{cases} f_p(p,q) = q+(1/p^2) = 0 \\ f_q(p,q) = p+(1/q^2) = 0. \end{cases}$$ Crit. pt.: $(-1,-1)$.

$f_{pp}(p,q) = -2/p^3$, $f_{qq}(p,q) = -2/q^3$, $f_{pq}(p,q) = 1$.   At

$(-1,-1)$, $D = (2)(2)-1^2 = 3 > 0$ and $f_{pp}(p,q) = 2 > 0$; thus

rel. min.   Ans. $(-1,-1)$, rel. min.

21. Profit per lb for A = p_A-60.

    Profit per lb for B = p_B-70.

    Total Profit = P = $(p_A-60)q_A + (p_B-70)q_B$.

    P = $(p_A-60)[5(p_B-p_A)] + (p_B-70)[500+5(p_A-2p_B)]$.

    $\begin{cases} \partial P/\partial p_A = -10(p_A-p_B+5) = 0 \\ \partial P/\partial p_B = 10(p_A-2p_B+90) = 0. \end{cases}$ Crit. pt.: $p_A=80$, $p_B=85$.

    $\dfrac{\partial^2 P}{\partial p_A^2} = -10$, $\dfrac{\partial^2 P}{\partial p_B^2} = -20$, $\dfrac{\partial^2 P}{\partial p_B \partial p_A} = 10$. When $p_A = 80$ and

    $p_B = 85$, then D = $(-10)(-20)-(10)^2 = 100 > 0$ and $\dfrac{\partial^2 P}{\partial p_A^2} =$

    $-10 < 0$; thus rel. max. <u>Ans.</u> $p_A = 80$, $p_B = 85$

25. c = $1.5q_A^2+4.5q_B^2$, $p_A = 36-q_A^2$, $p_B = 30-q_B^2$.

    Total Profit = Total Revenue - Total Cost

    $$P = (p_A q_A + p_B q_B) - c$$

    $$P = 36q_A-q_A^3+30q_B-q_B^3 - (1.5q_A^2+4.5q_B^2)$$

    $\begin{cases} \partial P/\partial q_A = 36-3q_A-3q_A^2 = 3(4+q_A)(3-q_A) \\ \partial P/\partial q_B = 30-9q_B-3q_B^2 = 3(5+q_B)(2-q_B). \end{cases}$

    Since we want $q_A \geq 0$ and $q_B \geq 0$, the crit. pt. occurs when

    $q_A = 3$ and $q_B = 2$.

    $\dfrac{\partial^2 P}{\partial q_A^2} = -3-6q_A$, $\dfrac{\partial^2 P}{\partial q_B^2} = -9-6q_B$, $\dfrac{\partial^2 P}{\partial q_B \partial q_A} = 0$. When $q_A = 3$ and

    $q_B = 2$, then D = $(-21)(-21)-0^2 > 0$ and $\dfrac{\partial^2 P}{\partial q_A^2} = -21 < 0$;

    thus rel. max. <u>Ans.</u> $q_A = 3$, $q_B = 2$

29. $y = (3x-7)/2$. $f(x,y) = -2x^2 + 5\left(\frac{3x-7}{2}\right)^2 + 7$. Setting the

derivative equal to 0 gives $-4x + 5(2)\left(\frac{3x-7}{2}\right)\left(\frac{3}{2}\right) = 0$. Thus

$-4x + \frac{15}{2}(3x-7) = 0$, $-8x + 15(3x-7) = 0$, $-8x + 45x - 105 =$

0, $37x = 105$, or $x = 105/37$. The second-derivative is

$37/2 > 0$, so we have a rel. min. If $x = 105/37$, then

$y = 28/37$.   <u>Ans.</u> $(105/37, 28/37)$, rel. min.

<u>EXERCISE 18.8</u>

1. $f(x,y) = x^2+4y^2+6$, $2x-8y = 20$.

      $F(x,y,\lambda) = x^2+4y^2+6 - \lambda(2x-8y-20)$.

$$\begin{cases} F_x = 2x-2\lambda = 0 & (1) \\ F_y = 8y+8\lambda = 0 & (2) \\ F_\lambda = -2x+8y+20 = 0. & (3) \end{cases}$$

From (1), $x = \lambda$; from (2), $y = -\lambda$. Substituting $x = \lambda$
and $y = -\lambda$ into (3) gives $-2\lambda-8\lambda+20 = 0$, $-10\lambda = -20$, so
$\lambda = 2$. Thus $x = 2$ and $y = -2$.
Crit. pt. of F: $(2,-2,2)$. Crit. pt. of f: $(2,-2)$.
<u>Ans.</u> $(2,-2)$

5. $f(x,y,z) = x^2+xy+2y^2+z^2$, $x-3y-4z = 16$.

      $F(x,y,z,\lambda) = x^2+xy+2y^2+z^2 - \lambda(x-3y-4z-16)$.

$$\begin{cases} F_x = 2x+y-\lambda = 0 & (1) \\ F_y = x+4y+3\lambda = 0 & (2) \\ F_z = 2z+4\lambda = 0 & (3) \\ F_\lambda = -x+3y+4z+16 = 0. & (4) \end{cases}$$

Eliminating x from (1) and (2) yields $y = -\lambda$. Substitu-

ting $y = -\lambda$ into (2) yields $x = \lambda$. From (3), $z = -2\lambda$.
Substituting $x = \lambda$, $y = -\lambda$, and $z = -2\lambda$ into (4) yields
$\lambda = 4/3$. Crit. pt. of F: $(4/3, -4/3, -8/3, 4/3)$.
Crit. pt. of f: $(4/3, -4/3, -8/3)$. <u>Ans.</u> $(4/3, -4/3, -8/3)$

9. $f(x,y,z) = x^2 + 2y - z^2$, $2x - y = 0$, $y + z = 0$. Since there
are two constraints, we use two Lagrange multipliers.

$$F(x,y,z,\lambda_1\lambda_2) = x^2 + 2y - z^2 - \lambda_1(2x-y) - \lambda_2(y+z).$$

$$\begin{cases} F_x = 2x - 2\lambda_1 = 0 & (1) \\ F_y = 2 + \lambda_1 - \lambda_2 = 0 & (2) \\ F_z = -2z - \lambda_2 = 0 & (3) \\ F_{\lambda_1} = -2x + y = 0 & (4) \\ F_{\lambda_2} = -y - z = 0. & (5) \end{cases}$$

From (1), $x = \lambda_1$. From (3), $z = -\lambda_2/2$. From (4) and (5),
$2x = -z$, so $\lambda_1 = \lambda_2/4$. Substituting $\lambda_1 = \lambda_2/4$ into (2)
yields $\lambda_2 = 8/3$. Thus $\lambda_1 = 2/3$, $x = 2/3$, and $z = -4/3$.
From (5), $y = -z$ and hence $y = 4/3$.
Crit. pt. of f: $(2/3, 4/3, -4/3)$. <u>Ans.</u> $(2/3, 4/3, -4/3)$

13. Want to minimize $c = f(q_1, q_2) = 0.1q_1^2 + 7q_1 + 15q_2 + 1000$
subject to the constraint $q_1 + q_2 = 100$.

$$F(q_1, q_2, \lambda) = 0.1q_1^2 + 7q_1 + 15q_2 + 1000 - \lambda(q_1 + q_2 - 100).$$

$$\begin{cases} F_{q_1} = 0.2q_1 + 7 - \lambda = 0 & (1) \\ F_{q_2} = 15 - \lambda = 0 & (2) \\ F_\lambda = -q_1 - q_2 + 100 = 0. & (3) \end{cases}$$

From (2), $\lambda = 15$. Substituting $\lambda = 15$ into (1) gives
$0.2q_1 + 7 - 15 = 0$, so $q_1 = 40$. Sustituting $q_1 = 40$ into (3)
gives $-40 - q_2 + 100 = 0$, so $q_2 = 60$. Thus $\lambda = 15$, $q_1 = 40$,

q_2 = 60.   **Ans.** Plant 1, 40 units; Plant 2, 60 units

17. $U = x^3 y^3$, p_x = 2, p_y = 3, I = 48 $(x^3 y^3 \neq 0)$.

We want to maximize $U = x^3 y^3$ subject to $2x + 3y = 48$.

$F(x, y, \lambda) = x^3 y^3 - \lambda(2x + 3y - 48)$.

$$\begin{cases} F_x = 3x^2 y^3 - 2\lambda = 0 & (1) \\ F_y = 3x^3 y^2 - 3\lambda = 0 & (2) \\ F_\lambda = -2x - 3y + 48 = 0. & (3) \end{cases}$$

From (1), $\lambda = (3/2)x^2 y^3$ and from (2), $\lambda = x^3 y^2$. Thus $x = (3/2)y$. Substituting this expression for x into (3) yields $y = 8$. Hence $x = 12$.   **Ans.** $x = 12$, $y = 8$

EXERCISE 18.9

1. $n = 6$, $\Sigma x_1 = 21$, $\Sigma y_i = 18.6$, $\Sigma x_i y_i = 75.7$, $\Sigma x_i^2 = 91$.

$$\hat{a} = \frac{(\Sigma x_i^2)(\Sigma y_i) - (\Sigma x_i)(\Sigma x_i y_i)}{n\Sigma x_i^2 - (\Sigma x_i)^2} = \frac{91(18.6) - 21(75.7)}{6(91) - (21)^2} = 0.98.$$

$$\hat{b} = \frac{n\Sigma x_i y_i - (\Sigma x_i)(\Sigma y_i)}{n\Sigma x_i^2 - (\Sigma x_i)^2} = \frac{6(75.7) - 21(18.6)}{6(91) - (21)^2} = 0.61.$$

Thus $\hat{y} = 0.98 + 0.61x$. When $x = 3.5$, then $\hat{y} = 3.12$.

Ans. $\hat{y} = 0.98 + 0.61x$; 3.12

5. $n = 6$, $\Sigma p_i = 260$, $\Sigma q_i = 329$, $\Sigma p_i q_i = 12{,}760$,

$\Sigma p_i^2 = 13{,}600$.

$$\hat{a} = \frac{(\Sigma p_i^2)(\Sigma q_i) - (\Sigma p_i)(\Sigma p_i q_i)}{n\Sigma p_i^2 - (\Sigma p_i)^2}$$

$$= \frac{(13{,}600)(329) - (260)(12{,}760)}{6(13{,}600) - (260)^2} = 82.6;$$

$$\hat{b} = \frac{n\Sigma p_i q_i - (\Sigma p_i)(\Sigma q_i)}{n\Sigma p_i^2 - (\Sigma p_i)^2}$$

$$= \frac{6(12{,}760) - (260)(329)}{6(13{,}600) - (260)^2} = -0.641.$$

<u>Ans.</u> $\hat{q} = 82.6 - 0.641p$

9.

Year (x)	1	2	3	4	5
Production (y)	10	15	16	18	21

$n = 5$, $\Sigma x_i = 15$, $\Sigma y_i = 80$, $\Sigma x_i y_i = 265$, $\Sigma x_i^2 = 55$.

$$\hat{a} = \frac{(\Sigma x_i^2)(\Sigma y_i) - (\Sigma x_i)(\Sigma x_i y_i)}{n\Sigma x_i^2 - (\Sigma x_i)^2} = \frac{55(80) - 15(265)}{5(55) - (15)^2} = 8.5;$$

$$\hat{b} = \frac{n\Sigma x_i y_i - (\Sigma x_i)(\Sigma y_i)}{n\Sigma x_i^2 - (\Sigma x_i)^2} = \frac{5(265) - 15(80)}{5(55) - (15)^2} = 2.5.$$

Thus $\hat{y} = 8.5 + 2.5x$.   <u>Ans.</u> $\hat{y} = 8.5 + 2.5x$

EXERCISE 18.11

1. $\int_0^3 \int_0^4 x \, dy \, dx = \int_0^3 xy \Big|_0^4 dx = \int_0^3 4x \, dx = 2x^2 \Big|_0^3 = 18$

5. $\int_1^3 \int_1^2 (x^2-y)\, dx\, dy = \int_1^3 \left(\frac{x^3}{3} - xy\right)\Big|_1^2 dy =$

$\int_1^3 \left[\left(\frac{8}{3} - 2y\right) - \left(\frac{1}{3} - y\right)\right] dy = \int_1^3 \left(\frac{7}{3} - y\right) dy =$

$\left(\frac{7}{3}y - \frac{y^2}{2}\right)\Big|_1^3 = \left(7 - \frac{9}{2}\right) - \left(\frac{7}{3} - \frac{1}{2}\right) = \frac{2}{3}$

9. $\int_0^6 \int_0^{3x} y\, dy\, dx = \int_0^6 \frac{y^2}{2}\Big|_0^{3x} dx = \int_0^6 \frac{9x^2}{2} dx = \frac{3x^3}{2}\Big|_0^6 = 324$

13. $\int_0^2 \int_0^{\sqrt{4-y^2}} x\, dx\, dy = \int_0^2 \frac{x^2}{2}\Big|_0^{\sqrt{4-y^2}} dy = \int_0^2 \frac{4-y^2}{2} dy =$

$\int_0^2 \left(2 - \frac{y^2}{2}\right) dy = \left(2y - \frac{y^3}{6}\right)\Big|_0^2 = \left(4 - \frac{4}{3}\right) - 0 = \frac{8}{3}$

17. $\int_0^1 \int_0^y e^{x+y}\, dx\, dy = \int_0^1 e^{x+y}\Big|_0^y dy = \int_0^1 (e^{2y}-e^y)\, dy =$

$\left[\frac{e^{2y}}{2} - e^y\right]\Big|_0^1 = \frac{e^2}{2} - e - \left(\frac{1}{2} - 1\right) = \frac{e^2}{2} - e + \frac{1}{2}$

21. $\int_0^1 \int_{x^2}^x \int_0^{xy} dz\, dy\, dx = \int_0^1 \int_{x^2}^x z\Big|_0^{xy} dy\, dx =$

$\int_0^1 \int_{x^2}^x xy\, dy\, dx = \int_0^1 \frac{xy^2}{2}\Big|_{x^2}^x dx = \int_0^1 \left[\frac{x^3}{2} - \frac{x^5}{2}\right] dx =$

$\left[\frac{x^4}{8} - \frac{x^6}{12}\right]\Big|_0^1 = \frac{1}{24}$

25. $P(x \geq 1, \ y \geq 2) = \int_2^4 \int_1^2 \frac{x}{8} \, dx \, dy = \int_2^4 \frac{x^2}{16} \Big|_1^2 \, dy =$

$\int_2^4 \left(\frac{4}{16} - \frac{1}{16} \right) dy = \int_2^4 \frac{3}{16} \, dy = \frac{3y}{16} \Big|_2^4 = \frac{12}{16} - \frac{6}{16} = \frac{3}{8}.$

Ans. $\frac{3}{8}$

CHAPTER 18 – REVIEW PROBLEMS

1. $2x+3y+z = 9$ can be put in
   the form $Ax+By+Cz+D = 0$,
   so the graph is a plane.
   The intercepts are $(9/2,0,0)$,
   $(0,3,0)$, and $(0,0,9)$.

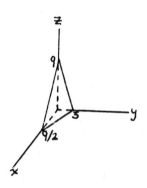

5. $f_x(x,y) = 2(2x)+3(1)y+0-0 = 4x+3y$

   $f_y(x,y) = 0+3x(y)+2y-0 = 3x+2y$

9. $f(x,y) = \ln \sqrt{x^2+y^2} = \frac{1}{2} \ln(x^2+y^2).$

   $\frac{\partial}{\partial y}[f(x,y)] = \frac{1}{2} \cdot \frac{1}{x^2+y^2}(2y) = \frac{y}{x^2+y^2}.$ Ans. $\frac{y}{x^2+y^2}$

13. $\frac{\partial}{\partial z}[f(x,y,z)] = (x+y)[2z].$ $\frac{\partial^2}{\partial z^2}[f(x,y,z)] = (x+y)[2].$

   Ans. $2(x+y)$

17. $\dfrac{\partial w}{\partial r} = \dfrac{\partial w}{\partial x}\dfrac{\partial x}{\partial r} + \dfrac{\partial w}{\partial y}\dfrac{\partial y}{\partial r} = (2x+2y)(e^r) + (2x+6y)\left(\dfrac{1}{r+s}\right)$

$$= 2(x+y)e^r + \dfrac{2(x+3y)}{r+s}$$

$\dfrac{\partial w}{\partial s} = \dfrac{\partial w}{\partial x}\dfrac{\partial x}{\partial s} + \dfrac{\partial w}{\partial y}\dfrac{\partial y}{\partial s} = (2x+2y)(0) + (2x+6y)\left(\dfrac{1}{r+s}\right)$

$$= \dfrac{2(x+3y)}{r+s}$$

21. In order to avoid confusion of the letter "l" with the number "1", we shall use "L" for the letter "l".

$P = 20L^{0.7}k^{0.3}$. Marginal productivity functions are given by $\dfrac{\partial P}{\partial L} = 20(0.7)L^{-0.3}k^{0.3}$ and $\dfrac{\partial P}{\partial k} = 20(0.3)L^{0.7}k^{-0.7}$.

Ans. $\partial P/\partial L = 14L^{-0.3}k^{0.3}$; $\partial P/\partial k = 6L^{0.7}k^{-0.7}$

25. $f(x,y) = x^2+2y^2-2xy-4y+3$.

$$\begin{cases} f_x(x,y) = 2x-2y = 0 \\ f_y(x,y) = 4y-2x-4 = 0. \end{cases}$$ Crit. pt.: $(2,2)$.

$f_{xx}(x,y) = 2$, $f_{yy}(x,y) = 4$, $f_{xy}(x,y) = -2$.   At $(2,2)$, D =

$(2)(4)-(-2)^2 = 4 > 0$ and $f_{xx}(x,y) = 2 > 0$; thus rel. min.

Ans. $(2,2)$, rel. min.

29. $f(x,y,z) = x^2+y^2+z^2$, $3x+2y+z = 14$.

$$F(x,y,z,\lambda) = x^2+y^2+z^2 - \lambda(3x+2y+z-14).$$

$$\begin{cases} F_x = 2x-3\lambda = 0 & (1) \\ F_y = 2y-2\lambda = 0 & (2) \\ F_z = 2z-\lambda = 0 & (3) \\ F_\lambda = -3x-2y-z+14 = 0. & (4) \end{cases}$$

From (1), $x = \dfrac{3\lambda}{2}$; from (2), $y = \lambda$; from (3), $z = \dfrac{\lambda}{2}$.

Substituting into (4) gives $-3\left(\dfrac{3\lambda}{2}\right) - 2\lambda - \dfrac{\lambda}{2} + 14 = 0$, from which $\lambda = 2$. Thus $x = 3$, $y = 2$, and $z = 1$.

Crit. pt. of F: (3,2,1,2).   Crit. pt. of f: (3,2,1).

Ans. (3,2,1)

33. $\int_0^4 \int_{y/2}^2 xy \ dx \ dy = \int_0^4 \left.\frac{x^2 y}{2}\right|_{y/2}^2 dy = \int_0^4 \left(2y - \frac{y^3}{8}\right) dy =$

$\left.\left(y^2 - \frac{y^4}{32}\right)\right|_0^4 = (16 - 8) - 0 = 8$

CHAPTER 18 — MATHEMATICAL SNAPSHOT

1. $y = Ce^{ax} + 5$, $y-5 = Ce^{ax}$, $\ln(y-5) = ax + \ln C$.

x	y	y - 5	ln(y - 5)
0	15	10	2.30259
1	12	7	1.94591
4	9	4	1.38629
7	7	2	0.69315
10	6	1	0.00000

$n = 5$, $\Sigma x_i = 22$, $\Sigma \ln(y_i - 5) = 6.32794$,

$\Sigma[x_i \ln(y_i - 5)] = 12.34312$, $\Sigma x_i^2 = 166$.

$$a = \frac{n\Sigma[x_i \ln(y_i - 5)] - (\Sigma x_1)[\Sigma \ln(y_i - 5)]}{n(\Sigma x_i^2) - (\Sigma x_i)^2}$$

$$= \frac{5(12.34312) - 22(6.32794)}{5(166) - (22)^2} \approx -0.22399;$$

$$\ln C = \frac{\Sigma(x_i^2)[\Sigma \ln(y_i - 5)] - (\Sigma x_i)\{\Sigma[x_i \ln(y_i - 5)]\}}{n(\Sigma x_i^2) - (\Sigma x_i)^2}$$

$$= \frac{166(6.32794) - 22(12.34312)}{5(166) - (22)^2} \approx 2.25113.$$

$C \approx e^{2.25113} \approx 9.50$.   Ans. $y = 9.50e^{-0.22399x} + 5$